SEEING AND
LATER MEDIEVAL WORLD

During the later Middle Ages people became increasingly obsessed with vision, visual analogies and the possibility of visual error. Exploring the writings of Roger Bacon, Peter Aureol and Nicholas of Autrecourt in light of an assortment of popular religious guides for preachers, confessors and penitents, including Peter of Limoges' *Treatise on the Moral Eye*, Dallas Denery illustrates how this interest in vision preoccupied medieval men and women on both an intellectual and practical level. This book offers a unique interdisciplinary examination of the interplay between religious life, perspectivist optics and theology. Denery presents significant new insights into the medieval psyche and conception of the self, ensuring that this book will appeal to historians of medieval science and those of medieval religious life and theology.

DALLAS G. DENERY II is Assistant Professor of History at Bowdoin College. He was the recipient of a NEH Award for Summer 2004 and is a member of the Medieval Academy of America.

*Cambridge Studies in Medieval Life and Thought*
*Fourth Series*

General Editor:

ROSAMOND McKITTERICK

*Professor of Medieval History, University of Cambridge, and Fellow of Newnham College*

Advisory Editors:

CHRISTINE CARPENTER

*Reader in Medieval English History, University of Cambridge, and Fellow of New Hall*

JONATHAN SHEPARD

The series Cambridge Studies in Medieval Life and Thought was inaugurated by G. G. Coulton in 1921; Professor Rosamond McKitterick now acts as General Editor of the Fourth Series with Dr. Christine Carpenter and Dr. Jonathan Shepard as Advisory Editors. The series brings together outstanding work by medieval scholars over a wide range of human endeavor extending from political economy to the history of ideas.

*For a list of titles in the series, see end of book.*

# SEEING AND BEING SEEN IN THE LATER MEDIEVAL WORLD

## Optics, Theology and Religious Life

DALLAS G. DENERY II

*Bowdoin College*

CAMBRIDGE
UNIVERSITY PRESS

CAMBRIDGE UNIVERSITY PRESS
Cambridge, New York, Melbourne, Madrid, Cape Town, Singapore, São Paulo, Delhi

Cambridge University Press
The Edinburgh Building, Cambridge CB2 8RU, UK

Published in the United States of America by Cambridge University Press, New York

www.cambridge.org
Information on this title: www.cambridge.org/9780521108935

First published 2005
This digitally printed version 2009

*A catalogue record for this publication is available from the British Library*

*Library of Congress Cataloguing in Publication data*
Denery, Dallas G. (Dallas George), 1964–
Seeing and being seen in the later medieval world : optics, theology, and religious life /
Dallas G. Denery II.
p.   cm. – (Cambridge studies in medieval life and thought ; 4th ser.)
Includes bibliographical references and index.
ISBN 0-521-82784-1
1. Vision–Religious aspects–Christianity–History of doctrines–Middle Ages, 600–1500.
I. Title.   II. Series.
BT745.D46   2005
261.5′15 – dc22   2004058560

ISBN 978-0-521-82784-3 hardback
ISBN 978-0-521-10893-5 paperback

*To my three mentors*
*Owen Carroll,*
*Robert Brentano*
*and especially*
*Amos Funkenstein*

# CONTENTS

# ACKNOWLEDGMENTS

This book began as a dissertation that I had hoped to write under the direction of Amos Funkenstein. Although Amos passed away just weeks before my oral examinations and, therefore, just weeks before I began that dissertation, this completed book still bears his imprint everywhere and would not exist without his influence and kindness. After Amos' passing, Robert Brentano enthusiastically agreed to direct my work. What doesn't bear Funkenstein's imprint certainly bears his. If I have succeeded at all, it is in finding a way to combine their very different styles of thought. I miss them both.

As I worked to complete this book I came in contact with other scholars, other specialists, all of whom were more than happy to lend me their support, and some of whom have since become friends. In particular I would like to thank Richard Newhauser for his many kindnesses and Katherine Tachau for her close reading of various versions of this work. In France, Christophe Grellard kindly shared copies of his own work on Nicholas of Autrecourt. At Berkeley, during those first enthralling seminars with Funkenstein, I made a number of friends, Greg Moynahan, Mike Whitmore, Jonathan Sheehan and Isaac Miller, each of whom contributed to the ideas that have finally found their way into this book. My colleague here at Bowdoin College, Stephen Perkinson, commented on drafts of this work and suggested ideas from his own vantage point as a scholar of medieval art history.

Before I came to Bowdoin College, Stanford University proved a valuable way station. Phillip Buc was unstinting in his support. Carolyn Lougee Chappell and the Stanford History Department made it possible for me to conduct final revisions for this book during the Summer of 2003. Hester Gelber, Paula Findlen, Brad Gregory and Meg Worley all contributed to making my time there profitable and pleasurable.

At Cambridge University Press, William Davies, Simon Whitmore and Alison Powell made the process of transforming this work from typescript into book something of a joy. Several anonymous readers provided useful feedback on earlier versions of the work. David Luscombe, then editor of

*Acknowledgments*

this series, read these pages with care and made many valuable suggestions (not to mention corrections), and this work is much the better for his attention.

My parents, my sister Celia and my brother John have all helped me in innumerable and important ways. Finally, there is my wife Lorry and our son Keegan, who likes to walk into the room when I am sitting at the computer and ask, "Are you still working Daddy?" When I respond, "That's what they call it," he laughs saying, "That's not what they call it!" And so to the two of them, and especially to Lorry, who has somehow put up with all these years of preoccupation and weekends with me off in some library, buried in some book, telling her I don't have the time to see a movie, go for a walk, go to the store, clean the house, wash the car (the unspoken academic perks finally revealed), thank you for allowing me to do whatever it is they call this thing I do (Keegan so far having chosen not to tell me) and now have done.

# INTRODUCTION:
## VISION AND VISUAL ANALOGY DURING
## THE LATER MIDDLE AGES

In some country everyone is blind from birth. Some are eager for knowledge and aspire after truth. Sooner or later one of them will say, "You see,
sirs, how we cannot walk straight along our way, but rather we frequently
fall into holes. But I do not believe that the whole human race is under
such a handicap, for the natural desire that we have to walk straight is not
frustrated in the whole race. So I believe that there are some men who are
endowed with a faculty for setting themselves straight."
> Nicholas of Autrecourt, *Exigit ordo* (ca. 1330)[1]

Tired of falling into holes, someone in a country where everyone is blind
from birth dreams of the ability to avoid falling into holes. Unfortunately,
nothing is foolproof and Thales, reputed to have been the very first of
the Presocratic philosophers and someone who, I imagine, could see as
well as the next person, still had his problems with holes. As an ancient
and probably apocryphal anecdote would have it, one day Thales fell
into a well while looking up at the stars. We know all this because a
witty servant girl just happened to be on the scene, ready with a quip
and eager to gossip.[2] Late in the sixteenth century, Michel de Montaigne
would include this anecdote in his *Apology for Raymond Sebond*. According
to Montaigne, Thales does not simply fall into the well. The servant girl
places a rock in the philosopher's path to teach him a lesson. Before he
worries about things in the clouds, he had better first worry about the
things around him. Montaigne, however, has doubts about the value of
the girl's advice. "Our condition," he writes, "makes the knowledge of
what we have in our hands as remote from us and as far above the clouds

---

[1] Nicholas of Autrecourt, *Exigit ordo executionis*, ed. Reginald O'Donnell, in *Mediaeval Studies* 1,
(1939), 189. *The Universal Treatise of Nicholas of Autrecourt*, trans. Leonard A. Kennedy, Richard E.
Arnold and Arthur E. Millard (Milwaukee: Marquette University Press, 1971). I have both relied
upon and emended this translation where necessary.

[2] The anecdote comes from Plato's *Theaetetus* 174a and is included in G. S. Kirk, J. E. Raven and
M. Schofield (eds.), *The Presocratic Philosophers*, 2nd. edn. (Cambridge: Cambridge University
Press, 1983), p. 80.

I

as that of the stars."[3] Had he been staring at the servant girl, Thales most likely would still have fallen in the well.

Nicholas of Autrecourt, who was undoubtedly among the most innovative and controversial of fourteenth-century thinkers, would have appreciated Montaigne's sentiments. After all, Nicholas did not generate his little thought experiment concerning the country of blind people in order to extol the virtues of sight, but rather to alert his readers to the potential insufficiency of vision and visual evidence. While the blind dreamer imagines a faculty that would allow him to somehow avoid the holes that all too frequently interrupt his walks, Nicholas tells us that his peers chastise him. "Your supposition goes right against experience," they say, "What would that faculty be? Not intellect, for we have that and we still do not walk straight. Not taste, not smell – these senses effect nothing." Perhaps experience provides no evidence for the existence of such a faculty, but does that mean it does not or could not exist? The blind man appeals to something Nicholas will call a "metaphysical argument," an argument that looks to non-evidential, non-experiential, criteria for its support. Given our natural desire to walk straight, he argues, it only makes sense that someone, somewhere, has this ability. The blind dreamer's argument is not evident and nothing his visually-impaired countrymen have ever experienced supports it. But then again, nothing they have experienced argues decisively against the existence of such a faculty. His supposition is possible and, given his metaphysical argument, it might even be probable. Nicholas believes there is a simple lesson to be gleaned from this anecdote – sensory evidence, all sensory evidence, is inconclusive for "many things can exist which are not naturally fitted to reach" the senses.[4] Maybe we, possessed of sight as we are, can see the holes and wells that block our paths, but that certainly does not mean we see everything or see things for what they really are.

Whether or not falling into a hole is a fit metaphor for the practice of philosophy, Nicholas was certainly not the only scholastic thinker to recognize that our senses sometimes deceive us. It was a topic of much discussion at Paris and Oxford during the fourteenth century, a topic most famously associated with the English Franciscan William Ockham. Imagine you are looking at a star. Now imagine that God, who can do anything, destroys the star while maintaining your vision of it. What you

---

[3] Michel de Montaigne, *The Complete Essays of Montaigne*, trans. Donald M. Frame (Stanford: Stanford University Press, 1965), p. 402.

[4] Nicholas of Autrecourt, *Exigit*, p. 189 (lines 16-25): "Dicet alius: tu ponis directe contra sensum; quale esset illud principium, non intellectus quia illum habemus, non tamen recte incedimus; non gustus, non olfactus; isti sensus nihil faciunt . . . et tamen ille habebit certitudinem per suum medium metaphysicum et sciet quod multa possunt esse quae non sunt nata pervenire apud sensum eorum, saltem non est repugnantia."

now see is a non-existent star. In other words, there is no necessary connection between the act of seeing and the seen object. What appears need not exist.[5] Three hundred years later, René Descartes would transform Ockham's omnipotent God into an evil demon and use this argument to great sceptical effect. With it, he thought he could clear away the deadweight of scholastic philosophy and build "a firm and permanent foundation in the sciences."[6] That Descartes ultimately failed is of less importance than that he tried and that he thought such an undertaking was both necessary and, in principle at least, achievable. For their part, scholastic thinkers had reacted quite differently to the problem of sensory error.

The distinction between what appears and what exists (however they phrased it, and they phrased it in a bewildering variety of ways) certainly fascinated scholastic theologians. Henry of Ghent, Duns Scotus, Peter Aureol and Walter Chatton are only a few of the academics during this period to devote large sections of their commentaries on Peter Lombard's *Sentences* to problems concerning vision and visual error. What is the relation between the intellect and its object? What is the relation between what appears to the senses and what exists in the world? Could God cause us to see a non-existent star and, if so, would we be deceived? Despite their almost obsessive interest in these sorts of questions and problems, medieval thinkers did not believe that the mere possibility of visual error posed the sort of absolute epistemological threat that Descartes thought it posed. While Nicholas was more than happy to overturn past authority and to argue that the senses could provide us with little certitude, he never considered this a problem that needed to be corrected. In the pages and chapters that follow, I hope to explain what made these different attitudes towards visual error possible.

No doubt these are the sorts of abstract philosophical questions Thales was warned against considering too deeply, at least not before looking where his next step was about to land. But falling in a hole can have its advantages, and sometimes when we are in a hole we can see things previously invisible to us. At least this was the opinion of Aristotle, who once observed that during the day, a man deep down in a well and

---

5 William of Ockham, *Quodlibeta* VI, quodlibet 6, in Gedeon Gál *et al.* (eds.), *Opera philosophica et theologica*, vol. 9 (St. Bonaventure: The Franciscan Institute, 1967–), p. 605. Philotheus Boehner, "The *Notitia intuitiva* of Non-Existents According to William Ockham," in Eligius Buytaert (ed.), *Collected Articles on Ockham* (St. Bonaventure: The Franciscan Institute, 1958), pp. 274-87, offers the clearest account of how Ockham situates this scenario within his broader epistemological and cognitive theories. Compare with Katherine Tachau, *Vision and Certitude in the Age of Ockham* (Leiden: E. J. Brill, 1988), pp. 115-29, for a somewhat different interpretation.
6 René Descartes, "Prima," in George Heffernan (ed. and trans.), *Meditationes de prima philosophia* (Notre Dame: University of Notre Dame Press, 1990), p. 86.

looking up could "sometimes see the stars."[7] While it is entirely beside the point that Aristotle's observation was wrong, it is not at all beside the point that, during the second half of the thirteenth century, Franciscan natural philosophers like Roger Bacon and John Pecham believed they had acquired and mastered a visual theory capable of explaining such peculiar (if occasionally specious) phenomena as the alleged visibility of stars during the day from the bottom of a well.[8] There is no doubt that the science of perspective (as this visual theory was commonly called) influenced theological debates concerning knowledge, vision and visual error, but the nature and extent of this influence is not at all straightforward.[9] It is undeniable, for example, that perspectivist theory provided a multi-faceted framework within which theologians worked to develop a wide-ranging theory of cognition.[10] There is, however, another complementary, if different way to approach this history of intellectual debate, one that does not treat these theologians in their role as cutting-edge natural philosophers, creatively mining the possibilities hidden within the ore of Roger Bacon's nascent perspectivist paradigm. Rather, it treats them as theologians (or theologians-in-training), as religious men immersed in the religious practices and concerns of their day, men who found in perspectivist thought a way to articulate the implications of those practices and concerns.

As a starting point for this approach, it is important to recognize that the problems that motivated theologians like Duns Scotus and Peter Aureol were at times incidental to or entirely independent of perspectivist theory. Whereas the perspectivists were interested in the actual causal processes that made human visual cognition possible, theological debates concerning the nature of vision and the relation between appearance and reality were often framed within quite different concerns. Theological debates, more often than not, began with ontological questions connected with

---

[7] Aristotle, *On the Generation of Animals*, in Jonathan Barnes (ed.), *The Complete Works of Aristotle: The Revised Oxford Translation* (Princeton: Princeton University Press, 1984), 780b. On the history of this commonly accepted and untrue belief, see Aydin M. Saylii, "The Observation Well," *Actes du VIIe Congrès international d'Histoire des Sciences* (Jerusalem, 1953), 542-50.

[8] See Roger Bacon, *Perspectiva*, Part 1, distinctio 1, chapter 1, in David C. Lindberg (ed. and trans.), *Roger Bacon and the Origins of Perspectiva in the Middle Ages: A Critical Edition and English Translation of Bacon's "Perspectiva" with Introduction and Notes* (Oxford: Clarendon Press, 1996), pp. 162-4.

[9] See David C. Lindberg, *Theories of Vision from Al-Kindi to Kepler* (Chicago: The University of Chicago Press, 1976), pp. 139-42 and Gabriella Federici Vescovini, "Vision et réalité dans la perspective au XIVe siècle," in *View and Vision in the Middle Ages* (Turnhout: Brepols, 1997), pp. 161-73.

[10] In her excellent study, Tachau, *Vision and Certitude*, p. xvi, writes, "At least as early as Roger Bacon . . . scholars perceived the whole range of optical concerns as lying not at the periphery but at the nexus of natural philosophy and epistemology (all ultimately at the service of theology). Hence from the mid-thirteenth century medieval intellectuals sought what might seem a 'unified field theory' of light, vision, cognition, and our expression of what we know to be true."

the principle of singularity, moral problems involving human free will, and theological problems arising from the nature of the beatific vision and God's omnipotence. In addressing these sorts of issues, theologians exploited perspectivist ideas and resorted to visual analogies. When considering some of the epistemological implications of his revolutionary ontology, for example, Duns Scotus suggests that in addition to sensory vision there must also exist an "intellectual vision."[11] The intellect and its capacities, in other words, are modelled after vision. Knowing something is somehow analogous to seeing something.

Before losing ourselves in the minutiae of these rather intricate medieval scientific and theological controversies, it might serve us well to step back from them for a moment in order to make a fairly broad observation. Whatever else it might indicate about later medieval intellectual life, the rise of perspectivist optics and the scholastic debates about the nature of sensory and intellectual cognition reveals a keen interest in vision and in the distinction between what appears and what exists. Not only were natural philosophers interested in the nature of vision, theologians found it useful to employ a rich variety of visual analogies to explain intellectual, spiritual and moral processes. Framing the issue in this way has the distinct advantage of cutting down on the glare of details that can all too easily blind us to whatever connection these arcane debates may have had to the rest of medieval society. After all, who besides a very few highly trained men at the universities in Paris and Oxford really cared whether vision occurred through the mediation of sensible species or through an immediate act of virtual attention or, for that matter, whether an intuitive cognition was similar to or radically distinct from an abstractive cognition? But if we put such complicated and terminologically daunting philosophical details aside for a moment, these seemingly abstract and rarefied debates can be seen as part of a much wider, more deeply felt set of concerns about the nature of appearances, about how the world appears to us and about how we appear to others and to ourselves.

Roger Bacon himself suggests some of these connections in the *Perspectiva*. Included as part of his *Opus maius*, a work he cobbled together around 1268 at the request of Pope Clement IV, Bacon's *Perspectiva* represents the first European effort to master the visual and optical theories of the Islamic natural philosopher Alhacen. As far as Bacon was concerned, the value of this science far exceeded all others. Vision, he claims, is the noblest of our senses. It is the sense upon which all human science depends. To understand how vision operates is to understand how

---

[11] Cited in Allan Wolter, "Duns Scotus on Intuition, Memory, and Our Knowledge of Individuals," in *The Philosophical Theology of John Duns Scotus* (Ithaca: Cornell University Press, 1990), p. 98.

human science is possible, how it can be improved and how errors can be avoided.[12] But to Bacon's mind the science of perspective was capable of much more. And so, towards the very end of the *Perspectiva*, Bacon writes, "Now, in conclusion, I wish to reveal how this science has inexpressible utility with respect to divine wisdom." The science of vision, quite simply, is the key to interpreting and understanding scripture. "For in divine scripture," he continues, "nothing is dealt with as frequently as matters pertaining to the eye and vision . . . and therefore nothing is as essential to [a grasp of] the literal and spiritual sense than the certitude supplied by this science." For example, we cannot hope to understand a passage like, "Preserve me oh Lord, as the pupil of your eye," Bacon explains, "unless we first consider how the preservation of the pupil is achieved, to the point where God would consider it worthy to preserve us in like manner."[13]

Now this rather odd approach to biblical interpretation might not really seem to move us all that far from the medieval university and its complicated theoretical debates. Admittedly, if it had never moved beyond the back pages of the *Perspectiva*, Bacon's plea for the spiritual significance of this science would be interesting, but not terribly representative of anything but the peculiarities of the medieval intellectual. However, Peter of Limoges, a prominent member of the Sorbonne (where he became a master in theology) and a fairly well-known astrologer, found Bacon's plea quite compelling. Peter was well versed in the newly emergent science of perspective and in the 1280s he put that knowledge to good use. The result was the *Tractatus moralis de oculo*, or *The Moral Treatise on the Eye*, a lengthy, at times repetitive, almost always fascinating attempt to articulate the moral and spiritual implications of perspectivist optics. Most significantly, the *Moral Treatise* was composed with an eminently practical goal in mind. Despite the occasional detailed foray into perspectivist theory, the *Tractatus* was first and foremost a preaching manual, a manual designed to assist preachers with their sermons. Divided into fifteen books, each one subdivided into numerous chapters and filled with illustrative exempla, Peter's manual proved popular throughout Europe, not only among members of the university, but also among the religious of all sorts. Over 150 manuscript copies still exist and records indicate that at least another 100 copies were made. It was still popular enough in the late

---

[12] Roger Bacon, *Perspectiva*, Part I, distinction 1, chapter 1, pp. 2-4 (lines 12-50).

[13] Roger Bacon, *Perspectiva*, Part III, distinction 3, chapter 1, pp. 320-2 (lines 21-5): "Volo nunc in fine innuere quomodo hec scientia habet ineffabilem utilitatem respectu sapientie divine . . . Cum enim dicitur, 'Custodi nos, Domine, ut pupillam oculi,' impossibile est scire sensum Dei in hoc verbo nisi primo consideret homo quomodo pupille custodia perficitur, quatenus ad eius similitudinem Deus nos custodire dignetur."

fifteenth century to justify several incunabula editions, including one translated into Italian.[14]

It would be too much to claim that the *Tractatus'* popular success indicated a general hunger for perspectivist theory. Nevertheless, its success is indicative of something quite interesting and quite important. Scholastic natural philosophers and theologians were not the only medieval Europeans interested in vision, in visual analogies and visual metaphors. At least one reason why the *Tractatus* resonated so loudly with the religious throughout Europe is that developments in religious practice and life had changed the way that many people understood both themselves and those around them. In many respects, people had come to think about themselves primarily in visual terms, in terms of a somewhat amorphous distinction between what appears and what exists. Perhaps Peter of Limoges' preaching aid most explicitly addresses these ideas, but they inform a wide variety of literature in a wide variety of ways. In particular, they inform two significant developments in medieval religious life: the growing popularity of personal confession and the rise of the mendicant religious orders.

Confessional treatises from as early as the late eleventh century, as well as thirteenth- and fourteenth-century religious *pastoralia* of all sorts, reveal an overwhelming and systematically conceived interest in appearances. Confessional manuals, for example, are full of instructions to ensure that penitents and their sins will be fully revealed to their confessors. Not only does the confessor see the penitent, the penitent is taught to see himself through the confessor's gaze. Likewise, Dominican and Franciscan training books constantly urge their members to adapt their appearance, their self-presentation, to the demands of the moment. Religious novices and preachers alike are taught how to behave and how to present themselves in any given setting, in the refectory, for example, in the library or on the road, before different sorts of audiences. "At no time should you ever be careless or secretive" writes the thirteenth-century Franciscan David of Augsburg in the *De institutione novitiorum*, "rather you should always maintain yourself with discipline and chastity in sight, taste, touch and in everything else, as if you were being watched by someone." According to David, the novice was, in fact, always under observation, if not by his

---

[14] Richard Newhauser, "Der *Tractatus moralis de oculo* des Petrus von Limoges und seine *exempla*," in Walter Haug and Burghart Wachinger (eds.), *Exempel und Exempelsammlungen* (Tübingen: Max Niemeyer Verlag, 1991), pp. 95-136 and "Nature's Moral Eye: Peter of Limoges' *Tractatus moralis de oculo*," in Susan J. Ridyard and Robert G. Benson (eds.), *Man and Nature in the Middle Ages*, Sewanee Mediaeval Studies 6 (Sewanee: University of the South Press, 1995), pp. 125-36. Given the sheer volume of surviving witnesses, Newhauser, pp. 133-4, remarks that Peter's manual was as popular as Thomas of Cantimpré's better remembered *Bonum universale de apibus*.

7

peers or his masters, certainly by the "holy angels who are always with us and who see every act we commit."[15]

None of this is meant to imply that an interest in vision and visual analogy was unique to people during the later Middle Ages, between say, 1150 and 1400. A great deal has been written in recent years concerning the power of visual metaphors and modes of thought throughout much, if not all, of Western history. Roger Bacon was only one in a long line of theologians, philosophers and scientists extending all the way back to the Presocratics to praise vision as the noblest and most useful of all the senses.[16] Aristotle gave particularly clear voice to this tradition at the very start of his *Metaphysics* when he wrote, "All men by nature desire to know. An indication of this is the delight we take in our senses; for even apart from their usefulness they are loved for themselves; and above all others the sense of sight. For not only with a view to action, but even when we are not doing anything, we prefer sight to almost everything else. The reason is that this, most of all the senses, makes us know and brings to light many differences between things."[17] However innocent such reflections on vision may appear at first glance, philosophers, historians and psychologists have long noted the many ways that this emphasis on vision has shaped and determined conceptions of truth and knowledge. The tendency to equate knowing with seeing has, among other things, fostered a Western intellectual predilection for the eternal over the temporal, being over becoming, and a peculiar distinction between knower and known that inevitably led to what John Dewey famously referred to as "the spectator theory of knowledge."[18]

---

[15] David of Augsburg, *De institutione novitiorum*, Part I, chapter 16, in Bonaventure, *Opera omnia*, vol. 12 (Paris: Vivès, 1868), p. 298: "Nunquam ita securus sis et absconsus, quin ita disciplinate et caste te habeas in visu, gestu, tactu, et in omnibus aliis, ac si ab aliquo videreris: quia sancti angeli, qui nobiscum sunt, semper vident omnia opera quae facimus: quorum aspectus debemus ubique vereri, et praesentiam revereri."

[16] For a comprehensive overview of this tradition from the Presocratics through to the European Enlightenment see, Martin Jay, *Downcast Eyes: The Denigration of Vision in Twentieth-Century French Thought* (Berkeley: University of California Press, 1993), pp. 21-147.

[17] Aristotle, *Metaphysics*, I.I, trans. W. D. Ross, in Barnes (ed.), *Complete Works*, vol. 2, p. 1552.

[18] John Dewey, *The Quest for Certainty* (New York: G. P. Putnam and Sons, 1980), p. 23, "The theory of knowing is modeled after what was supposed to take place in the act of vision. The object refracts light to the eye and is seen; it makes a difference to the eye and to the person having an optical apparatus, but none to the thing seen. The real object is the object so fixed in its regal aloofness that it is a king to any beholding mind that may gaze upon it. A spectator theory of knowledge is the inevitable outcome." Richard Rorty, *Philosophy and the Mirror of Nature* (Princeton: Princeton University Press, 1980), p. 39, who cites Dewey, popularized many of these themes. For a survey of contemporary studies on vision see the two volumes edited by David Michael Levin, *Modernity and the Hegemony of Vision* (Berkeley: University of California Press, 1993) and *Sites of Vision: The Discursive Construction of Sight in the History of Philosophy* (Cambridge: The MIT Press, 1997). The literature on this topic is immense and I will limit further citations to two classic and commonly referenced works, Hans Jonas, "The Nobility of Sight: A Study in the

Whatever such grand theorizing lacks in nuance, it certainly makes up for in the sheer breadth of its explanatory scope. It is, however, important to recognize that this overarching visual bias has revealed itself in any number of different ways since its initial appearance in ancient Greece. The precise development of this Western visual favouritism (or "ocular-centrism"), in short, can only be grasped through its specific historical manifestations, that is, through the various "scopic regimes" to which it has given rise and within which it has achieved its concrete historical reality.[19]

The specific historical manifestation that has most interested historians of western vision and visuality is one that seems to have coalesced during the fifteenth through seventeenth centuries. Erwin Panofsky did much to jumpstart this line of inquiry in his seminal work, *Perspective as Symbolic Form*, in which he argued that the rise of linear perspective during the fifteenth century marked "the conquest over the medieval representational principle." According to Panofsky, linear perspective of the sort described by Alberti and put into painterly practice by Masaccio and Piero della Francesca not only constituted a new way of artistically representing space (and objects in space) but was itself reflective of contemporary advances "in epistemology or natural philosophy." The homogeneous, geometrically organized space of a painting drawn in linear perspective went hand in hand with the overthrow of Aristotle's hierarchized cosmos and the establishment of the homogeneous, geometrically describable and infinite space of early modern science.[20] This pictorial "rationalization of sight," to borrow a phrase from another historian of perspective, William Ivins, is only one of many developments that historians have cited in arguing for a visual turn during these centuries.[21] In a work whose influence matches that of Panofsky's, Walter Ong has argued for a European-wide visual turn during this period, "a profound reorientation

Phenomenology of the Senses," in *The Phenomenon of Life: Toward a Philosophical Biology* (Chicago: The University of Chicago Press, 1982) and Maurice Merleau-Ponty, "Eye and Mind," in James M. Edie (ed.) and Carleton Dallery (trans.), *The Primacy of Perception* (Evanston: Northwestern University Press, 1964). Although Jay's book, *Downcast Eyes*, does not include a bibliography, the footnotes are full to overflowing with citations from much of the relevant literature.

19 Christian Metz, *The Imaginary Signifier: Psychoanalysis and the Cinema*, trans. Celia Britton, (Bloomington: Indiana University Press, 1982), pp. 61-3, introduced the expression "scopic regime" to name dominant and structuring relations between observer, image and object. The scopic regime of the cinema, for example, is defined by the absence of the seen object (which simply means when we see something on the silver screen, we really only see its projected image, not the thing itself).

20 Erwin Panofsky, *Perspective as Symbolic Form*, trans. Christopher S. Wood (New York, Zone Books, 1991), pp. 55 and 65. For a superb critique of Panofsky's theoretical claims, see James Elkins, *The Poetics of Perspective* (Ithaca: Cornell University Press, 1994), pp. 181-216.

21 William M. Ivins, Jr., *On the Rationalization of Sight: With an Examination of Three Renaissance Texts on Perspective* (New York: Da Capo Press, Inc., 1975), p. 7.

within the human spirit which made it possible to think of all the pos-
sessions of the mind, that is, of knowledge and expression, in terms
more committed to space than those of earlier times." Ong contends
that transformations in university curriculum and logic textbooks, the
rise of Humanism and the printing press attest to an increasing tendency
to perceive and, therefore, to reduce and think about all problems, as
problems of spatial relations and vision.[22]

Narratives about vision and visuality during the fifteenth through
seventeenth centuries, in other words, have long since become part and
parcel of the larger story of Europe's transformation from a medieval to
a Renaissance or (more recently) from a pre-modern to an early modern
society. According to this line of thought, early modern Europe bears
witness to, perhaps is even constituted through, a new scopic regime,
a new understanding of vision, its physics, its limits and its metaphorical powers to encompass, explain and control both the world and human
beings. It is, scholars contend, a regime made manifest in everything from
the rise of the individual and mercantile capitalism to the development
of the mathematical sciences and the centralized absolutist state.[23] Whatever problems these accounts may have (and whether we interpret them
as signs of rationalization or disenchantment, progress or decline), all of
them posit some sort of break or rupture with the past, with medieval
or pre-modern visual discourse.[24] There is a good reason to take these

---

[22] Walter J. Ong, *Ramus, Method and the Decay of Dialogue* (Cambridge: Harvard University Press,
1958), pp. 306-10. While Ong suggests that the real reorientation in the European "sensorium"
occurred during the fifteenth and sixteenth centuries, he acknowledges that a slowly growing
visual bias had long been underway and is already somewhat evident in medieval manuscript and
university culture. For his part, Alfred W. Crosby, *The Measure of Reality: Quantification and Western
Society, 1250-1600* (Cambridge: Cambridge University Press, 1997), has pushed back the actual date
of this transformation to the decades surrounding 1300. Citing innovations like monetization,
double-entry bookkeeping, and Giotto's paintings, Crosby writes, pp. 227-8, "Beginning in the
miraculous decades around the turn of the century (decades unmatched in their radical changes
in perception until the era of Einstein and Picasso) . . . Western Europeans evolved a new
way, more purely visual and quantitative than the old, of perceiving time, space, and material
environment." For a critique of these visualist approaches to early modern history, see Timothy
J. Reiss, *Knowledge, Discovery and Imagination in Early Modern Europe* (Cambridge: Cambridge
University Press, 1997), pp. xii-xiii and 127. Joel Kaye, *Economy and Nature in the Fourteenth Century*
(Cambridge: Cambridge University Press, 1998), circumventing all arguments about vision and
visuality, links the rise of science to the influence of a monetized European marketplace. Kaye
writes, p. 14, "Scholastic natural philosophers began to create a new model of nature, one that
could comprehend the order and logic of the marketplace - dynamic, self-equalizing, relativistic,
probabilistic, and geometrical - a nature constructed and bound together by lines in constant
expansion and contraction. It was within this new model of nature that science emerged."

[23] For a summary of these sorts of arguments see Jay, *Downcast Eyes*, pp. 57-69.

[24] Suzannah Biernoff, *Sight and Embodiment in the Middle Ages* (New York: Palgrave Macmillan,
2001), pp. 6-13, critiques the tendency to interpret the shift from medieval to later visual culture
in terms of a move from primitive or pathological modes to increasingly advanced or normalized
modes of seeing.

sorts of claims seriously. Visual and optical theory underwent a radical reformulation between 1550 and 1650, paintings created after 1400 often do look markedly different than paintings from the prior century, and the science and astronomy that grew up in the wake of Copernicus' theories really do make quite different assumptions about space and the things that occupy it than did Aristotelian science.

Part of the problem in assessing the real nature and degree of these changes, not to mention their significance, is that too often too little is taken into account of, perhaps too little is known about, the visual discourse that characterizes the *terminus a quo* of this transformative process. More often than not, the Middle Ages are read and interpreted in terms of later fifteenth-, sixteenth- and seventeenth-century developments, as if the only proper context for understanding medieval visual culture must be in terms of early modern culture. Crosby's highly readable narrative of Europe's visual turn, *The Measure of Reality*, suffers throughout precisely because of this sort of overly determined historical teleology. This becomes particularly evident in his analysis of the development of artistic perspective in Italian painting when he assumes that Giotto (who painted early in the fourteenth century) and Alberti and Piero della Francesca (both of whom flourished more than 100 years later) were all concerned with "the problem of 'seeing' geometrically." While this "problem" certainly became something of a mania for Italian artists of the fifteenth century, it is not at all clear that it ever concerned Giotto. Something similar occurs in Samuel Edgerton's work, *The Heritage of Giotto's Geometry*, which, despite its title, has nothing to say about Giotto's actual use and knowledge of geometry and is more concerned with his (or someone else's) creation of illusionistic effects in the modillion borders at the Assisi chapel. Whatever geometry is present in Giotto's paintings is read back into them in light of Alberti's fifteenth-century writings.[25] In other words, Edgerton reads these early fourteenth-century frescos as if they were the products of fifteenth-century artistic techniques and procedures.[26] Giotto undoubtedly influenced later painters; the question is whether Giotto's own work ought to be interpreted primarily in terms of its subsequent influence. It is worth noting that these problems of interpretive contextualization seem to haunt the study of Renaissance perspective itself. James Elkins has argued persuasively that the geometrical problems and challenges that interested Renaissance painters differ from the geometrical problems that interest historians of perspective. Renaissance artists, Elkins contends, did not paint pictures in

[25] Crosby, *Measure of Reality*, p. 176, and, more generally, pp. 165-97.
[26] Edgerton, *Heritage*, pp. 47-87.

perspective, but rather painted perspective into pictures. He refers to this as "the object-oriented purpose of much Renaissance picture making." While historians like Panofsky, Ivins and Edgerton, have emphasized the artistic development of a fully rationalized and geometrically coherent unified picture space, Elkins suggests that the attention of the artists themselves, "and their perspective methods, were focused on the delineation of particular objects."[27] Perspectival techniques were developed to allow for artistic displays of prowess and Renaissance paintings often became collections of objects painted from different, often contradictory viewpoints.

Jonathan Crary suggests a way around this sort of interpretive impasse with his approach to the formation and transformation of a seventeenth-century scopic regime by way of the "observing subject who is both the historical product *and* the site of certain practices, techniques, institutions and procedures of subjectification."[28] Another way to make Crary's valuable point is to note that vision and its effects are not simply biological givens, but are themselves elaborated through a wide array of social practices and discourses out of which they derive their cultural, philosophical and psychological significance. These elaborations must always begin with the one who sees, with how he is situated (and understood to be situated) within the visual act and with respect to the visual object. For his part, Crary is primarily interested in an early modern scopic regime that found its organizing metaphor in the camera obscura. With the observer removed from the world and placed within the dark room of the camera, indeed, only discovering the world through an image projected on a wall within that room, the camera obscura provided the perfect metaphor for quite a few early modern ideals connected with vision, representational theories of knowledge, and scientific empiricism. Most significantly, it provided the perfect metaphor for the best known version of the spectator theory of knowledge, namely the interiorized, individualized, self-enclosed, and disembodied subject of Cartesian philosophy.[29]

---

[27] Elkins, *Poetics*, p. 56.

[28] Jonathan Crary, *Techniques of the Observer: On Vision and Modernity in the Nineteenth Century*, (Cambridge: The MIT Press, 1991), p. 5.

[29] Crary, *Techniques*, pp. 27-9. Crary demonstrates that English rationalists and Continental idealists alike shared this ideal and model. This dualist and reductionist visual regime may not have been quite so hegemonic as Crary suggests. See Barbara Stafford, *Visual Analogy: Consciousness as the Art of Connecting* (Cambridge: The MIT Press, 1999), pp. 120-34, who traces a counter-visual discourse that stresses resemblance and analogy throughout the early modern period, particularly evident in Leibniz's writings. Also, Martin Jay, "The Scopic Regimes of Modernity," in Hal Foster (ed.), *Vision and Visuality* (New York: The New Press, 1988), pp. 10-20, who analyzes internal tensions within the regime of "Cartesian perspectivalism" and delineates several possible counter regimes or discourses.

Spectator theories of knowledge, however, require spectators and during the Middle Ages there were no spectators, at least not in the philosophically and politically pregnant sense that term would assume in the seventeenth century. The medieval discourse about vision and visual error, whatever resemblance it might occasionally seem to have to early modern discussions, ultimately reflects and takes its real orientation from a fundamentally different historical setting, a setting that gave rise to a fundamentally different understanding of the relation between the one who sees and what is seen. As a means of emphasizing these differences, I purposely use the slightly unwieldy expression "the one who sees" precisely because the religious practices that determined how people employed visual analogies during the thirteenth and fourteenth centuries were practices that indefinitely deferred the formation of an individual or subject (at least as it was envisioned in the seventeenth century). If early modern thinkers found it possible, even necessary, to "consolidate" the observer as a subject entirely removed, isolated and distinct from the objects of its perception, medieval thinkers recognized neither the need, nor the possibility for such consolidation.[30] The inner house of conscience, for example, a quite popular medieval metaphor, did not describe the essentially private abode of the self. It named the room in which penitent and confessor met and spoke. Likewise, medieval natural philosophers argued that visual perception did not occur through the mediation of representations that stood between subject and object, but by appearances that somehow united the one who sees with what he sees. Distinctions between knower and known existed, but they were different and more fluid than the distinctions that would develop during the seventeenth century.

There is no obvious medieval equivalent for the seventeenth-century metaphor of the camera obscura. However, the medieval engagement with vision and its effects can be captured through the practices of personal confession and public preaching, and a coherent narrative can be written that moves from these practices to fourteenth-century epistemological controversies concerning the nature of vision and the relation between what appears and what exists. Both these religious practices and academic debates were, in final analysis, concerned with knowledge and its limits. Not only were they organized around a variety of visual or

---

[30] Hans Blumenberg, *The Legitimacy of the Modern Age*, trans. Robert M. Wallace (Boston: The MIT Press, 1983), p. 196, locates Descartes' desire to consolidate the self in the increasing threat posed by theological absolutism, "Under the enormous pressure of the demands made upon it by theology, the human subject begins to consolidate itself, to take on a new overall condition, which possesses, in relation to the ambushes set by the hidden absolute will, something like the elementary attribute of the atom, that it cannot be split up or altered."

13

scopic relations (between preacher and audience, between penitent and confessor), but they also compelled people to think about themselves in visual terms, in analogies and metaphors that made issues relating to seeing and being seen absolutely central to religious and spiritual life. Most significantly, the very relations that these practices instituted between the one who sees and what is seen would reappear and organize university discussions of vision and visual error. Like Nicholas of Autrecourt's country of blind men, preachers, penitents and theologians inevitably and repeatedly fell into their own sorts of holes and even if they wished they could avoid them, there really was not all that much they could do about it. They recognized the essential limits of vision and visual evidence; it occasionally worried them, but they really had no choice but to accept them.

The following chapters, in short, will explore how late medieval religious practice fostered new forms of self-awareness and, therefore, a new understanding of one's relation to oneself, to others and to the world. More often than not medievalists have looked to the twelfth century for these sorts of developments. During the twelfth century, to borrow loosely from the title of Colin Morris' famous book, people discovered the individual, they began to think about themselves "without paying excessive attention to the demands of convention and the dictates of authority."[31] Although Morris' work has not gone uncriticized, most criticisms have taken the form of modifications to his basic thesis. John Benton recommends that the discussion employ a more precise terminology. The twelfth century did not discover the "individual" so much as it discovered the "self." People living during this period emphasized the value of self-exploration, developed practices that promoted self-awareness and generally tended to exhibit a greater appreciation for their inner, emotional lives than did their immediate and not so immediate ancestors. Regardless, this self-awareness did not extend to an awareness of the self as radically individual and independent. Among other things, medieval Latin lacks our modern notion of personality, and self-exploration was never undertaken as an end in itself, but always as a means

---

[31] Colin Morris, *The Discovery of the Individual: 1050-1200* (London: SPCK, 1972), p. 7. Morris is not alone in making these sorts of claims. The original source of this debate is, of course, Jacob Burckhardt, *The Civilization of the Renaissance in Italy*, vol. II, trans. S. G. C. Middlemore (New York: Harper & Row, 1929), p. 303, in which he claims that the great achievement of the Italian Renaissance was that it first discerned and brought "to light the full, whole nature of man." Displeased, C. H. Haskins jumped into the fray with *The Renaissance of the Twelfth Century* (Cambridge: Harvard University Press, 1927), in which he claimed that many of Burckhardt's fifteenth-century innovations had already been discovered three hundred years earlier, during the twelfth century. For a brief summary of the history of this debate, see Jean-Claude Schmitt, "La 'Decouverte de l'individu': une fiction historiographique?" in Paul Mengal (ed.), *La Fabrique, la figure et la feinte: fictions et statut des fictions en psychologie* (Paris: Vrin, 1989), pp. 212-36.

to union with God.[32] Indeed, for people in the twelfth and early thirteenth centuries, the turn inwards was understood as the best means for
more fully identifying with and conforming to a group. Increased self-
awareness was merely the first step in a larger process through which the
individual ultimately found the resources for his own salvation through
the assimilation to a pre-existing model of communal religious life.[33]

No doubt these goals and ideals carried over to the thirteenth and
fourteenth centuries, but they did not carry over unchanged. What it
meant to look within oneself, what one saw and what one could learn,
were no longer the same. Or perhaps it might be better to say that during
these centuries, as people worked out the implications of this new-found
twelfth-century interest in the individual and in the self, they simultaneously discovered how difficult it was to know oneself. While the ideal
of union with community and with God remained in place, the means
for achieving that ideal grew more and more inadequate. And it is here,
in this slippage between ideal and practice, that a uniquely late medieval
sense of self was forged, a sense of self as indefinitely deferred, infinitely
complex and unknowable to all but God. Although I locate the proximate
causes for these developments in the practice of personal confession and
in a variety of ideals and attitudes embodied in the mendicant religious
orders, there may well be other causes behind them. Indeed, it might
even be the case that other developments, other practices and discourses,
offered alternatives to the model I describe. It is, after all, entirely possible
for competing visual discourses to coexist.[34] All I claim is that at least one
group of significant and significantly interconnected medieval religious
practices reconfigured the ways in which people during the Middle Ages
could see and experience themselves, their faith and their fellows.

[32] John F. Benton, "Consciousness of Self and Perceptions of Individuality," in Robert L. Benson
and Giles Constable (eds.), *Renaissance and Renewal in the Twelfth Century* (Boston: Harvard University Press, 1982), pp. 284-5. Schmitt, "La 'Decouverte de l'individu,'" pp. 230-31, suggests
something similar when he both recommends replacing the term "individu" with "personne"
while simultaneously noting its multiple medieval uses. It should be noted that Morris anticipated
these sorts of caveats to his claims, even if he has a tendency to downplay them, see *Discovery*,
pp. 160-1. See Charles Taylor, *Sources of the Self: The Making of the Modernity* (Cambridge: Harvard
University Press, 1989), pp. 127-42, for a more extended discussion of the move inward as a means
of moving upward to God in Augustine's writings.

[33] Carolyn Walker Bynum, "Did the Twelfth Century Discover the Individual?" in *Jesus as Mother:
Studies in the Spirituality of the High Middle Ages* (Berkeley: University of California Press, 1982),
pp. 106–9. Also Aaron Gurevich, *The Origins of European Individualism*, trans. Katharine Judelson
(Oxford: Blackwell Publishers Ltd., 1995), p. 155, who emphasizes "the tense conflict between
the dominant principle of humility and anonymity [at work in the twelfth century], on the one
hand, and the ambitious aspirations in the work of an ever-growing number of authors and artists
to leave memorials behind them 'now and for evermore,' on the other."

[34] See above, note 29. Catherine Wilson, "Discourses of Vision in Seventeenth-Century Metaphysics," in Levin (ed.), *Sites of Vision*, pp. 117–38.

Considered architectonically, this study divides into halves, the first concerned with practice, the second with theory or speculation. This division, however, is replicated again within each chapter as practice inevitably leads to speculation on the assumptions and implications buried within those practices and as speculation returns us to practice. The first chapter is a close reading of two significant thirteenth-century Dominican instruction manuals, Humbert of Romans' *Liber de eruditione praedicatorum* and an anonymous late thirteenth-century novice manual, the *Libellus de instructione et consolatione novitiorum*. Both works reveal how the requirement to preach *ad extra*, that is, in the world among the laity, compelled Dominicans to conceive of themselves in terms of their appearance (both to their audiences and to themselves, and to God). It was a conception that introduced new sorts of tensions into religious life, tensions that earlier monks, such as twelfth-century Cistercians and Benedictines, had not experienced. Cistercian writing, for example, often situates the monk in a *narrative of progress* in which his love of God increases as he slowly assimilates himself to his order. Preachers, by contrast, could no longer simply focus on assimilating themselves to the daily routine of a monastery. They needed to constantly adapt themselves to an infinite range of new and ever-changing preaching settings. As a result, Dominican *exempla*, preaching handbooks and novice manuals emphasize a new sort of self-awareness, a *heuristics of adaptation* in which novices are taught to carefully weigh and balance their self-presentation, their appearance, to the demands of the moment. The stability that earlier monks found in the ordered life of the monastery gives way to a complicated and never-ending balancing act, as mendicants try to maintain an inner holiness even as they repeatedly adapt their self-presentation to the needs of a constantly changing audience. Dominican writing, however, demonstrates a growing inability to distinguish the two, indicating that, perhaps, there really is no clear distinction between interior self and its external presentation to others.

One visual setting replaces another as the preacher, raised above the crowd he observes even as it observes him, gives way to the more intimate setting of personal confession. It is a natural progression. Not only was preaching meant to inspire a desire for forgiveness, a desire to confess and to receive the Eucharist, but Humbert himself instructed his preachers to examine themselves often to make sure they were not being taken in by their self-presentation. Chapter two analyzes the structural development of personal confession beginning with its origins in the late eleventh century. The goal of confession was forgiveness through the recognition of and sorrow for one's sins. In order to accomplish this, the confessor and the penitent worked together to construct a narrative or representation of the individual penitent's life as a sinner. Using a wide array of twelfth- through fifteenth-century confessional *pastoralia* (handbooks designed to teach priests how to hear confessions), I argue that confessional practice emphasized self-knowledge while simultaneously undercutting the possibility that we could ever fully know ourselves. Unlike Cartesian self-examination, for example, which sought the certitude of the self's epistemic relation to itself, confessional self-examination denied the possibility of any such secure foundation. Rather, it opened up a terrain of potentially infinite investigation and questioning in which (paradoxically) the penitent was in no better position than his confessor to judge the truth of his confession. In the end, the penitent, just like the priest, came to know his life as a sinner through the confessional representation itself. Knowing oneself was more like knowing another. Self-knowledge was not intuitive and immediate. It was mediated through the social practice of confession. If preachers worried about the relation between their hidden selves and their self-presentation, confessional practice taught that even that hidden self was known only through its appearances, its real presence forever deferred (although never denied).

Chapter three and, more specifically, Peter of Limoges' preaching manual, the *Tractatus moralis de oculo*, provides the link between religious practice and university speculation. Peter's work makes explicit the often implicit visual analogies at work within medieval preaching and confessional manuals. For Peter, problems arising from within the practice of medieval religious life find their natural articulation in the language of perspectivist optics, as analogies of visual experience and visual cognition. The terms and concepts of this theory will, obviously enough, shape his interpretation of those experiences. But analogies and metaphors work both ways, and those same experiences, once interpreted as types of visual experience, will work from within to destabilize perspectivist theory. If knowing oneself as a sinner is somehow like seeing something, then seeing something must also have something in common with knowing oneself as a sinner. More to the point, medieval visual theorists like Roger Bacon assumed that in certain common, normative and paradigmatic circumstances, things could be seen and known for what they really are. The experience of preachers, penitents and confessors undermined this assumption, not by denying that such ideal circumstances might exist, but by demonstrating our inherent inability to recognize them when they occur. Distinguishing true perceptual experiences from false ones (or even more accurate experiences from less accurate ones) proved increasingly difficult and certain knowledge of objects disappeared within an endless proliferation of appearances.

Against this wider cultural backdrop, the controversies that raged throughout the universities of Europe between 1280 and 1350 can be seen as philosophical responses to problems associated with medieval religious practice. Although the epistemological and ontological aspects of vision commanded the attention of numerous thinkers, I focus primarily on two whose work proved enormously influential (in the one case) and controversial (in the other). Peter Aureol and Nicholas of Autrecourt explored the relations between the one who sees and what is seen, between what appears and what actually exists, with more subtlety than any of their peers. Not only does their work reveal a fundamentally different visual paradigm from the one that seventeenth-century theorists found so captivating, it is a paradigm that precisely mirrors the epistemological dilemmas present in Peter of Limoges' spiritual interpretations of perspectivist theory and, by extension, in the practice of personal confession and mendicant preaching. As Nicholas' work makes abundantly clear, it is a paradigm that disperses the one who sees into the unending flow of appearances, that is, it does not constitute the one who sees as a permanent ground and authority, as one who can impose order on what appears. Rather, it works to constantly upset any foundation, to render all human knowledge claims unverifiable. And here, speculation returns us to religious life itself, to confession and to preaching. After all, Nicholas believes that, once men realize that little certitude can be acquired from the natural appearances, they will quickly recognize the futility of their arcane scientific and philosophical debates. Inevitably, they will return to the study of scripture, holy law and the purification of their hearts "so as to live and appear, in the sight of the most glorious Prince of all nature, as spotless mirrors, and images of his goodness."[35] From the act of preaching to the speculative debates of university-trained philosophers and theologians, the dialectics of seeing and being seen provided the model and the tool with which people during the thirteenth and fourteenth centuries sought to articulate their spiritual lives and to achieve their spiritual salvation.

---

[35] Nicholas of Autrecourt, *Exigit*, p. 182 (lines 3–9): "Tandem in processu temporis apparerent divini quidam homines qui non totum tempus vitae suae consumerent in logicis sermonibus vel in distinguendo propositiones obscuras Aristotelis vel in quotando commenta Averrois, sed intellectum divinae legis manifestarent populo et radiis suae bonitatis undique diffusis sic viverent quod in conspectu gloriosissimi principis totius naturae apparerent sicut specula sine macula et imagines bonitatis illius."

# Chapter 1

# *PONDERARE STATERA MEDITATIONIS:* SELF AS SELF-PRESENTATION IN EARLY DOMINICAN RELIGIOUS LIFE

## CONTEMPLATION, SPECULATION, MIRACLE

In the *Vitae fratrum*, a collection of stories compiled during the 1250s concerning the formation and early growth of the Dominican Order, Gerard de Frachet relates the tale of a certain unnamed English friar. It seems this friar thought it might be a good idea to incorporate "as many philosophical reasonings and axioms as possible into the matter of his sermon." The night before he was to give his sermon, Christ appeared before him as he slept and handed him a bible covered in filth. When the friar asked for a reason, Christ opened the book and showed him that, despite its cover, the pages themselves were spotless. "My word is fair enough," Christ tells the Englishman, "but it is you who have defiled it with your philosophy."[1] The tale itself is not particularly unusual. It is only one in a series of short anecdotes scattered throughout the *Vitae fratrum* that point up a certain unease with studying, with philosophy and with teaching. Another, for example, concerns a friar whose "whole mind had been given to the pursuit of philosophy." One night God summoned him to the judgment chair and convicted him of being a philosopher, not a friar, "whereupon he was stripped and beaten without pity. When he awoke he felt the pains in all his limbs as if he had been scourged bodily."[2]

Of course, Dominicans were not alone in their ambivalence towards studying, nor in their recognition of its importance. A tradition extending back to the Bible itself had simultaneously warned of both the dangers and the importance of study. No less an authority than Bernard of Clairvaux had contrasted those who sought knowledge for its own sake ("and this is shameful curiosity") or for glory and money ("and this is shameful profiteering") with those who sought knowledge in order to be of service to others ("and this is charity") or to better themselves ("and

---

[1] Gerard de Frachet, *Lives of the Brethren of the Order of Preachers*, ed. Bede Jarett and trans. Placid Conway (London: Blackfriars, 1955), pp. 178–9.
[2] Gerard, *Lives of the Brethren*, p. 179.

this is prudence").[3] And Bernard's was an authority that the Dominicans were eager to repeat word for word.[4] Nonetheless, appearances can be deceiving, and the apparent continuity of concern that seems to unite Dominicans writing in the thirteenth century with Bernard, who had died in 1153, conceals a striking discontinuity. It is not a discontinuity at the level of words. Dominicans happily cite Bernard's sermons, letters and meditations (not to mention those of Bernard's fellow Cistercians, Benedictines and Regular Canons), but rather at the level of organization. The manner in which Dominicans organize their concerns, the form they impose on them, points to a context far removed from those that spawned the Cistercian ideals. Indeed, in this case contexts and settings are everything, not only for locating the source of a specifically Dominican discomfort with study and philosophy, but even for the determination of a Dominican understanding of self which is, in every instance, a self adjusting itself to different contexts and different settings.

The specifically Dominican ambivalence towards study reflects an uneasy inheritance. During the course of the twelfth century the activity of *speculatio* underwent a reinterpretation. For eleventh-century Benedictines such as Anselm of Bec, and even for twelfth-century Cistercians, *speculatio* meant "a gazing upon the divine" and was essentially a devotional exercise related to *contemplatio*.[5] Anselm's *Proslogion* and *Monologion*, despite their philosophical content, were written as meditative prayers designed to assist the monk in acquiring a more affective understanding of God.[6] The (ideally) complete assimilation of study to prayer, of intellectual to affective experience, was facilitated by the institution of the monastery itself in which every activity was always already interpreted

---

[3] Bernard of Clairvaux, *Sermones super cantica canticorum*, sermon 36, section 3, in J. Leclercq, C. H. Talbot and H. M. Rochais (eds.), *Sancti Bernardi opera*, vol. 2 (Rome: Editiones Cistercienses, 1958), p. 6: "Et sunt item qui scire volunt, ut scientiam suam vendant, verbi causa pro pecunia, pro honoribus: et turpis quaestus est. Sed sunt quoque qui scire volunt, ut aedificent: et caritas est. Et sunt item qui scire volunt, ut aedificentur: et prudentia est." *On the Song of Songs*, vol. II, trans. Killian Walsh and Irene Edmonds (Kalamazoo: Cistercian Publications Inc., 1982), p. 176.

[4] See, for example, *Libellus de consolatione et instructione novitiorum* in Raymond Creytens (ed.), "L'Instruction des novices dominicains au XIIIe siècle d'après le MS Toulouse 418," *Archivum fratrum praedicatorum* 20 (1948), 167.

[5] G. R. Evans, *Old Arts and New Theology: The Beginning of Theology as an Academic Discipline* (Oxford: Clarendon Press, 1980), pp. 93-5. Also, Paul Gehl, "Mystical Language Models in Monastic Educational Psychology," *Journal of Medieval and Renaissance Studies* 14, no. 2 (1984), 230-2.

[6] Consider the manner in which Anselm concludes the *Proslogion*, chapter 26, in Salesius Schmitt (ed.), *Opera omnia* (Stuttgart-Bad Cannstatt: Verlag, 1968), vol. I, pp. 121-2 (lines 22-3): "Meditetur interim inde mens mea, loquatur inde lingua mea. Amet illud cor meum, sermocinetur os meum. Esuriat illud anima mea, sitiat caro mea, desideret tota substantia mea, donec intrem 'in gaudium domini' mei, 'qui est' trinus et unus deus 'benedictus in saecula. Amen.'"

and organized for the sake of piety, the love of God.[7] Study was a form of prayer and devotion, as were manual labour and the chanting of the psalter. These connections were loosened during the course of the twelfth century. As the cathedral school supplanted the monastery as the centre of intellectual activity, *speculatio* became disentangled from *contemplatio*. It came, instead, to refer to a teachable activity of the mind independent of religious emotion.[8] Theology, in turn, became a professional academic discipline, a body of knowledge to be mastered and taught to others in the environment of the university classroom. While thirteenth-century scholars and theologians continued to condemn curiosity as a sin, the realities of university training made it all the easier to treat speculation as an end in itself.

The special calling of the Dominicans to be public preachers practically guaranteed that they would manifest the tensions inherent in the new institutional organization of learning more vividly than older orders. Although Dominic himself shared with the founders of other orders the desire to establish a school of contemplation in which his friars could work to perfect themselves before God, the additional emphasis or shift away from contemplation and towards preaching moved the activity of study more fully to the centre of Dominican life. After all, one cannot preach without doctrine, and doctrine must be learned.[9] As the Dominican Hugh of St.-Cher would note, "First the bow is bent in study, then the arrow is released in preaching."[10] Be that as it may, early Dominican constitutions and regulations included traditional clerical prohibitions against pagan philosophical works. During the course of the first half of the thirteenth century, as the Dominicans recruited heavily among university students at Paris and Oxford and in Italy, the order gradually assimilated itself to and mastered the intellectual environment of the thirteenth-century university.[11] And this assimilation, in turn, introduced the (potential) separation between study and prayer into the heart

[7] Jean Leclercq, *The Love of Learning and the Desire for God*, trans. C. Misrahi (New York: Fordham University Press, 1962), pp. 18–19. Also, Paul F. Gehl, "*Competens silentium*: Varieties of Monastic Silence in the Medieval West," *Viator* 18 (1987), 138–41.

[8] Evans, *Old Arts and New Theology*, p. 29 and generally, pp. 8–56, for the rise and effects of the twelfth-century cathedral schools. Also, Marcia Colish, "Systematic Theology and Theological Renewal in the Twelfth Century," *Journal of Medieval and Renaissance Studies* 18, no. 2 (1988), 154–5.

[9] William A. Hinnebusch, *The History of the Dominican Order: Origins and Growth to 1500* (Staten Island: Alba House, 1965), pp. 122–4.

[10] Cited in M. Michèle Mulchahey, *First the Bow is Bent in Study: Dominican Education before 1350* (Toronto: Pontifical Institute of Mediaeval Studies, 1998), p. ix.

[11] Mulchahey, *First the Bow is Bent*, p. 39, notes the essentially "scholastic" organization of the Dominican cloister: "The chapter of 1220 stipulated that no convent could be set up without a *doctor*, that is, a teacher, making every convent a school." Mulchahey's book offers a wonderful, and wonderfully lucid, account of Dominican education. For a brief survey, see Edward Tracy

of Dominican life itself. In the *Vitae fratrum*, Gerard de Frachet includes the telling anecdote of a German friar who regularly "would prostrate himself in spirit" before the blessed womb that bore Christ, the breasts which fed him and the hands which protected him. Before each he would say a "Hail Mary" in memory of the blessed Virgin's virtues. One day, while rapt in such prayer, the blessed Virgin appeared and granted him those very same virtues. "From that moment," Gerard continues, "he put aside all study and other pursuits, and gave himself up entirely to prayer." This did not go unnoticed by his fellow friars, who criticized him for neglecting his proper duty to study. The German friar then prayed that the Lord would convert some of his new found delights "into knowledge, so that he might benefit the souls of others to the glory of His name. His suit was granted, for his scanty store of learning was so increased that he preached fluently in German and Latin, and was endowed with a rare understanding." In the changed environment of the thirteenth century, a miracle is required to join prayer and study.[12]

### PREACHERS AND AUDIENCES

The tension between prayer and study, and the need for both, reappear in Humbert of Romans' *Liber de eruditione praedicatorum*. Humbert, who became the Dominican Order's fifth master general in 1254, most likely did not write the *Liber* until after he had stepped down from that post in 1263. The *Liber* itself was a peculiar book for its time. Unlike most manuals for preachers, it is not an *ars praedicandi*, that is, it is not a technical manual designed to teach preachers how to compose

Brett, *Humbert of Romans: His Life and Views of Thirteenth-Century Society* (Toronto: Pontifical Institute of Mediaeval Studies, 1984), pp. 39-56. In particular, Brett notes the not always peaceful, though ultimately thorough, incorporation of Greek philosophy into the system of Dominican studies. Also, Maura O'Carrol, "The Educational Organisation of the Dominicans in England and Wales 1221-1348: A Multidisciplinary Approach," *Archivum fratrum praedicatorum* 50 (1980), 23-62.

[12] Gerard de Frachet, *Lives of the Brethren*, pp. 142-3. John Van Engen, "Dominic and the Brothers: *Vitae* as Life-forming *exempla* in the Order of Preachers," in Kent Emery, Jr. and Joseph Wawrykow (eds.), *Christ Among the Medieval Dominicans* (Notre Dame: University of Notre Dame Press, 1998), p. 14, warns against interpreting these exempla as opposing study and miracle, as denigrating study in favour of a more simple faith. He writes, pp. 17-18, "Gerard never intended to disparage his fellow Preachers' learning, but to warn a community made up of former students and masters. A life of advancement and pride in learning, not subservient to the ends of preaching, represented potentially their chief temptation." I think Van Engen is mostly right on this point. The need to balance study and preaching, to organize the former strictly to the demands of the latter, however, is only one example of a more far-reaching Dominican demand to organize all aspects of one's life to the demand to preach. Within this context, Gerard's miracle stories reveal how difficult it was to maintain this balance. They reveal the tensions and difficulties that Dominicans experienced as they attempted to properly organize their lives and activities in accord with the novel institutional demands of their order.

sermons.[13] Rather, it is a sustained reflection on the nature of preaching and on the person of the preacher himself. Quite simply, it is a handbook designed to instruct Dominicans on how to conduct their lives as preachers.[14]

As a member of a religious order created specifically for the purpose of preaching, it is not surprising that Humbert begins with a demonstration of the nobility of preaching. Preaching is, at one and the same time, a divine, an angelic and an apostolic task.[15] It derives not from the mind of man, but from scripture, which is from God.[16] Regardless of its nobility, regardless of the benefits that the preacher accrues from preaching,[17] Humbert is quick to warn of the difficulty of preaching. And the difficulties he cites are difficulties that return us directly to the issues of prayer and study. "There are," Humbert notes, "and there have been many very well educated men, who have struggled for all their worth to acquire the grace of preaching, and yet, for all their effort, have not succeeded."[18] Unlike other arts, there is no direct correlation in preaching between study and success. The ability to preach is a gift from God and "what a man cannot acquire through his own effort, but must come to him from another, is very difficult."[19]

Although the grace of preaching "is strictly had by God's gift, nevertheless," Humbert warns, "a wise preacher ought to do what he can by studying what he has to preach, so that he performs in a praiseworthy

---

[13] See, James J. Murphy, *Rhetoric in the Middle Ages: A History of Rhetorical Theory from Saint Augustine to the Renaissance* (Berkeley: University of California Press, 1974), pp. 267-355, on the history and development of the *ars praedicandi*. Jean Longère, *La Prédication médiévale* (Paris: Études Augustiniennes, 1983), pp. 54-130, provides a summary overview of later medieval preaching.

[14] Simon Tugwell, "Humbert of Romans's Material for Preachers," in Thomas L. Amos, *et al.* (eds.), *De Ore Domini: Preachers and the Word in the Middle Ages* (Kalamazoo: Medieval Institute Publications, 1989), pp. 105-6 and Mulchahey, *First the Bow is Bent*, p. 476. For a brief sketch of Humbert's life see Brett, *Humbert of Romans*, pp. 3-11, and p. 11 for the importance and influence of his writings on preaching.

[15] Humbert of Romans, *Liber de eruditione praedicatorum* in Joachim Berthier (ed.), *De vita regulari* (Rome: A. Befani, 1888), vol. 2, p. 374. The *Liber* is translated as *The Formation of Preachers* in Simon Tugwell (ed. and trans.), *Early Dominicans: Selected Writings* (New York: Paulist Press, 1982). Apart from the occasional alteration, I have depended upon Tugwell's translation.

[16] Humbert, *Liber*, I.2, p. 375.    [17] Humbert, *Liber*, I.5, pp. 384-90.

[18] Humbert, *Liber*, I.7, p. 393: "Secundo ex conatu multorum ad istud officium: sunt enim et fuerunt multi magni in litteraturis multis, qui quamvis apposuerunt diligentiam multam, et conati sunt pro viribus ad habendam gratiam praedicandi, tamen ad hoc nunquam pervenire potuerunt."

[19] Humbert, *Liber*, I.7, p. 393: ". . . quae autem homo ex opere suo non potest, sed aliunde oportet venire, difficilius est." On the Order's gradual recognition that not all men are suited to preach, see Augustine Thompson, *Revival Preachers and Politics in Thirteenth-Century Italy: The Great Devotion of 1233* (Oxford: Clarendon Press, 1992), pp. 84-8. Franco Morenzoni, "Parole du prédicateur et inspiration divine d'après les *Artes praedicandi*," in Rossa Maria Dessì and Michel Lauwers (eds.), *La Parole du Prédicateur* (Nice: Centre d'Études Médiévales, 1997), vol. 1, pp. 273-83, provides a brief overview on medieval ideas concerning the relation between preparation and divine inspiration in successful preaching.

fashion"[20] Preparatory study for preaching must always be organized around what is useful for the creation of appropriate sermons. Humbert likens the preacher to a host who must prepare a meal for his guests. He should supply good food in the proper proportions so that his guests can digest it easily and with pleasure.[21] Accordingly, he must not waste his time studying and developing intricate subtleties and novelties (like the Athenians), nor should he base his sermons on strange and obscure texts "which are more likely to incur derision than edification."[22] Rather, the preacher must organize all his preparatory study around the needs of his audience. It is the preacher's duty to be constantly aware of his audience and adapt to it.

Much of what follows these opening remarks, concerning the nobility and difficulty of preaching, will deal with the various types of audiences which the preacher might confront and the circumstances in which the preacher might confront them. Quoting Gregory the Great's *Pastoral Rule*, Humbert notes that "there is no single exhortation which is suitable for everyone, because men are not all held by the same kind of morals. Often, what helps one man harms another."[23] Humbert, still borrowing from Gregory, then proceeds to list over seventy types of audiences or audience members. These types range from such relatively straightforward and clear cut distinctions as the ones between men and women, young and old, or rich and poor, to a wide range of more subtle and nuanced distinctions such as the one between "those who weep for actual sins" and "those who weep for sins committed only in the mind" or between those "who neither steal what is not theirs nor give away anything that is theirs" and "those who are generous with what is theirs, but also constantly steal what is not theirs."[24] Not only must he adapt the topic of his sermon to his audience, he must also adapt his words to his audience. He must speak "crudely to the uneducated" and "more subtly with the wise."[25]

---

[20] Humbert, *Liber*, I.7, p. 394: "Circa primum notandum est quod licet praedicationis gratia specialiter habeatur ex dono Dei, tamen sapiens praedicator debet facere quod in se est, diligenter studendo circa praedicationem faciendam, ut laudabiliter fiat."

[21] Humbert, *Liber*, I.7, pp. 395-6.

[22] Humbert, *Liber*, I.7, p. 396: "Solet autem accidere frequenter quod hujusmodi themata extranea non possunt aptari ad propositum nisi cum magna et incongrua extorsione sententiae, et ideo potius inducunt derisionem quam aedificationem."

[23] Humbert, *Liber*, IV.18, pp. 421-2: ". . . non una eademque cunctis exhortatio congruit, quia nec cunctos par morum qualitas astringit. Saepe namque aliis officiunt quae aliis prosunt . . ."

[24] Humbert, *Liber*, IV.18, pp. 422-3: ". . . aliter qui nec aliena rapiunt, nec sua largiuntur, aliter qui et ea quae habent sua tribuunt et aliena rapere non desistunt . . . aliter qui peccata deplorant operum, aliter qui cogitationum . . ." D. L. D'Avray, *The Preaching of the Friars: Sermons Diffused from Paris Before 1300* (Oxford: Clarendon Press, 1985), pp. 64-131, discusses the types of manuals which the mendicants employed to facilitate the adaptation of sermons to audiences and occasions.

[25] Humbert, *Liber*, IV.18, p. 424: "Item, modo loquendum est grosse cum rudibus; modo subtilius cum sapientibus."

Similarly, he must consider the circumstances of his audience: Are they tired? Sorrowful? Have they just eaten lunch?[26]

Adjusting and adapting the content, the form and the style of his sermon to the audience is only part of the preacher's duty. In addition to identifying and meeting the needs of his audience, so that the "word of his preaching is a kind of mirror . . . in which a man sees himself,"[27] the preacher must also consider the impression he himself makes on the audience. Even before founding the Order, Dominic had recognized the importance of the preacher's appearance. Jean de Mailly's *Life of St. Dominic* recounts the critical and famous meeting which Dominic and Bishop Diego had with a legate of Pope Innocent, a number of bishops and twelve Cistercian abbots "in the land of the Albigensians." When asked what was the best means of countering the spread of the Albigensian heresy, Diego recommended that they abandon "all their splendid horses and clothes and accoutrements" and that they adopt "evangelical poverty so that their deeds would demonstrate the faith of Christ as well as their words." Only if their deeds and appearances matched their words would they be able to "bring back to the true faith the souls which had been deluded by the heretics with their false appearance of virtue."[28]

---

[26] Humbert of Romans, *De officiis ordinis*, in *De vita regulari*, vol. 2, p. 371: "Item, vitet, quando bono modo potest, praedicare immediate post prandium: id enim tempus est tam audientibus quam loquentibus minus aptum; sed si oportet fieri, temperatius sumat cibum et potum." The difficulties facing the preacher are even more complex than Humbert allows for. As Thomas Aquinas notes in the *Summa contra gentiles*, I.2, trans. Anton C. Pegis (Notre Dame: University of Notre Dame Press, 1955), pp. 61-3. not everyone accepts the same holy books. When preaching to Jews, the preacher can only employ the Old Testament and, when preaching to the Muslims, who (according to Thomas) accept neither the Old nor the New Testament, he must employ natural reason. In other words, there are cases in which the preacher must employ the methods of the Athenians. In his introduction to the English translation, Anton Pegis, pp. 20-1, argues that the *Summa contra gentiles* was written with just this purpose in mind, as a "manual of apologetics for missionaries" working in Spain. Norman Kretzman, *The Metaphysics of Theism: Aquinas' Natural Theology in "Summa contra gentiles" I* (Oxford: Clarendon Press, 1997), pp. 43-5, argues that this interpretation is implausible and that the treatise is an analysis of "the interrelation of philosophy and Christianity."

[27] Humbert, *Liber*, V.24, p. 437: "Verbum enim praedicationis est sicut speculum . . . in quo homo cognoscit seipsum."

[28] Jean de Mailly, *The Life of St. Dominic*, in Tugwell (ed. and trans.), *Early Dominicans*, p. 54. Patricia Ranft, "The Concept of Witness in the Christian Tradition," *Revue Bénédictine* 102, no. 1-2 (1992), 22-3, contends that the Dominicans were the first religious order "to realize the vital connection between witness and the vita apostolica, and the importance of institutionalizing witness within the apostolic life." Caroline Walker Bynum, "The Cistercian Conception of Community," in *Jesus as Mother*, p. 74, notes that Benedictines and Cistercians did not possess a positive institutionalized understanding of example, witness or edification. She writes, "[E]ven the occasional references to edification found in Cistercian treatises usually occur within broader discussions which see the community as a setting for individual growth, not as an opportunity for service." Compare with Martha Newman, *The Boundaries of Charity: Cistercian Culture and Ecclesiastical Reform, 1098-1180* (Stanford: Stanford University Press, 1996), pp. 42-66.

Humbert addresses the issue of the preacher's appearance, how he appears to others, in a number of places in the *Liber de eruditione*. A preacher "should preach not only with his voice, but with all that he is."[29] Nonetheless, preaching is primarily an oral activity and the quality of the preacher's voice cannot be ignored. It is essential that the preacher have a facility with words and a sonorous voice.[30] "A great deal of the effectiveness of the sermon is lost," Humbert writes, "if the preacher's voice is so thin and feeble that he cannot be heard clearly."[31] In addition, a preacher must not possess any obvious or remarkable bodily deformity. Humbert notes that the Church has banned such people from public office for fear of public ridicule and scandal.[32] These seemingly more superficial concerns gradually give way as Humbert considers a more significant array of requirements centring around the quality of the preacher's life and his merit.

Echoing the sentiments of his order's founder, Humbert writes that a preacher must maintain "a certain radiance about his life. It does not suffice for a preacher to lead a good life; rather, his brilliance must shine before everyone so that he preaches not only with words, but also with deeds."[33] For Humbert there are both negative and positive reasons for this, as well as reasons pertaining, on the one hand, to the audience's well-being and, on the other, to the well-being of the preacher himself. Among other things, an audience will scorn a preacher whose deeds do not harmonize with his words. Not only do such preachers disgrace the office which they represent, but, as a result of their inadequacies, the salvation of the audience is itself placed at risk.[34] Successful preaching, by contrast, can result in any number of positive effects for the audience, including conversion, release from the devil's snares, sanctification and a desire to confess.[35]

---

[29] Humbert, *Liber*, IV.20, p. 429: "Item, non solum voce, sed se toto praedicet . . ."

[30] Humbert, *Liber*, II.1, p. 402.

[31] Humbert, *Liber*, II.1, pp. 402: "Item, sonoritatem in voce. Multum enim perit de fructu sermonis, cum praedicator propter vocis debilitatem non potest clare audiri." Angela Montford, "Fit to Preach and Pray: Considerations of Occupational Health in the Mendicant Orders," in R. N. Swanson (ed.), *The Use and Abuse of Time in Christian History* (Woodbridge: The Boydell Press, 2002), pp. 95–110, analyzes "health and fitness requirements for the friars of the Franciscan and Dominican orders" during the thirteenth century.

[32] Humbert, *Liber*, II.12, pp. 406-7.

[33] Humbert, *Liber*, II.8, p. 400: "Aliud est vitae luciditas. Non enim sufficit praedicatori ducere bonam vitam, sed debet sic lucere lux ejus coram hominibus, ut non solum verbo, sed et opere praedicet."

[34] Humbert, *Liber*, II.8, p. 400; VII.35, p. 456; and VI.26, pp. 441-2.

[35] Humbert, *Liber*, VI.28, pp. 444-5. This is found within a section entitled "The Fruits of Excellent Preaching," in which Humbert considers an entire spectrum of possible results ranging from none whatsoever to thoroughly good. He also considers the reasons for such variations. These include problems with the preacher, with his sermon and even with the audience.

The demand for good conduct is more than a demand aimed at improving the effectiveness of the preacher's sermons. Indeed, the division between preaching and non-preaching settings blurs, even vanishes, as Humbert considers the nature of the preacher's vocation in connection with the demand for good conduct. Humbert recognizes that preachers must attempt to win the salvation of others "in any way they can. And sometimes this is achieved better by good conduct than by words."[36] As a result, the command for good conduct becomes all encompassing. Humbert notes that the preacher's conduct "must not be good in just one respect, but totally, that is, with respect to everything" and this means in every sort of company, in every sort of place, and during every moment of the day. "Be Holy in all your way of life," Humbert concludes glossing 1 Peter 1, "all your way of life, that is, with regard to everything and everybody, in every place and all the time."[37] A preacher must always carry himself in such a manner that he is acceptable and likeable to people, must avoid behaving strangely, and must always be humble.[38] And these demands arise because all settings are, in effect, preaching settings, settings in which the preacher must present himself appropriately in word and in deed. A preacher, Humbert warns, must never be idle "in the presence of people he lives with. He should always be devoting himself to some chance of getting results."[39]

If all settings become preaching settings, then the preacher is enjoined at every moment to consider, adapt and adjust himself to his audience. Not only must he consider how he appears to his listeners, but also to his companions. More importantly, he must consider how he appears to God and even to himself. Although there are many things involved in a preacher's good conduct among men, his primary duty is to moderate his behaviour in the sight of God. "Otherwise," Humbert writes, "his whole public presentation would simply be hypocrisy."[40] When he is alone,

---

[36] Humbert, *Liber*, VII.35, p. 455-6: "Item, praedicatorum interest procurare salutem aliorum modis quibus possunt. Quandoque vero melius procuratur per bonam conversationem quam per verbum."

[37] Humbert, *Liber*, VII.35, p. 457: "Tertio quod non solum sit bona secundum quid, sed totaliter, idest quoad omnia. *Hebr. ult.*: In omnibus bene volentes conversari. Et quoad omnes; *Rom.* 12: Providentes bona non tantum coram Deo, sed etiam coram omnibus hominibus. Et ubique; 2 *Cor.* 1: In gratia Dei conversati sumus in hoc mundo. Non solum in parte una, sed continue; *Act.* 23: In omni conscientia bona conversatus sum apud Deum, usque in hodiernum diem. Ideo dicitur; 1 *Petr.* 1: Sancti in omni conversatione sitis: in omni, scilicet quoad omnia, et quoad omnes, et in omni loco, et in omni tempore."

[38] Humbert, *Liber*, VII.35, p. 457-8.

[39] Humbert, *Liber*, VII.35, p. 457: "Sexto quo sit fructuosa. Non enim convenit quod praedicator sit unquam otiosus apud eos inter quos conversatur: sed semper debet alicui fructui vacare . . ."

[40] Humbert, *Liber*, VII.35, p. 457: "Primo in hoc quod sit bona coram Deo. Alioquin totum quicquid exterius praetenderetur esset hypocrisis."

the preacher is required to treat himself as his audience and examine his conduct and his life. Preaching presents the preacher with specific dangers precisely because it is a public activity. Set loose from the confines of a monastery, the preacher is placed amid the temptations of the world. There is a constant threat that his motivations will slip slowly, perhaps unknowingly, from the desire to save souls to a desire for glory, that his preaching will arise out of vanity, ambition or a desire, stoked with envy, to surpass other preachers.[41]

Even as the division between preaching and non-preaching settings dissolves, so too does the division between public and private settings. Since the preacher must always consider himself in terms of how he presents himself (even when he is alone), he is, almost imperceptibly, transformed into a thoroughly public being. The preacher is always confronted by and must always adapt himself to some audience. He is always the object of somebody's gaze, and his conduct, his conscience, his intentions, must always be regulated by the demands to preach to that gaze, by the demand never to be idle. At points Humbert speaks as if the preacher is unable to hide anything from anyone. The words that a preacher employs (and by extension, the deeds he performs) reveal much about his true nature. Quoting Isidore of Seville, Humbert writes, "It is a man's tongue that publishes his character; the sort of mind he has is shown by the words he speaks."[42] And a little later, he adds, "The tongue can bring forth into speech only what is already there in the heart, and so a tongue which speaks fatuous words is evidence of a fatuous heart."[43] This ideal of visibility is particularly evident in an anecdote from the *Vitae fratrum* in which Gerard de Frachet relates the tale of an "exemplary religious and very capable" (if unnamed) Dominican friar who began to include rash novelties in his lectures. Despite the protests of his superiors, including those of the master general and the definitors of the general chapter, he refused to withdraw them. Later, Gerard notes, "a venerable and saintly prior, whose testimony is beyond all suspicion, testifie[d] that he saw a devil on this man's head as he stood in the chapter-house."[44] The preacher is marked by a visibility that transforms the interior taint of sin into a public announcement of its presence. Dominican emphasis on self-presentation, on a distinction between exterior appearance and inner truth, in other

---

[41] Humbert, *Liber*, III.14, pp. 413-15.

[42] Humbert, *Liber*, VII.38, p. 463: "Mores hominum pandit lingua; et qualis sermo ostenditur, talis animus comprobatur."

[43] Humbert, *Liber*, VII.39, p. 464: "Quandoque ex cordis vanitate. Lingua enim non educit de corde, nisi quod est in eo: et ideo vana loquens lingua vani cordis est indicium."

[44] Gerard de Frachet, *Lives of the Brethren*, p. 178.

words, did not compel them to imagine the two as radically distinct. Rather, they are bound together in a complicated, not to mention complicating, manner.

The preacher, accordingly, becomes the site of a continual self-disclosure, a regulated self-presentation aimed always at assisting, in as economic a manner as possible, an audience which never leaves him.[45] The peculiar difficulties that confront the preacher arise precisely from this constant demand to adjust his self-presentation to an ever-shifting array of settings. Humbert describes this as a need for the preacher to moderate (*mediocritatem*) his words, his entire life.[46] He must, for example, balance his involvement in secular affairs with the demand not to become too embroiled in them.[47] Nevertheless, he must not only worry about interior things. Occasionally he must worry about exterior things. "Therefore," Humbert observes, "the middle way is to be held" and the preacher learns this middle way through study.[48]

The preacher must possess eight kinds of knowledge. He must have knowledge of the holy scripture, of God's creatures, of historical stories, of church precepts and mysteries. He must have that knowledge which only comes from the experience of dealing with men's souls, he must possess discretion (when should he preach? how?) and knowledge of and from the Holy Spirit.[49] But even here there is a need for balance, for discretion. Anecdotes of friars tempted to over-philosophize and suffering the torments of Hell as a result of their philosophical studies point to the dangers the preacher faces when he fails to study with discretion. Discretion (as we have already seen), refers to the preacher's need to regulate his appearance to an audience that never leaves him, to adjust his self-presentation to the specific setting in which he finds himself and to the varying elements and needs which arise in that setting. It is, furthermore, linked to a conception of the preacher as thoroughly public and visible. And if this conception of the preacher as visible finds its ideal model in the "pre-eminence" of the preacher raised above the crowd to

---

[45] Humbert, *Liber*, VI.24, p. 437.

[46] Humbert, *Liber*, II.10, p. 403: "Item, mediocritatem in pronuntiando, ut non nimis celeriter, nec nimis morose pronuntiet. Praecipitatio enim obruit intellectum, morositas generat fastidium. Ideo dicit Seneca in *Epist.*: Philosophi pronunciatio, sicut et vita, debet esse composita. Nihil ordinatum est, quod praecipitatur et properat. Ex aequo illum stillare volo ut currere. Non extundat aures, nec obruat. Si autem hoc in philosopho propter mundanum laudem requiritur, quanto magis in praedicatore propter animarum utilitatem?"

[47] Humbert, *Liber*, VII.42, p. 473.

[48] Humbert, *Liber*, VII.42, p. 474: "Circa hoc ergo tenendum est medium. Ad quod tenendum debet praedicator cavere ne unquam se occupet circa negotia saeculum sapientia, ut est occupatio circa negotia carnalia carnalium amicorum . . ."

[49] Humbert, *Liber*, II.9, pp. 400-2.

whom he speaks,[50] it nevertheless recurs and is endlessly replicated within the Dominican priory itself where it becomes normative in establishing a Dominican conception of self.

## NOVICES

Little is known about the author of the *Libellus de instructione et consolatione novitiorum*. An anonymous Dominican novice master in Toulouse, he submitted his work to the 1283 chapter general meeting in Montpellier where it received official approval.[51] Regardless of this honour, the work exerted little influence. Only one copy appears to have been made and that copy travelled no further than to the Toulouse public library. Nevertheless (or perhaps because of these very factors) the work is of particular value as it is the only extant thirteenth-century Dominican treatise concerning the ascetic and spiritual formation and development of novices. Unlike such "disciplinary" works as Humbert's *De officiis ordinis* or Jean de Montlhéry's *Tractatus de instructione novitiorum*,[52] which primarily focus on the "large and small duties that go to make up the daily life of the Dominican novice,"[53] the anonymous *Libellus* focuses instead on the novice's spiritual formation and on the rightness and rectitude which he must observe during his first months as a Dominican.

As an organizational device for much of the work, the author looks to the organization of the Dominican priory itself, to the different places that go to make up a Dominican priory. In section two, for example, "On the Divine Dignity of Servitude," the author adopts the allegory of the cloister of the soul.[54] The soul is compared to the Dominican priory itself, the formation of its various affections tied to specific places and

---

[50] Humbert, *Liber*, II.8, p. 400: "Aliud est vitae excellentia. Sicut enim preadicans in alto stat, ita debet esse in alto statu vitae."

[51] Creytens, "L'Instruction des novices," pp. 149-52 and also, Mulchahey, *First the Bow is Bent*, pp. 114-15, who stresses that the general chapter's official approval indicates the anonymous treatise "was thought to speak with an authentic Dominican voice." The complete anonymous *Libellus* is preserved in Toulouse, Bibliothèque Municipale MS 418. Creytens edited significant portions of it and attached it to the end of his study as pp. 153-93. He included the *Libellus'* introduction and prologue (which includes a thorough review of the matters discussed in each chapter of the *Libellus*) as part of his study at pp. 122-30.

[52] Both Humbert of Romans' *De officiis ordinis* and Jean de Montlhéry's *Tractatus de instructione novitiorum* are edited in Humbert of Romans, *De vita regulari*, vol. 2.

[53] Creytens, "L'Instruction des novices," pp. 135-6. Also, Hinnebusch, *The History of the Dominican Order*, p. 293 and Mulchahey, *First the Bow is Bent*, p. 111.

[54] *Libellus*, p. 123, "In prima distinctione ostenditur quare dignum est ut Deo ab homine serviatur . . . In secunda distinctione ostenditur que dignitas exigitur in servo, vel ministro, *qui tanto Domino famulator* . . . In tertia distinctione ostenditur quod dignitas exigitur in ministrandi modo, *ut gratus a Domino habeatur* . . . In quarta distinctione agitur de claustro duplicis affectionis anime." Commenting on this section, Creytens, "L'Instruction des novices," pp. 130-1, writes, "Le grand nombre de pages qu'elle occupe . . . montre clairement que l'auteur a voulu donner

activities in the priory: the hidden lecture room of the soul's meditation, the refectory of devotion, the temple of the sanctification of the soul, the intimate chapter hall of inner correction and the dormitory of the soul's contemplation.[55]

Although he will drop the allegory of the soul's cloister when he turns to consider the novice's spiritual comportment in daily life, the anonymous author retains the same organizational strategy. He writes, "Since it has been told to you, servant of God, what justice you ought to pursue, whether in the monastery or in the cloister, with respect to God and to the prelate, with respect to yourself and to your fellow brother, now I think it ought to be shown to you what justice you ought spiritually to pursue in each office."[56] What follows is, in essence, a tour of a thirteenth-century Dominican priory. If the novice wishes to appear "with justice before God in church" he must consider how quickly he rushes to appear before mere men, be they religious or lay, and hurry all the faster to God in his church.[57] He cites Bernard's *Commentary on the Song of Songs* as an authority on how the novice ought to behave in church and in the choir.[58] He proceeds in a similar vein, citing other sources, to consider how the novice ought "to appear with justice" in the chapter hall, in the refectory, the dormitory, in the lecture room, in the infirmary and outside the priory's boundaries. Activities are also treated as settings in which the novice must always be aware of his appearance. He must consider the "justice which ought to be preserved in the

à l'éducation des affections intérieures la place principale dans la formation de ses novices . . . L'allégorisme du cloître était donc tout indiqué pour servir de véhicule à l'explication des mystères de la vie spirituelle. L'âme était un cloître, dont la composition et l'ordination matérielle symbolisait l'organisation du cloître spirituel. Les règles qui président à l'édification, l'entretien et l'embellissement du monastère, régiront de la même manière la construction de cet édifice spirituel qu'est l'âme du religieux. Chaque lieu régulier du monastère aura son application dans la vie spirituelle: le parloir, le réfectoire, l'église ou la chapelle, la salle du chapitre, le dortoir, l'hospice, la salle d'étude, le vestaire et l'infirmerie." Also, Mulchahey, *First the Bow is Bent*, pp. 117-22

55 *Libellus*, 124-5, "In septima distinctione agitur de locutorio secrete meditationis anime . . . In octava distinctione agitur de refectorio devotionis . . . In nona distinctione agitur de templo sanctificationis anime . . . In decima distinctione agitur de capitulo intime correctionis . . . In undecima distinctione agitur de dormitorio contemplationis anime . . ."

56 *Libellus*, 153-4, "Postquam, serve Dei, dictum est tibi quam iusticiam sectari debeas in monasterio seu in claustro quantum ad Deum et quantum ad prelatum et generaliter ad te ipsum et quantum ad proximum fratrem tuum, *nunc tibi arbitror ostendendum quam iusticiam sectari debeas spiritualiter in aliquibus officiis*." Unlike the novice manuals by Humbert of Romans and Jean de Montlhéry, writes Mulchahey, *First the Bow is Bent*, p. 123 when the anonymous novice master turns to external matters of discipline, that is, to how the novice ought to behave within the cloister, he is still "at pains to make explicit the connection between the inner man he has just described and the outer man."

57 *Libellus*, p. 154, "Si ergo, sicut coram tuo domino temporali, vis coram Deo in iusticia apparere et ei tribuere . . . statim ut audieris per campanam vocem Domini ad suum servitium te vocantis, surge velociter . . . ad ecclesiam ad Dominum sine mora."

58 *Libellus*, pp. 156 and 157.

study of wisdom,"[59] when serving his fellow brothers[60] or when reading in the refectory.[61] The Dominican priory, in other words, is broken into discrete places and settings. The novice's spiritual formation and comportment is explained in terms of how he should respond to those places.

After decomposing the priory into its various settings, the novice master proceeds to decompose the settings themselves. Concerning the justice which ought to be maintained in the chapter hall, he writes, "The Holy Spirit says to you those words already mentioned, 'Before a judgment prepare justice' before him who stands in the place of God in the chapter hall. Prepare, I say, justice with respect to yourself and to the prelate, with respect to your fellow brother and to the councils and meetings in the chapter hall."[62] The novice is expected to adapt his conduct, the justice he maintains, not only to the setting in which he finds himself, but also to the individuals he meets in those settings. With respect to himself, the novice is expected to make that "justice of confession" that consists in "accusing himself and responding without any veil of excuses or coverings, so transparent and open, that the prelate can judge clearly of those things which have been said."[63] With respect to his brothers, the novice is to maintain that "justice of correction" which springs from mercy.[64] Similar sorts of guidance are given for dealing with the prelate and council meetings.

Obviously, the anonymous novice master's strategy is not the only one for presenting the novice's spiritual formation and, perhaps more interestingly, it was not the strategy that his sources tended to employ. The contrast with the ascetic and spiritual writings of the twelfth-century Cistercian, William of Saint-Thierry, are valuable in this regard.[65] William,

---

[59] *Libellus*, p. 162, ". . . nunc aliquid tibi dicendum de iusticia quam debes in studio sapiencie conservare."

[60] *Libellus*, p. 174.

[61] *Libellus*, p. 176, "Si vero legis in refectorio, debes servare iusticiam in legendo, ut unicuique, quod suum est, illud des."

[62] *Libellus*, p. 158, "Et ideo de iusticia ista quam debes habere in capitulo, tibi Spiritus sanctus prepositum verbum dicit: 'Ante iudicium para iusticiam' coram eo qui tenet locum Dei in capitulo. Para, inquam, iusticiam et quantum ad teipsum et quantum ad prelatum et quantum ad proximum et quantum ad capituli consilium vel tractatum."

[63] *Libellus*, p. 158, "Et debet esse ista iusticia confessionis in accusando et in respondendo sine omni palliationis et excusationis velamine, ita lucida et aperta, ut de hiis que dicuntur, possit prelatus lucide iudicare."

[64] *Libellus*, p. 159, "Quantum vero ad proximum fratrem tuum debes habere in capitulo illam iusticiam correctionis quam dicebat Psalmista (140, 5): 'Corripiet me iustus in misericordia et increpabit me'. Et bene dicit: in misericordia; non est enim malicia, sed misericordia de hiis que in capitulo sunt dicenda."

[65] The anonymous novice master cites William's *Epistola* at *Libellus*, p. 187. Following established tradition, he thought William's friend, Bernard of Clairvaux, had written the letter. Beyond

a close acquaintance of Bernard of Clairvaux, composed the *Epistola ad fratres de Monte Dei* in the 1130s. After an introductory section in which he praises the Carthusians of Mont Dieu for introducing that "eastern light and ancient Egyptian fervour for religion to our western darkness and French cold, namely the pattern of solitary life,"[66] William proceeds with a narrative of spiritual development. He tells the story of the novice, new to his cell, and his slow progress towards perfection from the state of the animal man to that of the rational and, finally, to the state of the spiritual man. Interspersed throughout the temporal narrative and ordered by the demands of that narrative, William offers advice and prayers to the novice. For example, after describing the state of the animal man, his attempts to free himself from the dependence on bodily pleasure, and the various temptations and consolations that might be visited upon him,[67] William offers advice explicitly geared to the novice in this beginning state. He suggests obedience, daily self-examinations, adherence to a spiritual master and so on.[68]

In William's writings, the Carthusian cell and the Cistercian monastery appear as a single and unified setting in which a narrative of the individual monk's spiritual development unfolds. This narrative of progress seamlessly melds with a narrative of incorporation. As William would put it in a related work, the novice's "miserable soul and degenerate spirit, corrupted by the vice of sin"[69] must slowly be reformed and assimilated into the social structure of the religious community so that one and all "share the same order of life, living one rule, having nothing as their own,

---

this particular quotation, it is worth noting that in the *De officiis ordinis* (in *Vita regulari*, vol. II), p. 230, Humbert of Romans recommends that all Dominican novice masters have their charges read William's *Epistola*, which he also attributes to Bernard. He also recommends works by, among others, Hugh of St. Victor and Hugo of Fouilly (*De disciplina, De claustro animae*), Anselm (*Meditationes, Orationes*) and Augustine (*Confessionum, Abbreviata*).

66  William of Saint-Thierry, *Epistola ad fratres de Monte Dei*, in Paul Verdeyen (ed.), *Guillemi a Sancto Theodorico opera omnia*, vol. 3, p. 228, "Fratribus de Monte Dei, orientale lumen et antiquum illum in religione Aegyptium feruorem tenebris occiduis et gallicanis frigoribus inferentibus, uitae scilicet solitariae exemplar . . ."

67  William, *Epistola*, pp. 233-47.

68  William, *Epistola*, pp. 247-57. For an overview of William's thought and career, see the two works by Jean Déchanet, *Guillaume de Saint-Thierry: aux sources d'une pensee* (Paris: Editions Beauchesne, 1978) and *William of St. Thierry: The Man and his Work*, trans. Richard Strachann (Spencer: Cistercian Publications, 1972). For an examination of the theological ideas behind William's notions concerning spiritual ascent, see Odo Brooke, "William of St. Thierry's Doctrine of the Ascent to God by Faith," in *Studies in Monastic Theology* (Kalamazoo: Cistercian Publications Inc., 1980), pp. 134-207.

69  William of Saint-Thierry, *De natura et dignitate amoris*, chapter 1, in *Opera omnia*, vol. III, p. 177: "Et cum horum nichil a naturae suae tramite aberret, sola misera anima et degener spiritus, cum per se naturaliter eo tendat, peccati uitio corrupta nescit, uel difficile discit ad suum redire principium." *On the Nature and Dignity of Love*, trans. Thomas X. Davis (Kalamazoo: Cistercian Publications, Inc., 1981), p. 48.

not even their bodies or their wills in their own power."[70] The narrative finds its natural conclusion when that assimilation has been realized, when the Carthusian monk who "has been so affected centers himself upon [the good] in such a way as not to be distracted from it until he becomes one or one spirit with it" or when the Cistercian monastery becomes the School of Charity, Jerusalem on earth.[71]

No doubt the Dominican novice's complete incorporation into the order was also a central concern for Dominican novice masters. The regimen of daily life in the priory and the friar's obedience to his superior, "who stands before him as the representative of God himself,"[72] were both aimed at this incorporation. Manuals showing Dominic in different postures of prayer receiving or administering penance with wooden whips or iron chains were utilized as both devotional tools and behavioural models to heighten each friar's identification with Dominic and with the order he founded.[73] Nonetheless, in the *Libellus de instructione*, the Dominican priory, unlike the Carthusian cell or the Cistercian monastery, is not elaborated as the unified setting in which a narrative of progress and incorporation unfolds. Rather, the priory is elaborated into a number of discrete settings in which the novice always finds himself already confronted by an audience, by multiple audiences at once.

Of course, Dominicans were not the first religious order to consider the impression they might make on others and to include instructions on how a person should present himself in various situations. Similar advice crops up in a variety of twelfth-century works, particularly works by regular canons such as Hugh of St. Victor and Hugh of Fouilly. Hugh of St. Victor writes that the novice must learn how "to exhibit himself" and that this requires the "knowledge of discretion." Living a common

---

[70] William of Saint-Thierry, *De natura*, chapter 24, p. 195 (*Nature and Dignity*, p. 82): "Omnia quaecumque faciunt, *in nomine Domini* facientes; simul habitantes uno ordine, una lege uiuentes, nichil habentes proprium, nec ipsa corpora sua, nec uoluntates in potestate sua habentes."

[71] William of Saint-Thierry, *Epistola*, p. 284. *The Golden Epistle: A Letter to the Brethren at Mont Dieu*, trans. Theodore Berkeley (Kalamazoo: Cistercian Publications, Inc., 1980), pp. 98-9. William makes it clear that this spiritual incorporation with God includes participation in the common life of the monastery, *De natura*, p. 268. Making a similar observation with respect to twelfth-century religious life in general, Bynum, "Did the Twelfth Century Discover the Individual?" in *Jesus as Mother*, p. 108, "[T]he goal of development to a twelfth-century person is the application to the self of a model that is simultaneously, exactly because it *is* a model, a mechanism for affiliation with a group."

[72] Hinnebusch, *The History of the Dominican Order*, p. 129.

[73] Jean-Claude Schmitt, "Entre le texte et l'image: les gestes de la prière de Saint Dominique," in Richard Trexler (ed.), *Persons in Groups: Social Behavior as Identity Formation in Medieval and Renaissance Europe*, (Binghamton: Medieval and Renaissance Texts and Studies, 1985), pp. 209-11 and Van Engen, "Dominic and the Brothers," pp. 19-20. For an entertaining, if perhaps dated, overview of this sort of self-disciplining as both a penitential and devotional activity, see Louis Gougaud, *Dévotions et pratiques ascétiques du moyen âge* (Paris: Desclée de Brouwer, 1925).

life with his brothers, the novice must know how to behave before them, must teach them through his example.[74] The anonymous Dominican master would not have disagreed, but within the Dominican context the demand for discretion, to adapt one's self-presentation to a gaze, becomes absolutely central to the order's very self-understanding. This becomes particularly clear when we consider how the Dominican novice master reworks important elements in another of his sources, Hugh of Fouilly's *Cloister of the Soul*.[75] The Dominican novice master clearly knew Hugh's treatise. Not only does he occasionally cite it, he even transposes the organizational metaphor of the soul's cloister onto the Dominican priory. For all that, there are telling differences in how these two works structure their presentation of daily life. In his discussion of life within the material cloister, Hugh primarily is concerned with establishing and preserving harmony within the cloister, with teaching his readers how to create a stable environment "in which the exterior man is held," and within which the interior man can undertake the allegorical and contemplative exercises which he elaborates in the final sections of his treatise.[76] As a result, Hugh seems happy enough to jump around a variety of topics, from guidelines on food and dress to a concluding (and lengthy) discussion on the twelve abuses that throw a cloister "into the greatest turmoil."[77] And while all of this presupposes that the cloister is a social setting in which the canons work together for their salvation, it is only towards the very end of his discussion of life in the material cloister, when he turns his attention to shameful behaviour in the choir and before the altar, that he explicitly raises the idea that the canon is seen and must consider himself

---

74 Hugh of St. Victor, *De institutione novitiorum*, chapter 2, *PL* 176, col. 927b: "Quam timoratum, quam sollicitum, quam devotum ac religiosum in Dei servitio homo exhibere se debeat, quam spontaneum, quam hilarem, et quam paratum offerre in sublevandis necessitatibus proximorum . . ."

75 For a discussion of Hugh's treatise, see Bynum, *Docere verbo et exemplo* (Missoula: Scholar's Press, 1979), pp. 45-8. Despite Hugh's attention to instructing others through gestures, behavior and words, Bynum concludes, p. 48, that "Hugh's awareness of educational responsibility does not have an impact on the form of his treatise. The novice's 'teaching by example' and 'by word' is not carefully fitted into the hierarchy of activities Hugh discusses." See Gerhard Bauer, *Claustrum animae: Untersuchungen zur Geschichte der Metapher vom Herzen als Kloster* (Munich: W. Fink, 1973) and Christiana Whitehead, "Making a Cloister of the Soul in Medieval Religious Treatises" in *Medium Aevum* 47, no. 1 (1998), 11-29, for more general discussions of this allegory in medieval religious writing.

76 Hugo de Folieto, *De claustro animae*, Book I, prologue, *PL* 176, col. 1019: "Primus quidem quid noceat claustralibus vel mundo renuntiare volentibus, continet. Secundus vero claustri materialis ordinationem, in quo tenetur homo exterior, docet. Tertius animae claustrum ordinat. Quartus claustri non manufacti habitationem quae est in coelo, commendat appetendam. Summi quoque abbatis, scilicet Christi, pacem quam ibi habet cum sujectis [*sic*], hic hortatur cum fratribus exhibendam."

77 Hugo de Folieto, *De claustro animae*, II.11, col. 1058: "Duodecim autem sunt abusiones claustri, quibus tota religionis summa turbatur . . ."

as having an audience.[78] For his part, the Dominican novice master begins his discussion of life in the priory with a discussion of how the novice must present himself where he is most visible, when he is in the choir, and this emphasis on visibility continues and structures all that will follow. It is no wonder that the *Libellus*' author begins these chapters with a quote from *Psalms*, "And I will appear with righteousness before your gaze."[79] The Dominican novice is constructed as the object of a gaze, not as the subject of a narrative.

As the constant object of an audience's gaze, the novice is transformed into the subject of continual adjustments. Like the preacher *ad extra*, the novice in the priory must constantly be aware of his self-presentation, of how he appears to others. "Discretion" is the type of knowledge, according to Humbert, that the preacher needs in order to adapt himself to whatever audience confronts him. The anonymous author of the *Libellus* introduces a similar notion into the priory itself. Having discussed the value of silence in the lecture hall, he adds that "with respect to your words, it is necessary that you place a guard over your mouth . . . lest your tongue is in anyway ensnared by hurtful words."[80] However, sometimes the novice must speak, and when he must, the author offers this advice, "Before you speak, you ought to choose the words which you are to speak to others, indeed, you ought to weigh in your soul what you are to say and the reason for your speech . . . These are the conditions of speech which you ought to weigh in your soul and which one grasps in this little verse: When about to speak, ask: what, why, who you are, to whom you speak, what manner and when."[81] And then he adds, "Indeed, you

---

[78] Hugo de Folieto, *De claustro animae*, II.22, col. 1080: "Cum non solum in caeteris officinarum locis, verum etiam in omnibus motibus nihil fiat, quod cujusquam offendat aspectum, congruum mihi fore videtur, ut maxime in ecclesia cum ad opus Dei ventum fuerit, humilitatis honestas diligentibus observetur, ut qui in ecclesiam ante conspectum Dei convenimus, ne ibidem deteriores simus."

[79] *Libellus*, p. 153, "'Ego autem in iusticia apparebo in conspectu tuo'; in Ps. [16,15]." He even cites Hugh's treatise in his discussion of how to behave in the choir, p. 154.

[80] *Libellus*, p. 179, "Quantum ad verba tua, oportet quod ponas custodiam ori tuo, et 'hostium circumstancie labiis tuis', ne ad verba nociva lassetur aliquatenus lingua tua, ut sunt verba mendosa, verba sophistica vel duplicitatis, verba blasphemie, verba periurii . . .'"

[81] *Libellus*, p. 182, "Et ideo antequam loquaris, debes eligere verba que aliis es dicturus, debes siquidem in animo ponderare, quid es dicturus et causam propter quam es locuturus . . . Hee sunt scilicet conditiones locutionis, quas debes in animo ponderare, quas quidam in quodam versiculo comprehendit dicens: quid, cur, quis dicas, cui, quomodo, quando, requiras locuturus." Compare the *Libellus*' list of conditions with the list which Humbert supplies, *De officiis ordinis*, "De officio praedicatoris communis – Qualiter praedicandum," p. 371, "Denique tam in sermonibus publicis, quam in collationibus privatis, advertat praedicator circumstantias, quae continentur in hoc versu: Respice, quid, cur, ubi, cui, quomodo, quando loquaris." While these are, of course, simply the classical rhetorical circumstances, historians of medieval religion have paid little attention to them or the impact they had on religious life and experience when they began to be more regularly incorporated into religious *pastoralia* around 1200. For a general account of their introduction

ought to weigh in your soul with the balance of meditation whether those words which you wish to speak are good or evil, allowable, useful or useless so that, from out of this weighing you do what the Apostle Paul said, 'Never let evil words escape from your mouth, but only what is good for edification.'"[82] The novice manages his self-presentation through a weighing of options, through a constant series of calculations that harmonize his words and activities with whatever situation and audience confronts him (e.g., God, himself, the prelate, a fellow brother – these distinctions are repeated endlessly in the *Libellus*). The demand always to employ the "balance of meditation" is a demand that the novice recognize every setting as the site of a potential edification, be it of himself or of his fellow brothers. It is, likewise, a demand to imagine himself as the object of a continuous gaze that renders him completely "transparent and clear," that constructs him as the site of a constant self-disclosure of the truth, a truth revealed in the carefully managed presentation of his words and deeds.

### NARRATIVES OF PROGRESS/HEURISTICS OF ADAPTATION

If all settings are preaching settings, the Dominican priory can be no exception, and the demands and duties that apply to the preacher in the world, apply no less to the novice in the priory. The centrality of preaching in Dominican life, accordingly, forced Dominicans to conceptualize and construct themselves in new and unique ways. Unlike pre-existing monastic orders, unlike Cistercians and Carthusians, Dominicans did not have the luxury of representing themselves as the subject of a single unified narrative of spiritual progress. Whereas the final goal for these earlier monks, for men like William of Saint-Thierry, was complete assimilation of self to order (and, thereby, of self to God), the Dominican demand to preach *ad extra* diffused that goal. As the relatively self-enclosed and stable setting of the monastery gave way to the open-ended settings that the friar faced in his travels, the goal of assimilation became equally open-ended. It was not enough for the friar to be assimilated to his order, he also needed to assimilate himself to a potentially infinite range of preaching settings. Narratives of progress necessarily gave way to heuristics of adaptation.

---

into pastoralia, see D. W. Robertson, "A Note on the Classical Origin of 'Circumstances' in the Medieval Confessional," *Studies in Philology* 43 (1946), 6-14.

[82] *Libellus*, p. 182, "Siquidem debes in animo ponderare statera meditationis, utrum verba illa que vis loqui, sint bona vel mala, licita, utilia vel inutilia, ut ex hac ponderatione facias quod apostolus Paulus dicit: 'Omnis sermo malus ex ore vestro non procedat, sed si quis bonus est ad edificationem' [Eph. 4:29]."

This demand for constant adaptation, the demand to treat all settings as preaching settings, marked the friar as the site of a constant tension and, perhaps, unease. Sometimes, as remarked upon earlier, this unease manifested itself in an ambivalence towards study, philosophy and learning. But it is captured just as easily in the images they occasionally used to describe themselves, as when Thomas of Cantimpré borrows from Matthew 10:16 to describe young, newly converted preachers, "simple as doves among the cunningly malicious, but at the same time as prudent as serpents in the care of themselves."[83] The friar achieved holy simplicity by employing the scale of meditation, by employing a heuristics of adaptation, and this required wiles and cunning. He could present himself as a dove only by playing the part of the serpent. As a self constructed for an audience, even if that audience consisted only of God and himself, the friar constantly utilized this cunning to balance the various parts of his self-presentation. In an intellectual environment which had inadvertently fostered a degree of tension between study and prayer, for example, in which study was no longer always already inscribed as an inherently devotional activity, this required the friar to adapt his self-presentation when studying not only with respect to himself and to God, but also "with respect to his neighbors and with respect to the order or manner of studying."[84] The failure to adjust was always present and so too was the fear.

What applied to study applied to all settings. Wandering through and preaching in the world, and yet not a part of the world, the friar faced something of a dilemma. He needed to regulate his appearance, his self-presentation, so as both to edify those around him, without being contaminated by them. Humbert recognized the difficulty of achieving this when he noted the preacher's need to "wash away any defilement that he has incurred and repair anything that has got broken" in the course of preaching.[85] This act of cleansing, of self-examination and confession, was itself an act of preaching, of self-edification, and, therefore, also required careful observation, adjustment and adaptation. And for thirteenth-century Dominicans, having constructed a notion of the self as self-presentation, as the continuous object of an audience's gaze, these observations, adjustments and adaptations were everything.

---

[83] Thomas of Cantimpré, *Defense of the Mendicants*, in Tugwell (ed.), *Early Dominicans*, p. 135.

[84] *Libellus*, p. 162, "Si ergo tu studes in studio sapiencie salutaris, sapienciam concupiscens, oportet ut iusticiam habeas et conserves, et hoc quantum ad te ipsum, et quantum ad Deum, et quantum ad proximum, et quantum ad studendi ordinem sive modum."

[85] Humbert, *Liber de eruditione praedicatorum*, IV.19, p. 427, "Debet enim sapiens praedicator post praedicationes regressum ad se redire, et quae contigerunt subtiliter considerare, ut abstergat sordes si quas contraxit, et reparet dissipata . . ."

# Chapter 2

# THE DEVIL IN HUMAN FORM:
# CONFESSION, DECEPTION AND
# SELF-KNOWLEDGE

In his *Dialogue of Miracles*, Caesarius of Heisterbach tells the story of a woman who came to give her annual Lenten confession. Kneeling before the priest, she "began to pour forth all the good deeds she could remember ever having done" and every fast she had ever undertaken. When the priest asked why she did not confess her sins, the woman replied that she was not aware of having committed any. The priest asked her to name her profession and, learning that she sold bits of iron, he began to question her. "Do you ever mix smaller pieces in bundles of larger pieces?" She admitted that, yes, she sometimes did this. "There is one mortal sin for that is deceit. Do you tell lies, perjure yourself or speak poorly of your rivals?" Again she admitted that, yes, sometimes she did these things as well. "These too are mortal sins and unless you accept and carry out a severe penance, you will quickly go to hell." And the upshot of all this? Caesarius concludes his tale, "At these words the woman was frightened, realized that she had sinned and learned how she ought to confess for the future."[1] The story is a rather plain one. Lacking the supernatural or miraculous elements that characterize so many medieval stories about confession, that characterize so many of Caesarius' own stories, it simply tells the tale of a woman who was more than a little unclear about how to confess and of a priest who was more than happy to correct the error of her ways.

## PRIVATE CONTRITION AND PUBLIC DISCIPLINE

Mendicant preachers and novices were taught always to think about themselves in terms of how they appeared to others, to think about themselves in terms of their self-presentation. In one way, Caesarius' female iron seller is no different. The point of the tale, at least one of its points, is that she does not know how to present herself properly before

[1] Caesarius of Heisterbach, *Dialogus miraculorum*, III.46, Josephus Strange (Cologne: H. Lempertz & Comp, 1851), p. 165. *The Dialogue on Miracles*, trans. H. Scott and C. C. Swinton Bland (London: G. Routledge & Sons, 1929), pp. 185–6.

her confessor. This failure, however, points to a larger failure. She fails to make an adequate confession, fails to present herself before her confessor as a sinner, because she does not really know herself, does not realize that she is, in fact, a sinner. As we saw in the previous chapter, there are similar moments in the *Liber de eruditione praedicatorum*, moments in which Humbert of Romans begins to problematize the relation between the preacher's self-presentation and his real inner self. The preacher might present himself to others as holy while, slowly but surely, a desire and lust for worldly acclaim replaces true holiness. It is at these moments that Humbert advises the preacher to scrutinize his conscience and to confess. Confession, for both the preacher as well as for Caesarius' female iron-seller, marks an inward turn in which the emphasis on self-presentation gives way to an emphasis on self-knowledge, to a knowledge of one's own conscience and of one's own sins.

It is precisely because of its emphasis on self-knowledge that historians have often cited the rise of private or personal confession as evidence of a twelfth-century "discovery of the individual."[2] For increasing numbers of the religious and the more religiously inclined among the laity, the activity of private confession during that century seemed to involve the cultivation of a sort of private life, a personal experience of piety, and a sense of self as, in part at least, independent from others. "It is easy enough for anyone to confess his sins, to accuse himself, or even to mortify his body in outward show of penance," Heloise would write to her one-time lover, now spiritual mentor and always beloved, Abelard, "but it is very difficult to tear the heart away from hankering after its dearest pleasures."[3] Difficult or not, Heloise was hardly alone in thinking that those hidden yearnings of a private heart mattered more than mere words. They were the very fulcrum on which the success of the confessional enterprise rested. Already in the late eleventh century, the unknown author of the influential treatise *On True and False Penance* had said as much when he identified and examined these two elements of confession. All penance is sterile, he notes, which is not accompanied by "the tears of [the penitent's] mind."[4]

---

[2] Morris, *Discovery*, pp. 70–5. See pp. 14–15 for a fuller discussion of Morris' claim.

[3] J. T. Muckle (ed.), "The Personal Letters Between Abelard and Heloise," *Medieval Studies* 15 (1953), 80: "Facile quidem est quemlibet confitendo peccata seipsum accusare, aut etiam in exteriori satisfactione corpus affligere. Difficilimum vero est a desideriis maximarum voluptatum avellere animam." *The Letters of Abelard and Heloise*, trans. Betty Radice (London: Penguin Books Ltd, 1974), p. 132.

[4] Ps.-Augustine, *De vera et falsa poenitentia*, IX.24, *PL* 40, col. 1121: "Poenitentia enim vera ad Baptismi puritatem, poenitentem conatur adducere. Recte enim poenitens quidquid sordis post purificationem contraxit, oportet quod abluat saltem lacrymis mentis." On dating this treatise, see Sarah Hamilton, *The Practice of Penance, 900–1050* (Woodbridge: The Boydell Press, 2001), p. 15.

The evaluation of this inner sense of suffering or "contrition" throughout the twelfth century posed certain theological and institutional challenges. As writers continued to emphasize the role of contrition, it became increasingly difficult for them to explain why a penitent needed to confess his sins to a priest at all. To many, though certainly not to all theologians, the actual forgiveness of sins seemed to be an entirely private transaction between a contrite sinner and a merciful God.[5] While Peter Abelard, for example, never denied the value of confession to a priest, his account of sin and its relation to the soul made it almost impossible to locate any intrinsic reason why confession required priestly mediation. Abelard argued that since "nothing pollutes the soul except what is of the soul," it followed that only a cleansing disposition of the soul could remove that pollution.[6] It was for this reason that Abelard would locate absolution entirely in contrition, in the soul's own sorrow over its evil dispositions. Only the soul's remorse could remove its guilt before God and, in so doing, remove the penalty of eternal damnation. In his *Book of Sentences*, a treatise that would give shape to all subsequent scholastic theological discourse, Peter Lombard would go so far as to argue that even "without oral confession and the payment of exterior penances, sins are deleted through contrition and humiliation of heart."[7] Exiled from the actual process of forgiveness, the priest was relegated to a declaratory role. Having heard the confession, the priest merely indicates God's willingness to forgive the penitent.[8]

Interpreting motives is always a difficult matter and interpreting the motives behind twelfth-century theological discussions of confession is no exception. Some historians, for example, have suggested that the continuing emphasis that theologians like Abelard and Lombard placed on

---

5 Marcia L. Colish, *Peter Lombard* (Leiden: E. J. Brill, 1994), vol. 2, pp. 583–609, offers a concise account of how this debate appeared to Abelard's contemporaries. Also, Pierre-Marie Gy, "Les Bases de la pénitence moderne," *La Maison Dieu* 117 (1974), 66–8. Paul Anciaux, *La Théologie du sacrement de pénitence au XIIe siècle* (Louvain: Nauwelaerts, 1949), analyzes the issue at length for the entire twelfth century.

6 Peter Abelard, *Ethics*, ed. and trans. D. E. Luscombe (Oxford: Clarendon Press, 1971), p. 22: "Nichil ergo ad augmentum peccati pertinet qualiscumque operum executio, et nichil animam nisi quod ipsius est coinquinat . . ."

7 Peter Lombard, *Sententiarum libri quattuor*, book 4, distinctio 17, in *Sententiae in IV libris distinctae*, 3rd edn., rev., ed. Ignatius C. Brady (Grottaferrata: Collegii S. Bonaventurae ad Claras Aquas, 1971–81.), p. 610: "Sane dici potest, quod sine confessione oris, et solutione poenae exterioris peccata delentur per contritionem et humilitatem cordis. Ex quo enim proponit mente compuncta se confessurum, Deus dimittit: quia ibi est confessio cordis, etsi non oris: per quam anima interius mundatur a macula et contagio peccati commissi, et debitum aeternae mortis relaxatur."

8 Peter Lombard, *Sent.* 4, d. 18, p. 620: "Non autem hoc sacerdotibus concessit, quibus tamen tribuit potestatem solvendi et ligandi, id est, ostendendi homines ligatos vel solutos. Unde Dominus leprosum sanitati prius per se restituit, deinde ad sacerdotes misit, quorum judicio ostenderetur mundatus. Ita etiam Lazarum jam vivificatum obtulit discipulis solvendum. Quia etsi aliquis apud Deum sit solutus, non tamen in facie Ecclesiae solutus habetur, nisi per judicium sacerdotis."

contrition reveals their failure to create a complete sacramental theory. They failed, that is, to create a theory in which the "subjective" and "objective" components of confession were fully wedded, in which the penitent's contrition and the priest's absolution played an integral role.[9] While it is certainly true that no theologian during this period developed a fully integrated account of confession, it is by no means clear that this lack of integration, this supposed failure, would have bothered them. The continued interest in contrition may well indicate an entirely different motive, one that recalls the notion of a twelfth-century discovery of the individual. Far from attempting to bring contrition in line with the other elements of penance, other historians have contended that the ongoing valorization of contrition seems to represent a "theological manifestation of the longing for privacy." The emphasis on the penitent's inner sorrow might well be yet another example of a general desire for privacy and autonomy, a desire evident throughout twelfth-century culture.[10] This motive is particularly clear in the widely held distinction between exterior and interior sins. Towards the end of the twelfth century, for example, Alan of Lille noted that exterior sins, such as murder and theft, were sins against God and the community. These types of deeds offended God and provided a bad example to one's neighbours. While contrition appeased God, only the imposition and performance of private or public penance could make good the injury done to society. Interior sins, however, differed from exterior sins because they did not offer an "example of sinning to one's neighbour." To cultivate an awareness of these sins, to cry alone over them with the desire not to repeat them, was itself to perform a penance worthy of expiation. In other words, Alan employs the distinction between interior and exterior sins as the basis for a distinction between two different kinds of penance, one of which works independently of any priestly interference. It arises freely from within the penitent's heart and is in no way imposed from without by the church.[11]

---

[9] Bernhard Poschmann, *Penance and the Anointing of the Sick*, trans. Francis Courtney (London: Burns & Oates, 1964), p. 157, argues that the theological elaboration of penance during this period was undertaken for the sole purpose of determining "the intrinsic relationship of the different factors of penance to each other and then the subsumption of the entire process under the concept of a sacrament, which at that period had recently been worked out." Also, Pierre-Marie Gy, "Les Définitions de la confession après le quatrième concile du Latran," in *L'Aveu: antiquité et moyen-âge* (Rome: Ecole Française de Rome, 1986), p. 288.

[10] Mary Mansfield, *The Humiliation of Sinners: Public Penance in Thirteenth-Century France* (Ithaca: Cornell University Press, 1995), p. 37. Georges Duby, "Solitude: Eleventh to Thirteenth Century," in Georges Duby and Phillippe Aries (eds.), *A History of Private Life* (Cambridge: Belknap Press, 1987), vol. 2, pp. 511–14, discusses in rather broad terms the growing desire for privacy as witnessed in such things as the increased use of locks, the growing popularity of solitary religious professions and even in the intimacies glorified in the literature of courtly love.

[11] I follow closely Mansfield's interpretation of Alan of Lille, *Humiliation*, p. 37. Alan of Lille, *Liber poenitentialis*, III.3, ed. Jean Longère (Louvain: Editions Nauwelaerts, 1965), vol. 2, pp. 128–7.

Although the value of self-examination was never disputed among thirteenth-century theologians, the independent efficacy of a privately cultivated contrition (and the private life which could arise around it) certainly came under fire. While everyone agreed that contrition was necessary for absolution and that works of satisfaction performed without contrition were works performed in vain, it became more difficult for theologians to imagine contrition as an independent and private means of penance. Increasingly, it was conceived as a step in the process of confession depending ultimately upon the confessor who spoke the words, "I absolve you," and ending with some form of external satisfaction. Central to this transformation in the meaning and role of contrition were the rapid advancements that theologians made in more fully integrating contrition with the other two elements of penance, with oral confession to a priest and the performance of penance. Slowly, it would seem, the hidden world of contrition opened itself to priestly mediation. No doubt the Dominican theologian Thomas Aquinas was central in completing certain aspects of this transformation. In his commentary on Lombard's *Sentences*, Thomas contends that the efficacy of penance comes from the priest's absolution, which bestows a form on the penitent's contrition, confession and satisfaction, and, in so doing, makes them worthy of justification. While acts of confession and satisfaction attest to and signify the presence of contrition, Thomas also argues that these acts, when linked to the priest's absolution, actually cause contrition, the infusion of grace that allows the soul to reject sin and love God.[12] Even the Scotists, who argued that true contrition was possible outside of the sacrament of penance, emphasized the power of the priest's absolution to transform attrition (that sorrow for sin which, although genuine, is not as profound

A form of the distinction can already be found in Abelard, *Ethics*, p. 99, who differentiates faults of the mind from public and solitary deeds.

[12] Thomas Aquinas, *Sent.* book 4, distinction 22, question 2, article 1, solution 2, in *Opera omnia*, vol. 7: "Exterior autem poenitentia, quae est sacramentum tantum in poenitentia, est sacramentum ut signum tantum ex parte actus poenitentis, sed ut signum et causa simul, si conjungatur actus poenitentis cum actu ministri; et ideo interior poenitentia est res exterioris poenitentiae; sed ut significata tantum per actus poenitentis; ut significata autem et causata per actus eosdem, adjuncta absolutione ministri, per quam aliquo modo homo ad gratiam disponitur; sicut etiam in sacramento eucharistiae corpus Christi verum est res significata tantum per species panis et vini, sed causata per verba ministri; et illa duo simul conjuncta sunt signum et causa." On the division of the sacrament into matter and form see distinction 22, q. 2, a. 2, sol. 2: "Ad secundam quaestionem dicendum, quod in sacramentis in quibus est materia et forma, significatio est ex parte materiae principaliter, sed efficacia ex parte formae; et ideo cum actus poenitentis in hoc sacramento sint sicut materia, et absolutio sacerdotis sicut forma; principaliter hoc sacramentum quantum ad rationem significandi consistit in actu poenitentis; sed quantum ad efficaciam, in absolutione sacerdotis." Poschmann, *Penance*, pp. 168–83, from whose work I draw heavily for my understanding of the thirteenth- and fourteenth-century theological discussions of penance, offers a succinct account and criticism of Thomas' position.

as the sorrow of contrition) into contrition. The priest's absolution was necessary as a guarantee that the penitent had sorrowed enough.[13]

Just as the attention that writers like Peter Abelard and Peter Lombard paid to contrition is often taken as evidence for an increased sense of self or a renewed sense of personal privacy, the various transformations in the role of and access to contrition in the thirteenth and fourteenth centuries are often viewed as developments that slowed down, shut down or even reversed these advances. This transformation is sometimes seen as part of a hidden agenda to humiliate sinners, to render all sin and all penance public.[14] Or it is seen as part of the formalism and legalism that came to characterize confession as it moved from an activity of a devoted few to an activity imposed upon all Christians. After all, contrition cannot be mandated (not even if only once a year during Lent). Focus, therefore, was displaced from a hidden and private contrition to the penitent's avowal of sin before the confessor and the confessor's act of absolution.[15] The stage was now set, according to this line of reasoning, for confession to become a method of social control imposed by an increasingly hierarchical ecclesiastical structure.[16]

All of which brings us back to where we started, back to Caesarius' female iron seller and her patently insufficient confession. It should bring us back, because Caesarius' little tale points to yet another dimension of confession, a dimension that reveals something like the hidden logic and deeper affinities that unite confessional practice between, say, the late eleventh and fifteenth centuries. It is all too easy to lose sight of this dimension when we focus too narrowly on medieval debates concerning contrition or move too quickly towards the allegedly social and disciplinary ramifications of confession. One way to grasp these affinities is

---

[13] Gy, "Les Définitions de la confession," discusses many of these thirteenth-century developments.

[14] Mansfield, *The Humiliation of Sinners*, pp. 34–49.

[15] Jean Charles Payen, "La Pénitence dans le contexte culturel des XIIe et XIIIe siècles: des doctrine contritionistes aux pénitentiels vernaculaires," *Revue des sciences philosophiques et théologiques* 61 (1977), 418–22. Also, Jean Delumeau, *Sin and Fear: The Emergence of a Western Guilt Culture 13th–18th Centuries*, trans. Eric Nicholson (New York: St. Martin's Press, 1990), pp. 197–8.

[16] Thomas N. Tentler, *Sin and Confession on the Eve of the Reformation* (Princeton: Princeton University Press, 1977), pp. 345–9 and "The Summa for Confessors as an Instrument of Social Control," in Charles Trinkaus and Heiko A. Oberman (eds.), *The Pursuit of Holiness in Late Medieval and Renaissance Religion* (Leiden: E. J. Brill, 1974), pp. 109–13. Also, Lester K. Little, "Les Techniques de la confession et la confession comme technique," in *Faire croire: modalités de la diffusion et de la réception des messages religieux du XIIe au XVe siècle* (Rome: Ecole Française de Rome, 1981), pp. 97–8, Roberto Rusconi, "De la Prédication à la confession: transmission et controle de modèles de comportement au XIIIe siècle," in *Faire croire*, pp. 67–85 and R. N. Swanson, *Religion and Devotion in Europe, c.1215–c.1515* (Cambridge: Cambridge University Press, 1995), pp. 25–6 and 236–8. Lawrence G. Duggan, "Fear and Confession on the Eve of the Reformation", *Archiv für Reformationsgeschichte*, 75 (1984), 162, argues that there is no evidence pointing towards the *effective* use of confession as an agent of social control.

simply to recognize that penitents were never encouraged to look within themselves and report whatever they might find. Confession required a very specific sort of self-examination and the techniques employed in conducting that examination went quite a long way in determining the sort of self-awareness that it generated, the sort of self and inner privacy that it created and discovered. The iron seller quite clearly does not know how to conduct this kind of investigation. Realizing this, the confessor steps in and interrogates her in order to help her identify her sins more fully. The goal of this telling and questioning, of this questioning and retelling, is a complete and adequate statement of sins. The iron-seller and her confessor work together to create this statement. It is through this statement that the iron-seller discovers the truth about herself. And it is this statement that the priest uses to judge the penitent's sinfulness and to assign penance.

Seen in this light, confession is an epistemological practice. It is a carefully organized activity that links the penitent's spiritual well-being with the acquisition of a very particular form of self-knowledge.[17] As an epistemological practice, confession seeks to form its proper object out of the penitent's often scattered and disparate memories. The penitent's conscience, with all the sins it houses, is present to the confessor through this object, through this confession. The confessor comes to know the penitent by scrutinizing and examining her confession, by guiding and correcting her responses. But the same thing can be said about the penitent herself. She comes to know herself in precisely the same manner as the confessor comes to know her. She realizes she is a sinner through the activity of confessing to her priest, through reflecting on her own confession. Without this interaction, without the self-knowledge it generates, she would have had no reason to feel contrite because she would never have thought of herself as a sinner in the first place. With its complicated mix of introspective analysis and social interaction, the self-examination promoted by the practice of confession was anything but straightforward. Indeed, Caesarius' tale suggests that when it comes to the sort of introspection and self-examination practiced during the middle ages, knowing

---

[17] The term "practice" is a tricky one, capable of describing just about everything and, therefore, nothing. The most useful definition that I know of (and the one I have in mind here) comes from Alasdair MacIntyre, *After Virtue: A Study in Moral Theory* (Notre Dame: University of Notre Dame Press, 1981), p. 175, a practice is "any coherent and complex form of socially established cooperative activity through which goods internal to that form of activity are realised in the course of trying to achieve those standards of excellence which are appropriate to, and partially definitive of, that form of activity, with the result that human powers to achieve excellence, and human conceptions of the ends and goods involved, are systematically extended." Much of this chapter will consist in carefully describing the exact form of confessional practice and in charting whether that practice could lead the penitent to the practice's avowed goals.

oneself might not have been that different from knowing somebody else.

DECREES AND HANDBOOKS

In 1215, in Canon 21, the Fourth Lateran Council gave something of an official form to the idea and practice of private confession that had evolved during the course of the prior 150 years. It was not the first time church officials had addressed the importance, even the necessity, of confession. As early as the mid-eighth century, local synods had occasionally referred to confession, either suggesting, requesting or requiring certain classes of the faithful to confess once, twice, sometimes three times a year.[18] These, however, were local regulations whose impact is still a source of controversy.[19] Lateran IV's confessional decree was different. As the pronouncement of a universal church council, it embodied a particular interpretation of confession, an interpretation which was then disseminated throughout Europe as an ideal minimum which all the faithful, laymen and clerics alike, were expected to meet.

As a minimum standard, Canon 21 or *Omnis utriusque* (as it came to be known) certainly does not seem to have required much. On the one hand, it required "all the faithful of either sex, after they have reached the age of discretion," to confess once a year to their own priest and to perform certain required acts of satisfaction. Having confessed and barring other problems, they were also expected to receive the Eucharist each year, at Easter. Priests, on the other hand, were expected to inquire intelligently and diligently into the nature and circumstances of each penitent's sins. The entire process was conceived by analogy with medicine. The confessor was modelled after a doctor who was charged not only with curing the wound (of sin), but with isolating and eliminating its causes. The penitent was a patient whose spiritual illness was disclosed through confession. The confessor makes a diagnosis, imposes a specific cure (penance) and

---

[18] Poschmann, *Penance*, pp. 139–45. For example, around 760, Chrodegang of Metz required his canons, as well as the poor who were supported by his church, to confess at the beginning of Lent and in the autumn.

[19] Alexander Murray, "Confession before 1215," *Transactions of the Royal Historical Society*, 6th series, 3 (1993), 51–81, argues against the widespread practice of private confession prior to the twelfth century. It is possible, however, that this traditional view is slowly being supplanted. For a summary of recent work to this effect see Rob Meens, "The Frequency and Nature of Early Medieval Penance," in Peter Biller and A. J. Minnis (eds.), *Handling Sin: Confession in the Middle Ages* (Woodbridge: Boydell & Brewer Ltd.), pp. 35–61 and Hamilton, *The Practice of Penance*, pp. 207–10, who suggests that penitential practice was widespread and varied during the tenth and eleventh centuries, and that the apparent sudden popularity of personal confession during the twelfth century is really little more than a "trick of the evidential light," the result of greater manuscript production and survival.

makes suggestions to prevent a relapse. Implicit throughout the decree is the assumption that the priest plays more than a mere declaratory role in the process of forgiveness. He does not simply announce whom God has cured. He plays an active role in bringing about that cure. The constitution closes with a stern warning concerning the secrecy that must surround confession and the penalties any priest will suffer should he betray those secrets (deposition from the priesthood, confinement to a "strict monastery" and perpetual penance). However, should a priest need wise advice, the constitution does allow him to "seek it cautiously without any mention of the person concerned."[20]

All of this may seem fairly straightforward, but it probably would have been news to most laypeople (like Caesarius' iron seller) who did not know how to make an individual confession, not to mention to many priests who likely did not know how to interrogate a penitent. In order for the decree for annual confession to be implemented, not only did it need to be transmitted from council to bishop and from bishop to deacon and so on, all the way down the ecclesiastic hierarchy until it finally reached the parish priest whose duty ultimately it would be to hear the majority of confessions,[21] but priests themselves needed to learn how to conduct a confession. Lateran IV's universal pastoral demands, in

---

[20] Norman P. Tanner (ed. and trans.), *Decrees of the Ecumenical Councils* (Washington, DC: George-town University Press, 1990), vol. 1, p. 245. The full text of Canon 21 reads: "Omnis utriusque sexus fidelis, postquam ad annos discretionis pervenerit, omnia sua solus peccata confiteatur fideliter, saltem semel in anno proprio sacerdoti, et iniunctam sibi poenitentiam studeat pro viribus adimplere, suscipiens reverenter ad minus in pascha eucharistiae sacramentum, nisi forte de consilio proprii sacerdotis ob aliquam rationabilem causam ad tempus ab eius perceptione duxerit abstinendum; alioquin et vivens ab ingressu ecclesiae arceatur et moriens christiana careat sepultura. Unde hoc salutare statutum frequenter in ecclesiis publicetur, ne quisquam ignorantiae caecitate velamen excusationis assumat. Si quis autem alieno sacerdoti voluerit iusta de causa sua confiteri peccata, licentiam prius postulet et obtineat a proprio sacerdote, cum aliter ille ipsum non possit solvere vel ligare. Sacerdos autem sit discretus et cautus, ut more periti medici superinfundat vinum et oleum vulneribus sauciati, diligenter inquirens et peccatoris circumstantias et peccati, per quas prudenter intelligat, quale illi consilium debeat exhibere et cuiusmodi remedium adhibere, diversis experimentis utendo ad sanandum aegrotum. Caveat autem omnino, ne verbo vel signo vel alio quovis modo prodat aliquatenus peccatorem, sed si prudentiori consilio indiguerit, illud absque ulla expressione personae caute requirat, quoniam qui peccatum in poenitentiali iudicio sibi detectum praesumpserit revelare, non solum a sacredotali officio deponendum decernimus, verum etiam ad agendam perpetuam poenitentiam in arctum monasterium detrudendum." Gy, "Les Définitions de la confession," 288, suggests Canon 21 be read in conjunction with Canon 10, which required bishops to make sure there were adequate numbers of men in their diocese to act as preachers and confessors. The net effect of these two canons and much of thirteenth-century theological development was to more fully unite the practice of hearing confessions and imposing penance. On theological speculation concerning the requirement for annual confession, Pierre-Marie Gy, "Le Précepte de la confession annuelle (Latran IV, C. 21) et la détection des hérétiques," *Revue des sciences philosophiques et théologiques* 58 (1974), 444–50.

[21] H. Leith Spencer, *English Preaching in the Late Middle Ages* (Oxford: Clarendon Press, 1993), pp. 201–7, discusses the "cumbersome" apparatus through which council and synod statutes were passed on in medieval England.

short, created the need for a better educated clergy and to meet this need the religious of all sorts began composing treatises and handbooks at a remarkable rate.[22] These works varied in both style and size, ranging from huge and expensively bound academic texts like Raymond of Penafort's *Summa de casibus poenitentiae* to crib sheets consisting of little more than a few folds of vellum containing the briefest of guidelines to help a local priest fulfill his duties. Copied and recopied, revised and rewritten, often by anonymous scribes who produced "new" manuals by compiling selected sections from previous ones, these manuals exercised a decisive influence on how priests and laymen came to understand the importance and practice of confession, an influence that continued well into the fifteenth and sixteenth centuries as many of them became quite popular as printed texts.[23]

Despite this thirteenth-century upsurge in production, confessional treatises did not form a new genre. Early medieval penitentials or handbooks of penance, such as the Irish *Penitential of Finian*, which dates from the first half of the sixth century, are undoubtedly the ancestors of these post-1215 manuals.[24] Much less removed were the sorts of confessional works that began to appear in the mid-eleventh century, like *On True and False Penance* and Lanfranc's *De celanda confessione*. Not only do thirteenth- and fourteenth-century manuals repeatedly cite and borrow from these late eleventh- and twelfth-century manuals, there is also a clear continuity of ideas, interests and goals. The emphasis on discerning the circumstances surrounding a penitent's sin, the need for complete confessions, and even some of the methods suggested for drawing out confessions from reticent penitents are common to almost every manual written between the eleventh and early sixteenth century.

---

[22] Leonard E. Boyle, "The Fourth Lateran Council and Manuals of Popular Theology," in Thomas J. Heffernan (ed.), *The Popular Literature of Medieval England*, (Knoxville: The University of Tennessee Press, 1985), pp. 31–43, discusses the relation between Lateran IV and the "rash of aids for confessors" which appeared over the next several hundred years. The best overview of this vast pastoral literature is still Pierre Michaud-Quantin, *Sommes de casuistique et manuels de confession au moyen âge (XII–XVI siecles)*, Analecta mediaevalia namurcensia, 3 (Louvain, 1962) and his article "A Propos des premières *Summae confessorum*: théologie et droit canonique," *Recherches de théologie ancienne et médiévale* 26 (1959), 264–306. A more recent and quite excellent study is Joseph Goering, "The Internal Forum and the Literature of Penance and Confession," in W. Harmann and K. Pennington (eds.), *History of Medieval Canon Law* (Washington, DC: Catholic University Press of America, 2001), pp. 1–75.

[23] Tentler, *Sin and Confession*, pp. 46–9.

[24] John T. McNeil and Helena M. Gamer (eds. and trans.), *Medieval Handbooks of Penance: A Translation of the Principal "Libri poenitentiales" and Selections from Related Documents* (New York: Columbia University Press, 1938) provides a selection of these early manuals. Raymund Kottje (ed.), *Paenitentialia minora Franciae et Italiae saeculi VIII–IXe*, Corpus Christianorum, Series Latina, 156 (Turnhout: Brepols, 1994) contains critical editions of many of the early Continental manuals. Meens, "Frequency," pp. 39–47, examines their uses and intended audience.

None of this is meant to imply that confessional pastoralia manifest no development during the later middle ages. Over time their organization changes. The categories, lists and rubrics of interrogation expand. They occasionally exhibit a greater sense of psychological insight and a more explicit awareness of the problems involved in making and hearing confessions. These developments are neither opposed nor external to the structure and practice of confession as outlined in earlier manuals. Rather, they are often outgrowths of problems already present in those earlier manuals (if often left implicit or only briefly noted). It is in the recognition of these continuing problems, in the evolution of these internal possibilities, that confessional treatises can be read as something more than mere pedagogical tools. The very practices they describe, elaborate and adjust, reveal a set of epistemological presuppositions at work within the activity of confession itself. Simply put, confessional pastoralia are witnesses to an ongoing discussion in problems of practical epistemology and self-examination. And it is these practices (and the problems they generated), not the theological debates concerning contrition and priestly absolution, that determined the sort of self-awareness, the sort of self, that was discovered and created through the practice of medieval confession.

## THE IDEAL OF TRANSPARENCY

The penitent confesses his sins to the confessor. This is an act of disclosure and of revelation. The ideal confession is one in which the penitent makes a complete disclosure, in which he becomes transparent to himself and to his confessor. Hiding one's sins accomplishes nothing. There is no hidden thing, no "ulcer of perverse conscience," Peter of Blois warned during the second half of the twelfth century, that will not be revealed on the day of judgment.[25] It is with this sort of threat in mind that, over a century earlier, the author of *On True and False Penance* had recommended that "the penitent should represent his life to God through a priest and should anticipate God's judgment through confession."[26] When this occurs, when the penitent confesses fully, Lanfranc noted, "[t]wo consciences cross over into one, namely that of the confessant into [the conscience] of him to whom he confesses, and of the judge into

---

[25] Peter of Blois, *Liber de confessione sacramentali*, PL 207, col. 1079B: "Quare dissimulas mortiferum vulnus? Ulcus pravae conscientiae, quod nunc pallias, quandoque in multa tui confusione publice revelabitur, cum in conspectu omnium sanctorum ante tribunal tremendi Judicis stabis nudus; nihil enim occultum, quod ibi non reveletur."

[26] Ps.-Augustine, *De vera et falsa poenitentia*, chapter 10, PL 40, col. 1122: "Quem igitur poenitet, omnino poeniteat, et dolorem lacrymis ostendat: repraesentet vitam suam Deo sacerdotem, praeveniat judicium Dei per confessionem."

him whom he judges." Not only does the penitent find himself joined to his confessor in this act, but more significantly, "God and man come together within the same judgment, because he who judges himself at that very moment acts with God."[27] Unfortunately, differences remain between these two unions, between penitent and confessor and between penitent and God, and the history of personal confession can be read as the never-ending effort to overcome or at least somewhat mitigate that difference. After all, God can see directly into the penitent's heart, but the confessor certainly cannot. Access to the penitent's life as a sinner comes primarily from the penitent's confession itself, from what the penitent reveals and from what the confessor can discern and infer from those revelations. The confession stands between the penitent and confessor as the intermediary through which that hidden life of sin appears.

These eleventh-century texts influenced attitudes towards personal confession throughout the twelfth century and beyond. Nearly 150 years later, Robert Grosseteste, future Bishop of Lincoln, recognized the intermediary status of oral confession when he described confession as a narration (*narratio*) of one's sins. Naturally, some narrations are better than others, and a sufficient narration is one which is "true, complete, full, plain, bitter and modest."[28] By the time Grosseteste wrote, these criteria had for all intents and purposes become (depending on one's perspective) either clichés or well-established technical terms with rather specific meanings. Around the turn of the century, Alan of Lille had discussed them in his *Liber poenitentialis* and the London-born, Paris-educated, theologian William de Montibus had composed verses that he hoped would allow students to recall them with greater ease.[29] The unknown author of *On True and False Penance* had already written about many of them and

---

[27] Lanfranc, *Libellus de celanda confessione*, PL 150, col. 627A–B: "Duae conscientiae in unam transeunt, confitentis scilicet in ejus cui confitetur, et judicantis in ejusdem qui judicatur. Hanc unitatem imprecatur Filius Dei apud Patrem: *Ut et ipsi in nobis*, inquiens, *unum sint, sicut tu Pater in me, et ego in te (Joan.,* xvii, 21). Deus et homo in eodem judicio conveniunt, quia qui se judicat, jam cum Deo facit (*Aug. tract.* 12, *in Joan.* sub finem). Unde et latro in cruce cum dixisset: *Nos quidem digna factis recipimus (Luc.* xxiii, 41), quia cum Domino se judicavit, cum Domino in paradiso est."

[28] Robert Grosseteste, *Deus est*, in Siegfried Wenzel (ed.), "Robert Grosseteste's Treatise on Confession, 'Deus est'," *Franciscan Studies* 30 (1970), 247: "Poenitentia, cuius ut praeostenditur est pars prima omnium peccatorem sufficiens narratio. Sufficiens quidem erit narratio cum vera fuerit, integra, plana, nuda, amara, verecunda." Thomas Aquinas also alludes to confession as a narration and to the problems that arise out of its intermediary role in *Sent.*, book 4, distinctio 17, q. 3, a. 4, sol. 1: "Ad tertium dicendum, quod ille qui peccata quae habet, narrat, vere loquitur, et sic cor concordat verbis quantum ad substantiam confessionis, quamvis cor discordet a confessionis fine."

[29] William de Montibus, *Peniteas cito peccator*, in Joseph Goering (ed. and trans.), *William de Montibus (c. 1140–1213): The Schools and Literature of Pastoral Care* (Toronto: Pontifical Institute of Mediaeval Studies, 1992), pp. 119–20, lines 21–5: "Vera sit, integra sit, et sit confessio munda. /Sit cita, firma, frequens, humilis, spontanea, nuda, /Propria, discreta, lacrimosa, morosa, fidelis. /Peniteas plene si uere peniteat te, /Non per legatum, non per breue, set refer ipse." In his introduction

hardly a handbook or summa on confession to be written for the next several hundred years lacked some variant on this list.

Grosseteste, accordingly, was writing in something of the confessional mainstream when he went on to explain that a confession is true if the penitent confesses "those things which he did and not those things which he did not do." It is complete if "he tells everything he did to one person" (as opposed to telling certain sins to one confessor and the rest to another). It is full if he discloses "every circumstance which augments or diminishes the sin itself." It is plain (*nuda*), if it is told without "circumlocutions that whitewash sin." It is bitter if the penitent accuses himself of his deeds and does not excuse himself and it is modest if he uses confession to cleanse and purge himself of sin and not as an opportunity to brag about his failings.[30] Some confessional writings had much longer lists, some had fewer. Whatever their length, these lists marked the general criteria of a successful confession, a confession that truthfully represented the sinner to the confessor and to himself. The more fully these criteria were met, the more fully the confession represented what God saw immediately, without the need of any intermediary appearances or representations.

### STAGE SETTING

If handled improperly, confessions could all too easily go awry.

Having just given birth after a difficult pregnancy, weakened, ill and fearing for her life, twenty-year-old Margery of Kempe seeks out her confessor. It seems that Margery had for some time been too embarrassed, too ashamed and too scared to reveal a certain sin that daily troubled her conscience. The devil, Margery would later dictate to a priest who recorded her story in the 1430s, had encouraged this secrecy, advising her that even without confession, so long as she did penance on her own, God would forgive all. Before her pregnancy this self-imposed penitential regime had been enough to assuage the pangs of guilt, but now, imagining herself to be days, perhaps only moments away from death, she no longer much trusted the devil's words. She finally met with her confessor. But when Margery "came to the point of saying that thing which she had so long concealed, her confessor was a little too hasty and began sharply to reprove her before she had fully said what she meant, and so she would

to the poem, Goering, p. 107, notes that the *Peniteas cito* "was one of the mainstays of European primary education."

30 Grosseteste, *Deus est*, p. 247: "Vera quidem est, si ea quae fecerit se fecisse confiteatur et non ea quae non fecerit. Integra, ut omnia quae fecit uni dicat. Plana, non solum peccata numerando sed etiam peccati circumstantias omnes ipsum peccatum augentes et minuentes detegendo. Nuda, non in circumlocutionibus peccatum dealbantibus. Amara, se in quolibet accusando non excusando. Verecunda, ut causa purgationis et non ostentationis peccata enumerare praesumat."

say no more in spite of anything he might do." Margery left worse off than before, crazed with grief and the fear of damnation.[31]

Extreme or not, Margery's experience points to the inherently social and dialogic dimension of private confession. The writers of confessional handbooks realized this, realized that the ideal of a full, clear and complete confession depended upon creating a setting and environment in which the penitent could openly discuss his sins and, together with the confessor, construct an adequate, even transparent representation of his life as a sinner. The failure to create this environment could entirely undermine the confessional project. To prevent this from happening, handbooks were careful to specify where confessions were to be heard, the postures and gesture appropriate to both the penitent and the confessor, and even the topics to be discussed. In the *Confessionale*, a "little work" that the Franciscan Marchesinus of Regio Lepide compiled sometime around 1300, the proper setting for confession is the very first thing considered. Private confession has never been entirely private and it was certainly much less private before the development of the confessional booth in the mid-sixteenth century. During the middle ages, private confession occurred in a public place where both the confessor and penitent could be seen by all, but not heard.[32] There was a practical need for this requirement. If confessions were heard out of sight, behind curtains or shut doors, people might become suspicious about what was really happening. The confessor must not only avoid every kind of evil, he must avoid those situations that give even the appearance of evil. For these reasons, "the priest hearing confession," Marchesinus would write, "should sit in a public and honourable place, lest, if this be wanting, he may appear to be an adulterer."[33]

Although warnings to keep private confession visible were certainly designed to pre-empt unscrupulous priests from taking advantage of their position and to assist otherwise upright priests who might suffer an unfortunate moment of weakness during confession, the constant emphasis that priests avoid situations which might give rise to suspicion indicates a broader concern, a concern that ultimately touches on the content of

---

[31] Margery Kempe, *The Book of Margery Kempe*, I.1, trans. B. A. Windeatt (Harmondsworth: Penguin Books Ltd., 1985), p. 41.

[32] Odo of Sully, *Synodicae constitutiones*, chapter 6, *PL* 212, cols. 60–1: "Ad audiendum confessiones communiorem [*al.* eminentem] locum in ecclesia sibi eligant sacerdotes, ut communiter ab omnibus videri possint; et in locis abditis, aut extra ecclesiam, nullus recipiat confessiones, nisi in magna necessitate vel infirmitate." Also, Marchesinus of Regio Lepide, *Confessionale*, chapter 1, particula 1, in Bonaventure, *Opera omnia*, vol. 7, p. 360.

[33] Marchesinus of Regio Lepide, *Confessionale*, chapter 1, particula 1, p. 360: "[S]acerdos audiens confessionem, sedeat, ut dictum est, in loco publico et honesto, ne, quod absit, adulterum se ostendat."

the penitent's confession itself. A priest tempted in some way by the person confessing to him could easily fail to assist the penitent in making an adequate confession. His questions might become leading, concerned more with his own lusts than with the penitent's well-being. Similarly, a penitent's willingness to disclose his sins might be adversely affected if the priest were known or even suspected of being dishonest, indiscreet or incompetent. *Omnis utriusque* alluded to this problem when it allowed any lay person "for good reasons" to seek another priest. Although the practice clearly was discouraged, there were situations in which it was allowed, when, for example, the priest was known to reveal secrets learned in confession, when the priest had participated with the penitent in committing the very sins that needed to be confessed or when the priest's judgments were notoriously indiscreet.[34]

Confessional activity needed to be staged, not merely to avoid scandal, but to encourage open communication between penitent and confessor. Matthew of Cracow recognized this when he urged Dominican novices to "select a compassionate confessor, proven against temptation and exercising himself in a temperate life, to whom you should confess often and to whom you should reveal clearly and distinctly every defect and stimulus by which you are troubled. Let him be discrete, loving, humble and intelligent so that you may return to him confidently and he may know you have applied the remedy. For otherwise, if the blind are charged with leading the blind, both will fall into the pit."[35] During the first half of the fourteenth century, the Cistercian John of Heisterbach succinctly brought all of these concerns together when he recommended that a monk hearing confession "ought to sit with his face covered, neither looking at nor being looked at by the confessant, but only directing an ear towards the penitent's mouth, lest the confessor himself

---

[34] Magister Serlo, *Summa de penitentia*, in Joseph Goering (ed.), "The *Summa de penitentia* of Magister Serlo," *Mediaeval Studies* 38 (1976), 4: "In quibus casibus licet adire alium sacerdotem, scilicet in tribus: Primus est si sit revelator secretorum, quoniam Gregorius dicit deponendum cum hac conditione, ut omnibus diebus vite sue ignominiosus pergat, ut xxxiii Causa, quest. vi, in fine. Secundus casus est in peccati participatione; *ad Rom.* ii, dicitur tali sacerdoti qui particeps est criminis: In quo alium iudicas, te ipsum condempnas. Tertius est in iudicandi indiscretione, quia si cecus cecum ducat ambo in foveam cadunt, *Math.* xv. In aliis vero casibus non est subditi confessorem eligere et proprium prelatum vitare. Precipit enim beatus Petrus, *i epistula Petri*, ii cap.: non solum subdi prelatis modestis, set eciam discolis. Set hoc intellige quamdiu tollerat eos ecclesia sicut exponitur in canone." Murray, "Counselling," pp. 66–72, discusses reasons why a penitent might "shop around" for a different confessor.

[35] Matthew of Cracow, *De modo confitendi et de puritate conscientiae*, chapter 16, in Bonaventure, *Opera omnia*, vol. 7, p. 577: "Confessorem eligas compassivum, probatum in tentationibus, et in via continentiae se exercentem, cui saepe confitearis, et aperias omnes defectus clare et lucide, et stimulos quibus molestaris. Sit ille discretus, charitativus, humilis et intelligens, sic quod possis ad ipsum confidenter recurrere, et sciat tibi remedium adhibere. Aliter autem, si caecus caeco ducatum praestet, ambo in foveam cadunt."

be tempted by what he hears or he makes the confessant silent from shame."[36]

The instruction not to look at penitents was only the first in a number of guidelines concerned with alleviating the penitent's shame and embarrassment during confession. At the very least manuals and treatises advised confessors to behave humbly and discreetly during confession. Quite often they included more detailed instructions. An anonymous manual from the thirteenth century, picking up on the problem of embarrassed penitents, advised confessors "to behave humbly and devoutly in confession so that the confessant's face, and especially the face of a woman, does not blush" and then adds that the confessor "must not loathe [the penitent's] sins, but should listen compassionately."[37] Marchesinus intensified this advice when he stressed that the confessor ought not to loathe the revealed sins no matter how "enormous, repulsive, great, unheard of or strange" they might be.[38] Confessors were not to jeer or laugh at the penitent's sins, nor were they to spit during confessions, unless perhaps they needed to cough.[39] The confessor must behave in a fashion which would do nothing to discourage the penitent from revealing her sins.

Despite all of these precautions, a penitent still might be quiet and it was in just such cases that manuals offered confessors advice on how to encourage penitents to speak. Alan of Lille, drawing on the medical analogy, imagined the confessor as a spiritual doctor, the sinner as someone spiritually ill. He encouraged the confessor "to entice the sinner with words, soften with compliments, so that the invalid will most readily reveal his illness, most readily reveal his sin."[40] About a century later, Marchesinus provided what amounts to the same advice when he

---

[36] John of Heisterbach, *Auditorium monachale*, III.6, in Pierre Michaud-Quantin (ed.), "*L'Auditorium monachale* de l'abbé Jean de Heisterbach," *Cîteaux* 15 (1964), 142–3: "Ultimo sciendum est cuilibet confessori quod in audiendo confessiones debet sedere cooperta facie nec respicere faciem confitentis nec respici ab eodem, sed solum applicare aurem ori poenitentis, ne vel ipse tentetur ex auditis vel verecundiam tacendi faciat confitenti."

[37] Pierre Michaud-Quantin (ed.), "Deux formulaires pour la confession du milieu du XIIIe siècle," *Recherches de théologie ancienne et médiévale* 31 (1964), 53: "Sacerdos humiliter et devote debet se habere in confessione, ut vultus confitentis non erubescat, et maxime mulieris. Et non debet horrere peccata eius sed misericorditer audire."

[38] Marchesinus of Regio Lepide, *Confessionale*, chapter 1, particula 4, p. 360: "Non debet etiam confessor poenitentis horrere peccata, quantumcumque enormia, turpia, magna, inaudita, vel inusitata sint; quia, ut dicit Joannes: *Qui sine peccato est vestrum, primus in illam mittat* [John 8:7]. Aut enim confessor fuit, vel est, vel erit, aut esse potuit in similibus peccatis, vel majoribus."

[39] *Summa penitentie fratrum predicatorum* in Joseph Goering and Pierre J. Payer (eds.), "The *Summa penitentie fratrum predicatorum*, a Thirteenth-Century Confessional Formulary," *Mediaeval Studies* 55 (1993), 27 (lines 42–3): "Caveat autem a cachinno et risu et ne spuere velit cum audierit peccata, nisi forte tusseat."

[40] Alan of Lille, *Liber poenitentialis*, I.3, p. 26: "Sic sacerdos quasi spiritualis medicus, dum ad eum accedit peccator quasi spiritualis aegrotus. Primo, debet peccatorem verbis allicere, blandimentis mulcere, ut facilius aegrotus detegat morbum, detegat peccatum . . ."

recommended that the confessor speak "piously and sweetly" in order to lead the confessant to a "simple and plain confession." The priest ought not to begin the proceedings with an abrupt command like, "Tell your sins!" Rather, he should begin by speaking pleasantly of the value of confession.[41] One of the earliest Dominican manuals provides lines of dialogue to assist the confessor. If a penitent should appear "to fret, as if thoroughly racked with nervousness," the manual recommends the priest say something like this, "Brother, you may securely say whatever you wish because God is with you." The manual even warns priests not to chide sinners immediately for enormous and horrible sins, since each time a sinner blushes he will leave something out of his confession. "Therefore," the text continues, "the sinner ought not be immediately disturbed. But as soon as he has said everything, he ought then to be shown the magnitude of his sins. Indeed, rather than piercing the fleeing dragon by hand, he should provoke the penitent to say everything; let him warn him, moreover, if he sees him speaking haltingly."[42]

Early in the fifteenth century, the Parisian theologian Jean Gerson imbued many of these psychological tactics with additional degrees of nuance. In the popular *On the Art of Hearing Confessions*, Gerson urged confessors to seek nothing in confession but the health of the penitent's soul. The confessor must be careful not to be too austere, saddened or rigid from the start. Otherwise the "frightened sinner's mouth may quickly close." Gerson suggests the priest speak affably with the penitent and, if necessary, perhaps even discuss things unrelated to sin, so that the penitent might feel more comfortable with the confessor. Once a "certain familiarity has been established," the priest can then show "how it is unreasonable and the worst sort of hypocrisy to wish to hide anything

---

[41] Marchesinus, *Confessionale*, chapter 1, particula 5, p. 361: "Exinde debet confessor pio ac suavi alloquio, ipsum confitentem ad veram compunctionem, et ad nudam et expressam confessionem inducere, non statim ex abrupto, si tempus sufficit, inferre: 'Dic peccata tua;' sed dulciter ei proponere aliqua de confessionis utilitate . . ." Thomas of Chobham, *Summa confessorum*, article 6, question 1a, ed. F. Broomfield (Louvain: Editions Nauwelaerts, 1968), p. 240, used a similar example during the first decades of the thirteenth century, "Circa primum attendendum est quod non debet sacerdos statim ex abrupto dicere penitenti; dic peccata tua, sed debet prius multipliciter eum instruere, et multa ab eo inquirere ut devotius et melius confiteatur."

[42] *Summa penitentie fratrum predicatorum*, pp. 27–8 (lines 45–57): "Sacerdos, si uiderit penitentem cespitare et dubitare et quasi palpando pertransire, dicat ei, 'Frater, dicas secure quicquid uolueris quia Deus uobiscum est.' Et si uoluerit, cum penitens dixerit ei aliquod enorme peccatum uel modicum, poterit ei dicere, 'Dominus dimittat tibi,' ut postea cetera <familiarius> dicat; melius tunc permittat eum dicere. Et caueat sacerdos multum ne cum peccator dixerit aliquod enorme peccatum uel orribile statim uelit eum increpare. Aliquando enim erubescunt peccatores et sic in confessione quedam relinquunt. Non ergo statim est confundendus peccator. Set postquam dixerit omnia, tunc est magnitudo peccatorum ostendenda. Quin potius 'obstetricante <manu> educendus est coluber tortuosus,' ut sacerdos, quasi lenigando peccata, prouocet penitentem dicere omnia; moneat cum etiam si uidet dicere inpedite."

in confession before God and how such an act is nothing but vicious self-deception." Far from merely warning priests not to become offended by what they hear, Gerson believes priests should "applaud a person speaking the truth about their faults however much more enormous and worthy of abomination they seem." By praising penitents for their disclosures, Gerson believes they will boldly proceed "to other matters, hesitating at nothing."[43]

It was not enough to create a comfortable environment. Confessions needed to be complete. Sins left undisclosed in confession had a way of sooner or later making themselves known. Some penitents might intentionally omit a sin. In the thirteenth-century collection of Dominican exempla, *Lives of the Brethren*, Gerard de Frachet included the story of a brother in Bologna. Standing before the altar during prayer, the devil suddenly dragged him along the ground to the middle of the church. A number of his fellow brothers seeing this and hearing his screams, ran to him. They sprinkled him with holy water to no avail. Finally, they managed to drag him to St. Nicholas' altar where he "confessed a mortal sin he had concealed in confession and he was immediately freed." Other penitents might accidentally pass over a sin in confession like the novice in Lausanne who believed he had made a "good and careful confession." On the eve of communion, however, he saw the devil in human form holding a piece of paper. "You fancy you have made a good confession," the devil taunted, "but for all that there is much on this paper that makes you mine." The novice asked to see the paper. The devil refused and hurried away. In his haste, he stumbled over a stoup for holy water, dropped the piece of paper and vanished. Rushing over to the paper, the novice found a list of sins which he had, in fact, forgotten to confess.[44] Miracles of this sort were probably somewhat scarce outside the pages of exempla collections and it was up to confessors themselves to make sure that the confessions they heard were complete. If the initial narration of sins seemed inadequate or insufficient, then the priest needed to make good the defective confession, "to investigate the sins which the penitent omitted."[45]

---

[43] Jean Gerson, *De arte*, section 11, in P. Glorieux (ed.), *Oeuvres complètes*, vol. 7 (Paris: Desclee & Cie, 1960–), p. 13, "Applaudat confessor dicentibus veritatem super delictis suis, quanto magis enormissima et abominanda videbuntur. Collaudentur de veritate, de religione, de timore Dei, de zelo propriae salutis, de confidentia ad sacerdotem, et similibus; et quod audacter pergant ad alia nihil haesitantes."

[44] Gerard de Frachet, *The Lives of the Brethren*, pp. 147–8.

[45] Alexander of Stavensby, *Quidam tractatus de confessionibus*, in F. M. Powicke and C. R. Cheney (eds.), *Councils and Synods with other Documents Relating to the English Church: AD 1205–1313*, vol. 2 (Oxford: Clarendon Press, 1964), p. 221: "Auditis omnibus debet querere ab eo si plura reducit ad memoriam. Si dicit quod sic, dicat ergo. Si dicit quod non, tunc debet sacerdos supplere

Unlike the priest in another of Caesarius' tales who confessed his parishioners in groups of six or eight, having them recite prepared confessions in which men and women, young and old, together admitted to adulteries, thefts, robberies, perjuries and many other crimes, the good confessor needed to realize that not all penitents were the same.[46] He needed to determine what sort of individual this particular person was and adapt his interrogation accordingly. A manual derived from Humbert of Romans' *Liber de officiis*, was particularly clear on this point when it divided confessional inquiry into two broad categories. There are those questions that pertain "to the person of the confessant himself" and those questions that pertain "to the person's actions."[47] It was a common, though often implicit, tactic. If a penitent were unknown to the priest, he was advised to first inquire where the penitent had been born, to which parish he belonged and whether he was under excommunication. The priest then needed to determine the penitent's social and economic status. Generally, the questions were phrased in an either/or fashion. "Are you a cleric or a layman?" If he was a cleric, the priest then needed to determine whether the penitent was a religious or a secular and so on. Should the penitent answer that he was a layman, the priest needed to know if he was married or unmarried, a soldier, a townsman, a merchant, a peasant, a tanner, rich, poor and so on. "All of these things and similar ones ought to be asked," the manual concludes, "so that later the priest may know how much and in what ways he who confesses was able to sin and how much satisfaction he could sustain."[48]

And so it was that active encouragement would slowly give way to active interrogation.

### TRANSPARENCY LOST

The interrogation could not proceed haphazardly. The recollection of sins needed to follow an order that guaranteed that "every corner of

---

deffectum confitentis, iuxta quod scriptum est: Iustus in principio accusator est sui; venit amicus eius et investigabit eum. Iustus, id est confitens, primo debet accusare seipsum. Postea amicus, id est sacerdos, debet investigare peccata que omisit."

[46] Caesarius of Heisterbach, *Dialogus miraculorum*, distinction 3, chapter 45, p. 164.

[47] Namur, Musée Archéologique, Fonds de Ville, MS 87, 151rb: "Circa secundum etiam vero notandum quod duo sunt genera interrogationum que a peccatore confitente querendae sunt. Quaedam enim pertinent ad ipsam personam confitentis, quaedam ad facta personae." Thomas of Chobham, *Summa confessorum*, article 3, distinctio 2, question 2a, p. 48, draws on the same distinction which he explicitly takes from Cicero's *De inventione*: "Tullius autem in prima rhetorica apertius et expeditius dividit circumstantias in duo membra, scilicet attributa persone et attributa negotio, quod quomodo sit, commodum est breviter investigare. . . ."

[48] *Summa penitentie fratrum praedicatorum*, p. 26 (lines 20–3): "Hec omnia et hiis similia sunt querenda ut postmodum cognoscat sacerdos quantum et quibus peccare potuit ille qui confitetur et quam satisfactionem poterit sustinere."

conscience" would be uncovered and scoured.[49] To accomplish this goal, several manuals recommended that confession follow "the order of vices rather than the order of places and times lest the hearing and memory of confessors be confused."[50] It is a significant piece of advice. The narration of sin needed to reveal the penitent in as straightforward a manner as possible so that the priest could easily and efficiently judge the penitent's narration. Be that as it may, theologians confronted some rather intractable problems whenever they began to consider just how to construct such a thorough interrogatory schema. Confession, after all, was an essentially negative enterprise.[51] It was not concerned with recognizing one's adherence to the faith, but in delineating each and every deviation from it, and there was an endless number of ways to deviate. Grosseteste faced the challenge head on when he announced his plan to enumerate "in order the type and species of every sin," and then catching himself, as if recognizing the inherent impossibility of such a task, added, "since evil has no order in itself except with respect to the good, of which it is either a superabundance or diminution, it is necessary to order the virtues according to their origin so that, through the order of these virtues, a sufficient enumeration of vices may be revealed."[52] Evil presents no positive features. There is no one set of questions which can guarantee that every sin has been represented. Indeed, as Grosseteste's manual demonstrates, there is no theoretical limit to the number of questions needed to capture the infinite array of possible sins.[53]

Completeness also required specificity. Lateran IV gave something of an official form to this requirement when it ordered priests "to inquire

---

[49] Peter of Blois, *De confessione sacramentali*, cols. 1084a–b: "Tuam igitur conscientiam solerti revolve scrutinio, explora omnes angulos ejus, nihilque in ea remaneat indiscussum." It was a common image and also appears, for example, in Alan of Lille, *Liber poenitentialis*, IV.1, p. 161.

[50] Magister Serlo, *Summa de penitentia*, chapter 6: "Confitendum autem est secundum ordinem viciorum potius quam secundum ordinem locorum et temporum ne confundantur auditus et memoria confessorum." A similar bit of advice appears in Robert of Flamborough, *Liber poenitentialis*, II.2, ed. J. J. Firth (Toronto: Pontifical Institute of Mediaeval Studies, 1971), p. 62. See also, Rusconi, "De la Prédication à la confession," pp. 79–80.

[51] Michaud-Quantin, *Sommes de casuistique*, pp. 107–8.

[52] Grosseteste, *Deus est*, p. 248, "Quia ergo de singulis interrogare utile est tam audienti poenitentiam quam poenitenti, ne quem ignorantia excuset vel impediat, ordine peccatorum omnium genera et species enumerabimus et cuiusmodi homines quibus magis maculentur peccatis. Hoc enim fuit principale intentum. Sed quia malum in se ordinem non habet nisi respectu boni, cuius vel superabundantia vel diminutio est, oportet virtutes ordinare secundum originem, ut in ipsarum ordine pateat sufficiens vitiorum enumeratio iuxta ipsas sumptorum. Sic enim ipsorum vitiorum ordinem sumere necesse est."

[53] Michel de Montaigne, "Of Liars," in *The Complete Essays*, p. 24, recognized this problem when he wrote: "If falsehood, like truth, had only one face, we would be in better shape. For we would take as certain the opposite of what the liar said. But the reverse of truth has a hundred thousand shapes and a limitless field. The Pythagoreans make out the good to be certain and finite, evil infinite and uncertain. A thousand paths miss the target, one goes to it."

about the circumstances of both the sinner and the sin, so that he may prudently discern what sort of advice he ought to give and what remedy to apply . . ."[54] The sins themselves, just like the person of the penitent, needed to be specified and individualized, their every detail laid bare. It is a requirement that can already be found in the eleventh-century treatise *On True and False Penance* and in numerous works from the twelfth century. It had long been recognized that the severity of any given sin was linked to the unique circumstances surrounding its occurrence: Was it committed in a church? during a holy festival? by a priest? by a peasant? Depending upon the circumstances, venial sins might well become mortal, and it was the confessor's job to make these determinations or at least recognize when such determinations were beyond his competence.[55]

Beginning in the early thirteenth century, discussions of the circumstances tended more and more to draw (sometimes knowingly, other times no doubt unknowingly) from a rhetorical tradition beginning with Cicero and moving through Boethius to such twelfth-century grammarians as Thierry of Chartres and John of Salisbury. Within this tradition, dialectic and rhetoric were distinguished in terms of subject matter. Dialectic dealt with theses or *propositiones*, that is, with general questions. Rhetoric dealt with hypotheses or *causae*, that is, with questions concerning the specific circumstances of persons and events.[56] Thomas of Chobham was one of the first writers to exploit openly this particular classical rhetorical tradition. "Since the circumstances are more fully and completely distinguished in secular writings," he wrote after a lengthy reproduction of the pseudo-Augustine's discussion of the circumstances, "it is useful to know what the philosophers say about these things."[57] And what the philosophers had to say about these things soon became what the authors of confessional manuals had to say about them. "According to Cicero," Bartholomew of Chaimis noted in the *Confessionale* of 1474, "there are seven circumstances through which sin is aggravated or

---

[54] Tanner, *Decrees of the Ecumenical Councils*, vol. 1, p. 245.

[55] Thomas Aquinas, *Summa theologica*, I–II, question 73, article 7, ed. P. Caramello (Turin and Rome: Marietti, 1952) and Bonaventure, *Commentaria in quatuor libros Sententiarum Magistri*, part 3, article 2, question 3 (Quaracchi: Collegii S. Bonaventurae, 1882–1902), vol. 4, offer clear explanations concerning the ways in which circumstances can alter a sin's gravity. It is worth noting that Thomas' opinion was cited approvingly towards the end of the fourteenth century by the Franciscan Bartholomew of Chaimis and Bonaventure's opinion was cited in a late thirteenth-century anonymous Dominican manual.

[56] D. W. Robertson, "A Note," pp. 6–14, and Michael C. Leff, "Boethius' *De differentiis topicis*, Book IV," in James J. Murphy (ed.), *Medieval Eloquence: Studies in the Theory and Practice of Medieval Rhetoric* (Berkeley: University of California Press, 1978), pp. 9–15.

[57] Thomas of Chobham, *Summa confessorum*, p. 47, "Sed quia circumstantie plenius et perfectius distinguuntur in secularibus litteris, quid de eis dicant philosophi utile est intelligere."

alleviated and they are contained in this little verse, 'who, what, where, with whom, why, how, when.'"[58] Cicero had not phrased the circumstances as questions nor, for that matter, had he said anything about sin, but no one really seemed to worry too much about this discrepancy. The practice of phrasing the circumstances as questions probably began with Victorinus in the fourth century; Boethius had followed suit early in the sixth, and by the time Bartholomew wrote in the fifteenth century there were dozens of variations (albeit minor) to this list. Another common one ran, "Quis, quid, ubi, per quos, quotiens, cur, quomodo, quando. Quilibet attendat anime medicamentum dando."[59] Some lists contained seven circumstances, others eight. Again, no one seemed to worry too much about these deviations and everyone felt confident that there were seven or eight circumstances because there were seven or eight "singular conditions pertaining to human acts."[60]

The incorporation of this rhetorical tradition into confessional literature provided for a simpler, more systematic and more mnemonically satisfying presentation of the circumstances. Prior discussions had quite often had a less comprehensive tone about them. Alan of Lille, for example, began his discussion of the circumstances with a qualification, "Although there are many circumstances of sins, we are accustomed to find ten in the Bible." Concluding in a similar vein, he wrote, "And this having been said about the circumstances should suffice: for the prudent reader will infer others from these."[61] Alan's admittedly incomplete list is not unlike lists found in *On True and False Penance* and in the writings of Peter of Blois. Justifying each circumstance with a passage or anecdote from the Bible, Alan contends that the priest should consider such circumstances as when and where the sin was committed, the sinner's rank, his worth, whether he was under any religious vow or knew he was committing a sin, how often and for how long he dallied in sin, the sinner's status and the manner in which the sin was committed. While not entirely dissimilar in content or intent from the lists derived from the rhetorical

---

[58] Bartholomew of Chaimis, *Confessionale*, III.2 (Augsburg, 1491): "Ad primum dicendum quod circumstantie quibus peccatum aggravatur vel alleviatur. Secundum Tullium sunt septem et continentur in hoc versu. Quis: quid: ubi: quibus: cur: quomodo: quando."

[59] Guido de Monte Rocherii, *Manipulus curatorum*, part 2, tractatus 2, chapter 5 (Strassburg, 1490). The same verse appears almost 100 years earlier in Namur MS 87, 154vb, an anonymous Dominican manuscript from the late thirteenth century.

[60] Bartholomew of Chaimis, *Confessionale*, III.2: "Ratio autem istius numeri est quia septem sunt conditiones singulares vel proprietates quibus aggravatur vel alleviatur peccatum ut supra: et circumstantie sunt conditiones singulares res actuum humanorum."

[61] Alan of Lille, *Liber poenitentialis*, I.37, p. 36: "Cum multae sint circumstantiae peccatorum, decem in sacra pagina invenire solemus," and p. 37, "Hae et aliae circumstantiae circa res in quibus, vel in quas peccamus, sunt considerandae. Et haec de circumstantiis dicta sufficiant: prudentis enim lectoris erit, ex his alia conjectare."

tradition, Alan's circumstances are redundant. Rank, worth, status and vow, for example, all fall under the heading of "who?" (*quis*) and could more effectively be taken up as examples of how a person's position might affect the sin's gravity.

What is more interesting, however, is that none of Alan's circumstances easily graft onto the question "Why?" In the thirty-two sections devoted to explaining these circumstances (mostly through examples), only two really begin to address the causes of sin. Confessors are instructed to consider the "origin and cause of sin" and to determine "by what cause the sinner was deceived." In cases of fornication, did the penitent stir up his desire or was he moved by desire? "He sins more gravely," Alan notes, "who stirs up his desire than he who is moved by it."[62] Turning to the problem of deception, he adds, "He sins more gravely who is seduced by the smell of lucre or sweet caresses, than if he is deceived through drunkenness."[63] No doubt there are implicit distinctions at work here, distinctions between penitents who are more or less responsible for their actions and, therefore, more or less culpable. Alan, for his part, does little to flesh them out. Although he holds the door open for a more far-reaching investigation into the causes of sin ("Similarly, [the confessor] ought to inquire concerning the causes and origins of other sins"), he never explicitly addresses the complex issue of motivations and intentions, of the reasons why a penitent might have been compelled to sin or of what he had hoped to achieve through sin.

The introduction of the rhetorical circumstances brought the implicit problem of intention and motivation to the foreground. Thomas of Chobham notes that the question "Why?" allows the confessor to inquire into the causes of sin. In particular, the confessor should consider and distinguish between an impulsive cause (*causa impulsiva*) and a reasoned cause (*causa rationativa*). Impulses are incitements which immediately, perhaps uncontrollably, rise up in a man and cause him to sin, when he sins because he is drunk, for example, or in love. Reason, however, pertains to the final cause "according to which something is done so that through great deliberation and foresight that final cause has long been anticipated."[64]

---

[62] Alan of Lille, *Liber poenitentialis*, I.11, p. 29: "Praeterea consideranda est peccati origo et causa, ut si fornicatus fuerit reus, inquirendum est utrum moverit concupiscentiam, vel motus fuerit a concupiscentia. Quidam enim movent concupiscentiam, quidam moventur ab ea. Gravius autem peccat qui movet concupiscentiam, quam qui movetur ab ea."

[63] Alan of Lille, *Liber poenitentialis*, I.12, p. 29: "Praeterea inquirendum est utrum seductus fuerit a concupiscentia vel deceptus fuerit pecunia, vel peccati dulcedine, vel ebrietate. Gravius enim peccat si odore lucri, vel dulcedine blandimenti seducitur quam si ebrietate decipitur. Simili modo, de causa et origine alterius peccati inquirendum est."

[64] Thomas of Chobham, *Summa confessorum*, article 3, distinction 2, question 2a, pp. 56–7: "Per 'cur' intelligitur causa peccandi per quam factum ipsum magis vel minus aggravatur. Et licet multe sint

The final cause of sins must be diligently examined, Thomas concludes, "because a person sins less who steals in order to feed his father, than he who steals so that he may live lavishly."[65] Alan most likely would not have disagreed, but he certainly never addressed the issue of intention as directly as did later writers whose orientation to the circumstances was primarily formed through the rhetorical tradition.

For some writers, intention would become the predominant circumstance. When Bartholomew of Chaimis explained the various circumstances, he began with "Why?" even though it was it was fifth in his mnemonic list (*who, what, where, with whom, why . . .*), "because among all the circumstances, it is the first." The end or goal of any action, Bartholomew contends, is two-fold. When considering the goal of any action, the confessor must distinguish between the deed and the intention governing the deed. A man might work to build a house, Bartholomew offers by way of an example, but the intention governing the work is to make a habitation. The question "Why?" insofar as it pertains to human acts, is only concerned with the intention, whether for example, a person intended to perform a good act for evil reasons or vice versa.[66] The question "What?" considers the deed in and of itself.[67] Guido de Monte Rocherii, the fourteenth-century Spanish curate, concurred when he noted that a sin could be mortal in two ways, because the deed itself is sinful (and here he cites fornication) or because of the intention governing the deed. "To sing in church," he offers by way of example, "is not

cause, tamen hic specialiter due considerande sunt, scilicet causa impulsiva et causa rationativa. Causa impulsiva est que subito nata impellit hominem ad aliquod scelus, ut ebrietas, ira, amor, forma muliebris, fames, sitis, nuditas et similia. Causa rationativa est causa finalis propter quam aliquid fit, ita quod per/ deliberationem magnam et providentiam illa causa finalis diu previsa est; ut si fecit furtum propter ampliandam substantiam suam, vel ad destruendum vicinum suum vel similia."

[65] Thomas of Chobham, *Summa confessorum*, article 3, distinction 2, question 2a, p. 57: "Diligenter etiam considerande sunt cause finales propter quas peccatum committitur, quia minus peccat ille qui propter alendum patrem furatur quam ille qui furatur ut habeat unde voluptuose vivat. Et ita de ceteris intellige."

[66] Bartholomew of Chaimis, *Confessionale*, III.2: "Prima circumstantia consideratur ex parte finis: et talis dicitur Cur quia inter omnes circumstantias est principalis. Ubi nota quod duplex est finis scilicet operationis et intentionis: exempla gratia, forma domus est finis operationis domus: et habitatio est finis intentionis. Sic a simili finis operationis hominis non est finis qui dicitur circumstantia sed finis intentionis qui quandoque ex malo actu bonum intendit et econtrario, et hic finis dicitur circumstantia, nam a fine intentionis in moralibus actus speciem recipit unde intentio operi tuo finem imponit."

[67] Bartholomew of Chaimis, *Confessionale*, III.2: "Secunda circumstantia consideratur ex parte operis scilicet quid: nec consideratur quantum ad substantiam facti scilicet quod occidit vel furatus est vel fornicatus sed quantum ad conditionem facti, id est, proprietatem: qualitatem et quantitatem facti: puta quod occidit patrem: cognovit virginem vel maritatam et sic hec circumstantia non consideratur prout est substantia actus sed prout est conditio actus. Nam quid aut actus sunt idem in specie nature qui differunt in specie moris sicut fornicatio et concubitus coniugalis."

a mortal sin, indeed it can be meritorious. But to sing in order to please a woman and entice her to sin is a mortal sin."[68]

So far so good and it might seem like yet another example of the standard axiom that the circumstances surrounding a sin can aggravate or alleviate its seriousness. But just as Grosseteste's effort to elaborate each and every type of sin opened itself up to a theoretically endless cataloguing of deviations from the norm, the refined focus on intentions likewise opened up a limitless terrain of potential investigation and inquiry. Having made his point about the importance of intentions, Guido concludes, "Since human intentions are nearly infinite, no certain rule can be given concerning which deeds are sins from intention."[69] Bartholomew of Chaimis recognized the severity of the problem, "It is impossible to confess every circumstance of sin, and this is the reason: while the singular circumstances of sins are nearly infinite, no one is obligated to confess those things which can proceed into infinity because concerning such things there is no art and no science."[70] An infinite regress of intentions would undermine confession as an epistemological practice. Knowledge is knowledge of causes and principles and these causes and principles cannot be infinite in number because "the intellect is incapable of understanding the infinite as infinite."[71]

## THE OPACITY OF EMOTION

Augustine had long before recognized the difficulties of knowing oneself and they were difficulties profoundly connected to the ever deepening

---

[68] Guido de Monte Rocherii, *Manipulus curatorum*, part 2, tractatus 2, chapter 9: "Sciendum tamen quod peccatum potest esse mortale dupliciter. Uno modo ex natura sua: sicut fornicari est peccatum mortale ex natura sua. Alio modo aliquis actus potest esse peccatum mortale ex intentione: sicut cantare in ecclesia non est peccatum mortale: immo potest esse meritorium sed cantare ut placeat mulieri et alliceat eam ad peccandum est peccatum mortale."

[69] Guido de Monte Rocherii, *Manipulus curatorum*, part 2, tractatus 2, chapter 9: "Et quia intentiones humane sunt quasi infinite ideo de his que sunt peccata ex intentione non potest certa regula dari, loquimur ergo hic de his que sunt peccata mortalia ex natura sua." Murray, "Confession as a Historical Source," p. 277, quotes a manuscript in which Grosseteste actually suggests that "he who wishes to confess fully should subject the whole treasury of his memory to careful scrutiny, extracting from his past acts, and passing them all in review before his mind's eye. The review should be thorough, orderly and conducted chronologically; that is, considering what one did in the first year one can remember, then in the second, and so on."

[70] Bartholomew of Chaimis, *Confessionale*, III.2: "Primo enim omnes peccatorum circumstantias confiteri est impossible cuius ratio est: quia cum singulares circumstantie peccatorum sint quasi infinite sed nullus obligatur ad confitendum ea que in infinitum possent procedere quia de talibus non est ars neque scientia ergo nullus tenetur omnes confiteri."

[71] Thomas Aquinas, *In Metaphysicam Aristotelis commentaria*, II.4, ed. M.-R. Cathala (Turin: Marietti, 1935), p. 326. Guido offers his dizzyingly circular solution at *Manipulus curatorum*, part 2, tractatus 2, chapter 9: Bartholomew, *Confessionale*, III.2, offers a "solution" that simply states and then willfully ignores the problem.

recesses of memory. "See the broad plains and caves and caverns of my memory," he wrote in his *Confessions*, "the varieties there cannot be counted, and are, beyond my reckoning, full of innumerable things . . . I run through all these things, I fly here and there, and penetrate their working as far as I can. But I never reach the end."[72] The practice of personal confession as it came to be elaborated from at least as early as the late eleventh century transformed Augustine's hard won insights about the nature of memory into the necessary consequence of a few easy-to-follow techniques. Caesarius of Heisterbach himself alluded to the problem in his *Dialogue on Miracles* when he wrote, "It seems to me a more miraculous thing to know the hidden things of the heart and to reveal a man's secret thoughts than to raise the dead . . . for to know a man's inward thoughts belongs to God alone."[73] These hidden and inward thoughts were not only forever inaccessible to the confessor, but even to the penitent himself. As a methodologically open-ended activity, confessional practice always extended the complete truth about the penitent's soul just beyond the confessor's most probing questions and the penitent's deepest self-scrutiny. Though a penitent would obviously be in a better position to know if he were intentionally deceiving his confessor, just like his confessor, he could never be sure if he had employed enough interrogatory rubrics, if he had specified enough circumstances, to encompass every sinful act and to discriminate every mortal from every venial sin.[74]

A specific form of anxiety could arise out of this situation. Theologians referred to it as "scrupulosity." The scrupulous penitent, fixated on the uncertainty of intention, saw sin everywhere forever undisclosed and doubted the efficacy of any confessional interrogation that did not guarantee complete and total disclosure. "At long last," Antoninus of Florence would warn in the fifteenth century, "the scrupulous conscience

---

[72] Augustine, *Confessions*, X.18, trans. Henry Chadwick (Oxford: Oxford University Press, 1992), p. 194.

[73] Caesarius of Heisterbach, *Dialogus miraculorum*, III.33, pp. 151–2: "Si nosti adhuc aliqua de hoc converso, precor ut edisseras mihi, quia magis videtur miraculosum, occulta cordium nosse, et cogitationum secreta revelare, quam mortuos suscitare . . . Verum quidem dicis, quia scire interiora hominis, solius Dei est." Abelard, *Ethics*, p. 40 (lines 7–11), makes a similar point, "Non enim homines de occultis, sed de manifestis iudicant, nec tam culpae reatum quam operis pensant effectum. Deus uero solus qui non tam quae fiunt, quam quo animo fiant adtendit, ueraciter in intentione nostra reatum pensat et uero iudicio culpam examinat."

[74] Guido de Monte Rocherii, *Manipulus curatorum*, part 2, tractatus 1, chapter 5, for example, discusses the ways in which sin might be forgotten and recommends a general sadness for forgotten sins since it is probable that the penitent will not remember and confess every sin: "Sed voco conteri in generali conteri sub extimatione probabili debet enim hoc probabiliter homo credere quod in multis offendit deum quorum non recordatur." Guido's opinion derives directly from Bonaventure, *Sent.*, book 4 distinction 16, article 2, question 2, response.

brings forward the tempest of desperation . . ."[75] Desperation itself was a rather serious sin and so the cycle continued. Whether or not scrupulosity understood as a psychological condition reached anything like epidemic proportions in later medieval Europe, the possibility of scrupulosity is of fundamental importance for appreciating confession as an epistemological practice.[76] The possibility of scrupulosity as the logical outcome of confessional self-examination reveals the structural situation within which the penitent discovered his inner life. In a very real sense, confessional self-examination removed the penitent outside of himself, the opacity of intention rendering true self-knowledge and one's true self always just out of reach.[77] Like his confessor, the penitent looked on himself as if he were someone else, not immediately but through the mediation of the confessional representation itself.

A similar displacement occurred with respect to the penitent's relation to his emotions, to those inner yearnings of the heart that Heloise wrote of with such beauty. The success of any confession depended not only on its completeness (a now constantly receding ideal), but on its bitterness. "A confession is a simulation and entirely false," Peter of Blois wrote, "if it does not proceed from a bitterness of heart."[78] This feeling of bitterness was most often linked to contrition, to that particular sorrow for having offended God which was necessary if the sinner's guilt were to be erased. Alan of Lille, for example, defined contrition as "a bitterness of mind by which someone grieves for perpetrated sins with

75 Antoninus of Florence, *Summa theologica*, chapter 10, part 9, p. 194: "Inducit demum scrupulosa conscientia tempestatem desperationis, a qua liberari se petebat." Although she never uses the term, Karma Lochrie, *Covert Operations: The Medieval Uses of Secrecy* (Philadelphia: University of Pennsylvania Press, 1999), pp. 24–55, seems to connect scrupulosity to confessional practices of secrecy. She writes (as part of a discussion of *Gawain and the Green Knight*), pp. 52–3, "Gawain verbalizes the central paradox of the confessional technology of secrecy as Foucault, de Certeau, and others have characterized it: that secrecy is the precondition for endless talk, confession, and disclosure and the the discovery of the secret does not end the process of verbalization."

76 Delumeau, *Sin and Fear*, pp. 314–21, contends that scrupulosity began to attract attention in the fourteenth century and by the fifteenth century "had already become a phenomenon of European civilization, at least at a certain social and cultural level." Bernt Hamm, "Normative Centering in the Fifteenth and Sixteenth Centuries: Observations on Religiosity, Theology, and Iconology," in *Journal of Early Modern History* 3.4 (1999), 307–54 agrees with Delumeau, but stresses the various measures the Church took to ease the anxieties of conscience. Along these lines is Antoninus's suggestion (citing Petrus Palude), *Summa theologica*, vol. 3, part 3, chapter 21, p. 979, that it is precisely because "no man knows whether he has ever made a perfect confession" that every confession should end with a general confession such as, "concerning every other venial and mortal sin, confessed and not confessed, I acknowledge my guilt."

77 Evelyn Birge Vitz, *Medieval Narratology and Modern Narratology: Subjects and Objects of Desire*, (New York: New York University Press, 1989), pp. 85–6, makes a related point concerning thirteenth-century fictional representations of the self.

78 Peter of Blois, *De confessione sacramentali*, p. 1085: "Simulatoria itaque est, et falsa prorsus confessio, si ex cordis amaritudine non procedit."

the intention of not returning (to them)."[79] Without this bitterness a confession was not really a confession at all. Rather, it was an excuse to brag, an exercise in temptation, a danger, not to mention a waste of time. A true and heartfelt confession was an expression of the penitent's contrition, arose out of that contrition and made the confession and subsequent acts of penance valid and useful.[80] It was for this very reason that most penitents were not allowed to confess in writing, through proxies or through messengers. Jesus ordered the lepers to "show themselves" to the priests, argues the author of *On True and False Penance*, in order to demonstrate that "sins ought to be confessed in person, not made manifest through messengers, nor through writing," adding that "you who have sinned through yourself, should grow ashamed through yourself."[81] It was as if confessors believed the truth of the confessional representation could be read off the penitent's face, that the truth of the sorrowfully worded narration of sins could be judged against the reality of the contrition made manifest in the penitent's posture, sighs and tears.

Interestingly enough, when Grosseteste defines bitterness, he defines it entirely in terms of its narrative or representable qualities. The penitent accuses himself. He does not excuse himself.[82] In other words, Grosseteste attempts to define bitterness in terms of specific elements of

---

[79] Alan of Lille, *Liber poenitentialis*, IV.4, p. 164: "Contritio est mentis amaritudo qua aliquis dolet de perpetratis peccatis cum intentione non relabendi, malens omnia mortis subisse pericula quam tali laborasse culpa. Vel sicut: contritio est cordis compunctio, quae nascitur ex recordatione praeteritorum malorum." In other words, the confession had to be sincere. Compare this with, John Martin, "Inventing Sincerity, Refashioning Prudence: The Discovery of the Individual in Renaissance Europe," *The American Historical Review* 102, no. 5 (1997), 1328–30, who suggests that the modern notion of sincerity has its roots in Renaissance culture and is one of the hallmarks of the invention of the modern individual.

[80] William of Auvergne, *Tractatus novi de poenitentia*, chapter 22, in *Opera omnia*, vol. II (Paris, 1674), p. 239: "Quaedam autem poenitentia est exterior quae non prodest sine interiori, propter quod dicit Propheta, *Scindite corda vestra, & non vestimenta vestra*."

[81] Ps.-Augustine, *De vera et falsa poenitentia*, chapter 10, col. 1122: "Praecepit enim Dominus mundandis, ut ostenderent ora sacerdotibus: docens corporalia praesentia confitenda peccata, non per nuntium, non per scriptum manifestanda. Dixit enim, Ora monstrate: et omnes, non unus pro omnibus. Non alium statuatis nuntium, qui pro vobis offerat munus a Moyse statutum: sed qui per vos peccastis, per vos erubescatis." Thomas of Chobham, *Summa confessorum*, article 5, question 13a, p. 220, makes this principle particularly clear when he discusses the confessions of mutes. Although the mute penitent was, according to Thomas, allowed to confess in writing, he was still required to be present when his confession was read, as a means of demonstrating that he himself confessed the written sins and that he "suffers over them in his heart": "Sciendum est tamen quod mutus si sciat scribere bene potest confiteri peccata sua scripturam, quia non habet aliud os per quod loqui possit. Ita tamen debet hoc fieri quod cum sacerdos legerit peccata illa scripta, debet mutus aliquo signo ostendere quod ipse confitetur peccata illa et corde dolet de illis."

[82] Grosseteste, *Deus est*, p. 247.

his self-presentation. Bitterness no longer refers directly to the immediate presence of sorrow in the penitent's heart. Rather, it refers to specific elements in the penitent's self-presentation, aspects of his confession through which the confessor can infer the true presence of bitterness. No doubt, from the perspective of the confessor, watching, listening and questioning the penitent, this only makes sense. The confessor can only come to know the penitent, his sins and sorrows, through this narration, through the words, gestures, sighs and tears that go to make it up. Of course, this narration can be false. A penitent's contrition may well be a complete fabrication or simply not as profound as it appears. Tears may indeed be a "great sign of an interior fire," but then again, they may not, and a lack of tears need not be held to signify a complete lack of sorrow over one's sins.[83]

If tears were no sure sign for the confessor, neither were they for the penitent. Perhaps some penitents were truly contrite, sorrowful for their every sin, but certainly not all. Some penitents were contrite for certain sins and not for others. Some penitents were not contrite at all, but merely attrite. Since the entire success of the confessional enterprise depended upon a complete and thorough sadness for all one's sins, these were in no way inconsequential distinctions.[84] Nonetheless, there was no easy way, perhaps no way at all, for the penitent to determine if *this* pain was sufficient. This is not to say that manuals lacked descriptions of contrition. They simply were not that useful at the practical level for discriminating one experience of pain from another. Angelus de Clavasi followed years

---

[83] William of Auvergne, *Tractatus novi*, p. 239: "Igitur in amaritudine moretur oculus poenitentis, & in cubili cordis sui conpungatur, ut nubes tristitiae, & interioris doloris in pluviam lachrymarum erumpat, & ex sumo compunctionis lachrymas extorqueat: magnitudo enim sumi signum est ignis interioris, & magni hospitis." Alan of Lille, *Liber poenitentialis*, IV.10, p. 168, however, warns that tears alone do not signify true repentance unless they are accompanied by a contrition of heart: "Ecce quidem adhuc, ut si vera poenitentia, concurrit mentis contritio, nec sufficit exterior satisfactio vel crebra lacrimarum profusio, nisi ex cordis fonte procedat." Guido de Monte Rocherii, part 2, tractatus 1, chapter 2, notes that people often cry more for the loss of temporal things than for the spiritual losses incurred through sin, and that few people, even sorrowful people, ever actually cry over their sins. At part 2, tractatus 2, chapter 6, he warns priests to be on the alert for penitents who confess fabulous sins. When hearing such a confession, the priest must immediately interrupt saying, "Although you pretend contrition and penitence on your face, nevertheless you keep malice in your soul." For all that, Guido offers no advice for distinguishing true from false contrition.

[84] Ps.-Augustine, *De vera et falsa poenitentia*, chapter 9, already discusses these distinctions. He does not, however, employ the terms "contrition" and "attrition." Anciaux, *La Théologie*, pp. 463–89, discusses the theological distinctions between contrition and attrition during the late twelfth century. Alfred Vanneste, "La Théologie de la pénitence chez quelques maitres parisiens de la prèmiere moitié du XIIIe siècle," *Ephemerides theologicae lovanienses* 28 (1952), 40–2, surveys early thirteenth century attitudes and concludes that the distinction hinged on the presence or absence of grace in the soul. Psychological factors were not emphasized.

of tradition when he defined contrition as a perfect sadness for sins, attrition as an imperfect sadness. What distinguished the one from the other? Perfect sadness is a sadness informed by grace whereas imperfect sadness is a sadness without grace. How can these states be distinguished? Angelus does not exactly say. He does add that attrition and contrition are "materially the same." Attrition is like the "light at daybreak which rising up becomes noon, and that is contrition," which, while going all the way in asserting the difference between the two, says little about when the one becomes the other.[85] The same sort of problem appears in the *Manipulus curatorum* when Guido contends that contrition possesses seven conditions, one of which is bitterness and then proceeds to separate out the various degrees of bitterness. "Contrition ought to be bitter," he writes, "because the sinner delighted in illicit thought. It ought to be more bitter should he consent and most bitter should he perpetrate that illicit deed." But again, nothing is said to assist the confessor or penitent in determining whether one's contrition is bitter as opposed to more bitter, or whether this bitterness is merely attrition and not contrition at all.[86]

What was the consequence of this inability to identify the exact nature of one's suffering, of the inability to weigh and determine its intensity? Louis IX recognized it when, according to his biographer Joinville, he warned, "When a man dies his body is healed of leprosy; but if he dies after committing a mortal sin, he can never be sure that, during his lifetime, he has repented of it sufficiently for God to forgive him."[87] Hugh of St. Victor and Thomas Aquinas agreed,[88] as did Guido who urged penitents and confessors alike not to perplex themselves with such

---

[85] Angelus de Clavasi, *Summa angelica de casibus conscientiae*, "Contritio" (Chivasso: Jacobinus Suigus, 1486): "In quo differt contritio ab attritione. Ratio patet Fran< > et alios theol< > quod in duobus. Primo quod attritio est dolor imperfectus. Contritio vero est dolor perfectus. Secundo quod attritio est dolor sine gratia gratum faciente sed non contritio. Et immo contritio et attritio materialiter idem scilicet sicut domus obscura et illuminata. Attritio quippe est lux aurore quae crescendo fit meridies id est contritio." Here I follow Tentler, *Sin and Confession*, pp. 254–5, who notes that the "most important attributes of contrition and attrition, according to this passage, are theological, not psychological."

[86] Guido de Monte Rocherii, *Manipulus curatorum*, part 2, tractatus 1, chapter 3: "Amara debet esse contritio: quia peccator delectatus fuit in cogitatione illicita. Amarior: quia consensit. Amarissima: quia opus illicitum perpetravit . . ."

[87] Joinville, *The Life of Saint Louis*, in Joinville and Villehardouin, *Chronicles of the Crusades*, trans. M. R. B. Shaw (London: Penguin Books, 1963), p. 169.

[88] Hugh of St. Victor, *De sacramentis*, II:4, chapter 2, *PL* 176, col. 555: "Quomodo scire possum quando condigna sit poenitentia mea? Quia hoc scire non potes, ideo necesse habes semper poenitere. Melius est ut plus facias quam minus." Thomas Aquinas, *Sent.*, book 4, distinction 17, question 2, article 5, solution 2, ad primum: "Ad primum ergo dicendum, quod aliquis non potest esse certus quod contritio sua sit sufficiens ad deletionem poenae et culpae; et ideo tenetur confiteri et satisfacere maxime cum contritio vera non fuerit, nisi propositum confitendi habuisset annexum; quod debet ad effectum deduci etiam propter praeceptum quod est de confessione datum."

irresolvable questions.[89] Bishop Antoninus of Florence, however, located the structural source of the problem when, in a related discussion, he noted that penitents can judge themselves to have a right conscience if they sense and taste "the sweetness of divine goodness, which sweetness is God" and then immediately qualified this assertion by adding, "Nevertheless, this knowledge is not gained through an infallible medium, but through signs."[90] Simply put, the penitent's relation to his contrition, just like his relation to the truth of his life as a sinner, was not intuitive, but mediated and, therefore, open to the very sorts of problems inherent in the attempt to construct a complete narration of sins. Perhaps the eleventh- and twelfth-century writers were never so clear on this point as Antoninus, but when the pseudo-Augustine distinguishes a bitterness that arises due to our transgressions against the faith from that sorrow we feel simply because we suffer,[91] or when Peter of Blois distinguishes grades of sadness and warns, "If you should sense in yourself the grace of compunction and an outpouring of tears, you should not immediately judge yourself reconciled to God,"[92] it should be clear that even the penitent's emotional life, his tears of contrition and solace, do not provide a special source of self-knowledge. Rather, they must be placed within the representational framework of confession itself. They must be read as signs and symptoms in which attempts to know oneself look very much like attempts to know someone else.

SELF-KNOWLEDGE

The private life that Heloise, Abelard, Peter Lombard and the early theologians of contrition promoted could never have remained private, perhaps never was private in any essential sense. The practice of confession

---

[89] Guido de Monte Rocherii, *Manipulus curatorum*, book 2, tractatus 1, chapter 3, "Et causa quare sic debet durare contritio semper est: quia nemo est certus adminus de lege (*) si peccatum est sibi per contritionem remissum: quia nescit si contritio fuit sufficiens." Also, chapter 2, "Sed quid si verus penitens nunquid vellet plus sustinere quacumque penam temporalem sicut penam inferni vel mortem vel quamcunque aliam penam quam peccare vel peccasse. Dico quod nullus in mente sua debet sibi ponere talem questionem nec etiam alicui alteri: qua istud esse se vel alium ponere in temptationem ut mens humana est multum infirma ex parte sensualitatis . . ."

[90] Antoninus of Florence, *Summa theologicae*, III.10, p. 192: "Quinti experiuntur se habere gratiam a bona conscientia, sicut illi, qui sentiunt dulcedinem divinae bonitatis in oratione, & gustant quam suavis est Dominus. . . . Ista tamen cognitio non est per medium infallibile, sed per signa." Robert Courson, *Summa*, I.2, solutio, in V. L. Kennedy (ed.), "Robert Courson on Penance," *Mediaeval Studies* 7 (1945), 299, discusses the sorts of signs through which a penitent might detect the presence of charity in his own soul.

[91] Ps.-Augustine, *De vera et falsa poenitentia*, chapter 13, col. 1124 : "Et non sit satis quod doleat, sed ex fide doleat, et non semper doluisse doleat."

[92] Peter of Blois, *De confessione sacramentali*, col. 1088b: "Si ergo senseris in te gratiam compunctionis et effluentiam lacrymarum, non tamen ideo te statim arbitreris Domino reconciliatum."

denied the penitent any privileged epistemological and private access to himself. Unlike seventeenth-century Cartesian self-examination, for example, which would claim to discover the self's unique and transparent relation to itself in the (supposedly) self-verifying statement, "I think, I exist," confessional self-examination made no such claims.[93] Confessional practice did not proceed through the logical elimination of all less than certain beliefs, but through the careful construction of a representation which in principle was never complete, whose truth only God could ascertain. The penitent was in no better position than the priest to judge the truth of this representation, the efficacy of this feeling of bitterness, and, as a result, the door was always already open to move the private life of contrition in to the public order of socially constructed representations and institutionally authorized judgments.

The authors of confessional pastoralia practically said as much themselves. Confession, according to them, was both a medical and a legal procedure, because sin was both an illness and a crime. Confessors, accordingly, were both doctors and lawyers of the soul.[94] The medical analogy was ubiquitous, appearing with little change or variation from early texts like *On True and False Penance* through the writings of Alan of Lille in the twelfth century to Guido de Monte Rocherii in the fourteenth century. The penitent revealed his illness to the confessor through confession and the confessor, in turn, diagnosed and prescribed the appropriate cure of penance.[95] The legal analogy appeared sporadically throughout the twelfth century, more often than not in discussions concerning the qualities that a spiritual judge, that is, the confessor, should possess.[96] Beginning in the thirteenth century, theologians began to exploit the legal analogy both more fully and more frequently. Confession was imagined as a legal proceeding. Whereas criminals presented their case and were tried in the external or outer forum, sinners were tried in the penitential or inner forum of confession. Bartholomew of Chaimis referred to

---

[93] René Descartes, *Philosophical Letters*, ed. and trans. Anthony Kenny (Minneapolis: University of Minnesota Press, 1970), p. 93: "I claim that we have ideas not only of all that is in our intellect, but also of all that is in the will. For we cannot will anything without knowing that we will it, nor could we know this without an idea; but I do not claim that the idea is different from the action itself."

[94] Nicole Bériou, "La Confession dans les écrits théologiques et pastoraux du XIIIe siècle: médication de l'ame ou démarche judiciare?" in *L'Aveu: antiquité et moyen-age*, (Rome: Ecole Francaise de Rome, 1986), pp. 261–82.

[95] On beliefs concerning the actual connection between sin and illness during the middle ages see Darrel W. Amundsen, *Medicine, Society and Faith in the Ancient and Medieval Worlds* (Baltimore: The Johns Hopkins University Press, 1996), pp. 187–8.

[96] Ps.-Augustine, *De vera et falsa poenitentia*, chapter 20, col. 1129. Alan of Lille, *Liber poenitentialis*, III.46, pp. 154–5.

it as the "soul's forum."[97] In confession, Antoninus noted, the penitent stood as both the accuser and the accused.[98] The confessor was the judge, standing in place of God, mediating between penitent and God.[99]

Both the medical and judicial analogies served to place the penitent outside of himself and both modelled self-examination on more public models of vision. The soul's forum was not a private room to which only the penitent had access. It bore little likeness to the interior depths of a uniquely accessible subjectivity. The practice of confessional examination itself defined the soul's forum, a practice that always presupposed the presence of another who listened to and judged the penitent's self-accusations, and that defined the penitent as another with respect to himself. It is worth noting, moreover, that private confession was private only in the sense that priests were not to reveal secrets learned in confession. Beyond that they were surprisingly public. Confessors could discuss difficult cases with their superiors and write interesting confessional tales in collections of exempla. Other parishioners could see the confession take place (even if out of earshot). Depending upon the sorts of penance imposed, neighbours and acquaintances could probably guess the sorts of sins confessed.[100] More importantly, the forum in which the penitent's soul revealed itself was a social forum, a forum defined by the penitent who submitted to this interrogation and to this confessor (and the entire institutional complex and practices which he carried with him into this personal encounter). The practice of confession, from its setting and requirements for completeness, specificity and clarity, to its interrogational techniques and its emphasis on intentions, defined self-knowledge as an intrinsically social and public affair.

[97] Bartholomew of Chaimis, *Confessionale*, I.1: "Et dīcitur proprius sacerdos omnis qui habet curam alicuius ordinariam sive delegatam in foro anime." During the first half of the twelfth century, Honorius of Autun, *Elucidarium*, II.20, *PL* 172, col. 1150, made rather full use of the legal analogy: "Duo sunt judicia Dei: unum hic per confessionem; aliud in ultimo die per examinationem; in quo ipse Deus judex erit, diabolus accusator, homo reus. In isto vero sacerdos, Christi vicarius judex; homo et accusator et reus: poenitentia est sententia." Few contemporaries followed Honorius' lead. The contrast between inner and outer fora was an innovation of thirteenth century. Mansfield, *Humiliation of Sinners*, pp. 49–55, distinguishes this innovation from the earlier distinction between interior penance (contrition) and exterior penance, and links it to the increasing legalism that characterized confession after its mandatory universal imposition in 1215.

[98] Antoninus, *Summa*, XVIII.1, p. 943: "Et quia in foro poenitentiae idem est actor & reus, inde est, quod idem potest seipsum accusare coram quocumque confessore de communibus, qui illum possunt absolvere de crimine ubicumque commisso."

[99] Guido de Monte Rocherii, *Manipulus curatorum*, part 2, tractatus 2, chapter 1: "Ex secundo scilicet ex hoc quod confessio ordinatur ad reconciliationem faciendam deo et eius ecclesie patet etiam quod debuit institui in lege nova ideo enim confessio sit homini ut homo sit iudex et arbiter inter deum et peccatorem."

[100] Little, "Les Techniques de la confession," pp. 89–90 and Murray, "Confession as an Historical Source," pp. 281–6.

Behind these techniques, simultaneously organizing them and responding to them, was the ideal of contrition, the actual experience of bitterness in which the soul grieved and rejected sin, rejoiced and turned to God. Theologians like Abelard, Lombard and Alan of Lille attempted to mark this experience off from external intervention. While priests could signify its presence in a penitent, they played no part in creating it. Contrition named the private and inviolate relation between sinner and God, a relation known to exist, they believed, because these tears and these sighs were its product. Unfortunately, the mere experience of bitterness could not bear the epistemological burden imposed upon it. The experience of bitterness could arise for any number of reasons and could signify any number of things about the state of the penitent's soul. Tears are nice, but in the final analysis they are only tears and nothing more. What revealed itself in the soul's forum was not the penitent's soul itself, but its appearance, and no appearance can guarantee its own truth, no specification of the traits present to an appearance can guarantee the reality of what never appears in and for itself.

Considered as an epistemological practice, personal confession could never have coherently sustained an essentially private interpretation of the self and of self-knowledge. Paradoxically, the emphasis placed on the individual penitent and on her contrition served to displace both the penitent and the priest from any privileged vantage point. There were no special tools, no special practices, that they could employ to learn the truth hidden away in the recesses of soul. God knew that truth immediately and intuitively, everyone else approached it through signs and stories that continued on endlessly. From this perspective, the history of confession beginning with the thirteenth century might be read as a continuing effort to overcome the epistemological deficit arising from the practice of confession itself. The growing emphasis on the causal efficacy of the priest's words of absolution points to the broader contexts in which confessions were made and heard. The actual rite of confession picked up where human knowledge failed. Thomas Aquinas argued that the priest's absolution coupled with the penitent's confession and acts of satisfaction actually helped to generate contrition in the sinner. Duns Scotus argued that the rite of confession could transform attrition into contrition, and many Thomists were to follow suit with this "easier" road to forgiveness. It was within this broader context that penitents and priests alike were urged not to perplex themselves with unanswerable questions about how much bitterness they needed to experience, or whether they had confessed enough, analyzed enough, to ensure their forgiveness. The form of the sacrament itself served to fill in the gap between appearance and reality, to guarantee that the confessional narrative conformed with the truth buried away in the penitent's heart. All things being equal, this confession was enough.

Once attention is switched to the sacramental aspect of confession, it only makes sense to emphasize the inherently public character of confession. The goal of confession was for the penitent, isolated through sin, to be readmitted to the community of the faithful through acts of reconciliation and the reception of the Eucharist.[101] This move from private to public, that is, from a private or (perhaps) personal analysis of sins to a public reception of the Eucharist, might seem to confirm interpretations of twelfth- and thirteenth-century religious life in which increased self-awareness was cultivated for the sake of more fully identifying with a group, an intent which is seen to undercut any awareness of the self as radically individual.[102] No doubt this is in part true. But confession differed from other sacraments. Robert Courson, the early thirteenth-century disciple of Peter Cantor, expressed this when he noted that baptism and the Eucharist did not require any special knowledge from the priest. All that mattered were the "form of the words and the order and substance of the elements." Penance, however, required "a most wise and discreet deliberation in accordance with the authorities of the fathers and a knowledge of scripture."[103] Just as sick people needed good doctors if they hoped to recover from an illness, sinners needed wise confessors if they hoped to receive forgiveness. Unfortunately, no confessor could be wise enough to uncover every sin and, as a result, the goals and ideals of the sacrament always remained external to the logic of confession as an epistemological practice.

As a methodologically open-ended activity, personal confession always contained the potential to divorce itself from its broader connections with the Eucharist and to become an end in itself. It is in this possibility, in this slippage between practice and ideal, that self-awareness quietly makes room for a sense of self as increasingly individualized, individualized

---

[101] John Bossy, *Christianity in the West* (Oxford: Oxford University Press, 1985), pp. 45–9, emphasizes the original social function of private penance. He suspects that the role of confession shifted sometime around 1400. One indication of this shift, he speculates, is Gerson's belief that children ought to confess. He writes, "[I]f young children were to be considered suitable for the sacrament it could not have as a prime purpose the settlement of social conflicts." Peter Biller, "Confession in the Middle Ages: Introduction," in Biller and Minnis (eds.), *Handling Sin*, pp. 22–3, contrasts various heretical conceptions of confession (Waldensian and Cathar) with Catholic attitudes to demonstrate the confessors' social concerns.

[102] Bynum, "Did the Twelfth Century Discover the Individual?" in *Jesus as Mother*, pp. 106–9.

[103] Robert Courson, *Summa de penitentia*, p. 305: "Et secus est de baptismate et de confectione quam de confessione et penitentia quia in celebratione tam baptismatis quam eucharistie non requiritur maior aut minor scientia sed tantum forma uerborum et ordo et substantia elementi. Sed in penitentia iniungenda coexigitur sanius et discretius consilium secundum auctoritatem patrum et intelligentiam scripturarum."

through the theoretically endless enumeration of sins and circumstances that serve to define the unique truth of this particular sinner. Nonetheless, the individual constructed in confession was not the private self which has so inspired or aggravated modern philosophers. Rather, it was the individual self understood through its endless self-presentations, the individual as taken up into and formed through the very system of interrogation which could then claim to have discovered that individual as an object for consideration in the first place. Confessors and penitents alike sought the individual; they had to settle with its infinitely changing appearance, its infinitely deferred presence.

# Chapter 3

# PETER OF LIMOGES, PERSPECTIVIST OPTICS AND THE DISPLACEMENT OF VISION

## PETER OF LIMOGES AND THE *TRACTATUS MORALIS DE OCULO*

Towards the very end of the *Perspectiva*, his influential treatise on vision, the thirteenth-century Franciscan natural philosopher Roger Bacon proclaims the wonders and powers of mirrors. They can make one man appear to be many men and one army to appear to be many armies. Some people, he adds, believe that demons can transform the air into a kind of mirror with which they reveal and betray hidden military encampments. Indeed, legend has it that the philosopher Socrates used mirrors to locate an evil dragon within its mountainous hiding places, a beast whose foul breath had poisoned both animals and men. "Anything," Bacon concludes, "that has been hidden away in some concealed place in cities, armies and the like can be brought to light through reflected vision."[1] As it turns out, mirrors can even reveal secrets hidden in the pages of sacred scripture.

Imagine that an eye is placed in the centre of a spherical, concave mirror. The natural properties of this mirror are such that wherever that eye looks, it will see only itself. Now imagine that another eye, placed somewhere else, anywhere else but the mirror's centre, looks at the mirror. It will never see the reflected image of that other eye. One eye sees itself everywhere while remaining entirely invisible to the other – ubiquitous, yet hidden. These are peculiar phenomena, but well enough known during the second half of the thirteenth century. Bacon discussed them in his *Perspectiva*, as did several others who took up, defended and spread this newly emergent science of vision, including Peter of Limoges.[2]

---

[1] Roger Bacon, *Perspectiva*, part 3, distinction 3, chapter 3, p. 330 (lines 165–7): ". . . et possunt per visionem reflexivam omnia occultata in locis abditis in civitatibus, exercitibus, et huiusmodi deduci in lucem." I would like to thank Richard Newhauser and A. Mark Smith for their generous assistance with this chapter.

[2] Bacon, *Perspectiva*, part 3, distinction 1, chapter 4, p. 272 (lines 242–9): "Cum autem oculus est in centro speculi concavi, ipse sibi tantum apparet, nulla enim reflectitur in centrum nisi que egreditur a centro; sola quidem perpendicularis in se redit. Si autem ponatur oculus in periferia vel extra, ipse sibi non apparet, sed est reflexio in partem oppositam. Si vero ponatur infra periferiam,

Peter was a scholar. He received degrees from the arts and theology faculties at the University of Paris. He was also a well known preacher, an astrologer and an early supporter of Ramon Llull. Peter undoubtedly knew Bacon's work, as well as a number of the Greek and Arabic sources that Bacon had studied and from which Bacon had so freely borrowed. Most significantly, in the visual phenomena associated with the concave mirror, Peter did not merely see a natural wonder, but also a wondrous revelation of God's relation to His creation and of our relation to God.

"It is proved in the science of perspective," Peter writes in the *Tractatus moralis de oculo*, a preaching manual he composed sometime around 1280, "that if an eye placed at the centre of a concave and spherical mirror looks at the mirror, it will see only itself." Peter follows this observation with a brief explanation that borrows succinctly and accurately from the science of perspective, the most advanced visual theory of the day. He then suggests that God's vision can be likened to the visual relations established within the concave mirror. After all, Peter continues, didn't Alan of Lille once note that "God is an intelligible sphere whose center is everywhere"? And doesn't scripture report that "God is a mirror without stain"? Like the eye placed at the center of the mirror that finds itself reflected everywhere, so too is the divine eye present everywhere, as if it exists in the very center of all things, seeing everything most intimately.[3] For our part, we are like that other eye, displaced from the centre of the concave mirror, distanced from God by this mass of sinful flesh, forever unable to see the divine essence that exists everywhere, that sees everything and is nowhere to be seen.[4]

---

nichil apparet eorum que sunt in semidiametro in quo est. Si autem visibile aliquod ponatur in centro, videri non potest reflexione, eius enim species non reflectitur nisi supra se." Also, John Pecham, *Perspectiva communis*, II.40–2, in David C. Lindberg (ed. and trans.), *John Pecham and the Science of Optics* (Madison: The University of Wisconsin Press, 1970), pp. 192–4. On Peter's life see, Newhauser, "Nature's Moral Eye," pp. 127–30. David L. Clark, "Optics for Preachers: the *De oculo morali* by Peter of Limoges," *Michigan Academician* 9.3 (1977), 330, incorrectly identifies Peter as a Franciscan.

3 Peter of Limoges, *Tractatus*, VI.8: "Probatum est in scientia perspectiva quod oculus existens in centro concavi sperici speculi si respiciat speculum videt se tantum. Unde si totum celum esset speculum oculus existens in centro si respiceret celum solummodo se videret. Quod sic probatur. Cum non res extra centrum posita radios habeat super superficiem speculi cadentes oblique cum eciam equales sint anguli reflexionis et incidencie: sequitur quod radii non in ipsum centrum sed ad partem oppositam reflectantur. Sic eciam suo modo est videre in deo. Ut enim dicit Alanus, 'Deus est spera intelligibilis cuius centrum est ubique.' Eciam est speculum sine macula ut dicit *Sapientia* vii. Divinus igitur oculus quasi in centro omnem existens presentissimus cuius omni rei sit intimus in seipso tanquam in speculo seipsum tetum intelligit per seipsum."

4 Peter of Limoges, *Tractatus*, VI.9: "Probatur eciam in dicta sciencia quod res existens in centro speculi sperici concavi ab oculo extra centrum posito respiciente speculum non videtur. Sic quamdiu in hac vita incolatus noster prolongatus est et mole carnis oppressi a deo distamus videre diuinam essenciam non valeamus."

The themes of vision and visibility, of seeing and being seen, inform Peter's treatise from beginning to end. Priests are warned against setting bad examples for their parishioners. Students are urged not only to appear industrious and attentive before their teachers, but to read and study on their own. And everyone is reminded not to confuse the poverty of worldly success with the real riches of spiritual happiness. Vices, sins and every sort of moral laxity are explained in terms of perception, as problems arising with the sinner's spiritual vision. Quite simply, the central problems of spiritual life are, when all is said and done, visual problems, problems with how things are seen and with how they appear. Just as God's ubiquity can be understood through an analogy with concave mirrors, so too can our distance from Him and our inability to see Him. Throughout the *Tractatus*, Peter will repeatedly tread this path from the science of perspective to its spiritual analogue. More often than not he will present some *notabilia* or theory culled from late thirteenth-century optical theory and give it a "spiritual" or "moral" interpretation, an interpretation motivated and fleshed out by passages from scripture, the church fathers, pagans like Seneca, as well as more recent authorities like Anselm of Canterbury and Bernard of Clairvaux. For example, according to the science of perspective, the pupil is protected by the eye's seven parts. Similarly, Peter writes, "for the spiritual pupil, that is the perfect custody of the soul, seven things are necessary."[5] Namely, the seven virtues. Knowledge of the eye's anatomy and powers provides the key to unlock the divine wisdom hidden within scripture.

The idea of drawing spiritual lessons from vision and visual phenomena certainly did not originate with Peter. Visual analogies appear sporadically in the early twelfth-century pseudo-Anselmian treatise *De similitudinibus*, and again towards the end of the century in Alexander of Neckham's treatise *Concerning the Nature of Things*. For all that, Peter's use of optical phenomena differs markedly from these earlier examples. Considering the refractive property of water, for example, Alexander writes, "Moreover, a fish or anything placed in water seems larger in the water than out of it. Thus a dog swimming in water holding a piece of meat in its mouth is deceived seeing a shadow and lets go of the meat that it was holding in its mouth, hoping to secure a larger piece for itself, but in vain. Let the waters represent tribulations; martyrs placed in tribulations were greater than in time of peace."[6] Whereas in passages like these, Alexander's strategy is

---

[5] Peter of Limoges, *Tractatus*, I.2: "Modo consimili pro spiritualis pupille id est anime perfecta custodia septem sunt nobis necessaria scilicet septem virtutes principales, tres scilicet theologie et quatuor cardinales."

[6] Pseudo-Anselm, *De similitudinibus*, chapter 99, PL 179, cols. 664–5. On the connection between this treatise and Anselm's own writings and ideas see R. W. Southern and F. S. Schmitt (eds.),

simply to note some optical phenomena before immediately proceeding to his allegorical interpretation ("Let the water's represent . . ."), Peter tends to incorporate the perspectivist explanation of the phenomena into the allegorical reading itself. That is, he does not merely allegorize the phenomena, but also the scientific explanation behind the phenomena.[7]

In his desire to allegorize both optical phenomena and their scientific explanation, Peter seems to follow the lead of Roger Bacon himself, the first European thinker to assimilate fully the science of perspective. Bacon had, after all, concluded the *Perspectiva* with a defence of the science's spiritual significance. "Nothing in divine scripture is expounded as much as those things that pertain to the eye and vision," Bacon wrote (and Peter liked these words enough to paraphrase them unascribed into the prologue of his own work), "and therefore nothing is more necessary for [an understanding of] the literal and spiritual sense of scripture than the certitude of this science."[8] And like Peter nearly twenty years later, Bacon argued that the spiritual significance of a phrase like, "Preserve me, oh Lord, as the pupil of your eye," can only be grasped if we first understand the eye's seven-fold anatomical structure.[9]

Precedent aside, Peter's treatise takes the spiritual implications of vision and visual theory more seriously than did any of his predecessors. Whereas Bacon had merely promised his readers that the science of perspective could have great spiritual value, Peter fulfils that promise and gives it a practical application. And here it is important to realize that, despite its frequent recourse to scientific explanation, the *Tractatus* is not and

---

*Memorials of St. Anselm* (London: Oxford University Press, 1969), pp. 12 and 110. Peter cites the pseudo-Anselm at *Tractatus*, VI.1. See Edward Grant (ed.), *A Source Book in Medieval Science* (Cambridge: Harvard University Press, 1974), pp. 380–4, for a translation of the relevant sections of Alexander of Neckham's *Concerning the Nature of Things*. The example of the dog and the martyrs is found at p. 384.

7  This contrast was first noted by Gudrun Schleusener-Eichholz, "Naturwissenschaft und Allegorese: Der *Tractatus morali de oculo* des Petrus von Limoges," *Frühmittelalterliche Studien*, 12 (1978), 258–309.

8  Roger Bacon, *Perspectiva*, part 3, distinction 3, chapter 1, p. 322 (lines 15–18): "Nam in scriptura Dei, nichil tantum multiplicatur sicut ea que pertinent ad oculum et visionem, ut manifestum est perlegenti; et ideo nichil magis necessarium est sensui litterali et spirituali sicut huius scientie certitudo." Compare with Peter's version, *Tractatus*, prol.: "Si diligenter volumus in lege domini meditari facillime perpendimus ea que pertinent ad visionem et oculum pre ceteris frequencius in sacris eloquiis recitari." On Bacon's notions concerning the proper relations between pagan science and Christian wisdom see, David C. Lindberg, "Science as Handmaiden: Roger Bacon and the Patristic Tradition," *Isis* 78 (1987), 518–36 and Jeremiah Hackett, "Philosophy and Theology in Roger Bacon's *Opus maius*," in James R. Long (ed.), *Philosophy and the God of Abraham* (Toronto: Pontifical Institute of Mediaeval Studies, 1991), pp. 55–69.

9  Bacon, *Perspectiva*, part 3, distinction 3, chapter 1, p. 322 (lines 21–25): "Cum enim dicitur, 'Custodi nos, Domine, ut pupillam oculi,' impossibile est scire sensum Dei in hoc verbo nisi primo consideret homo quomodo pupille custodia perficitur, quatenus ad eius similitudinem Deus nos custodire dignetur." Peter's interpretation varies insignificantly from Bacon's.

could never have been mistaken for a scientific treatise. It is, first and foremost, a preaching manual, a manual designed to assist preachers to compose sermons.[10] Not only is Peter's use of scientific theory always subordinated to that purpose, but that purpose complicates and enriches the treatise's relation to its thematic material in such a way that it cannot even simply be a book about the spiritual implications of perspectivist optics. The preacher was the pre-eminently visible member of the medieval church, raised above his parishioners as he spoke, looking out on an audience that returned his gaze, an audience whose salvation or damnation depended upon what they saw and what they heard. As the thirteenth-century Dominican Humbert of Romans makes abundantly clear in his own preaching manual, *De eruditione praedicatorum*, an awareness of this interplay of gazes is crucial to the preacher's success. The adaptation of the preacher's self-presentation (of his gait, his demeanour, even of his vocal inflections and vocabulary) to the demands and needs of his audience is central to the practice of preaching and, ultimately, to the preacher's conception of himself and of his relations to others.[11] Not only was preaching a thoroughly visible and public activity, but Humbert urged his preachers to always think of themselves as if they were on public display, even when they were alone. Peter would have known all of this at first hand. A renowned homilist who once preached before the king at the Sainte-Chapelle on Maundy Thursday 1273,[12] Peter himself would have participated in these visual relations, and his book, a preaching manual, is, at one and the same time, a product of those relations, a reflection on them, and a tool for engaging in them.

The sort of religious life in which Peter participated was structured around visual relations and the interplay of seeing and being seen – between preacher and audience, novice and novice master, penitent and confessor. What, then, is vision and how does it occur? What is the relation between what appears and what exists? In an institutional and cultural environment that increasingly framed the most basic religious and social relations in visual terms, these are natural questions to ask, and Peter asks and examines them throughout his manual. They are potentially dangerous questions as well. Dominican exempla like the ones we considered from Gerard de Frachet's *Vitae fratrum* in the first chapter, exempla concerning friars tempted by the desire for superfluous knowledge, spending unnecessary hours reading books of pagan philosophy

---

[10] Newhauser, "Nature's Moral Eye," p. 135, emphasizes that "a functional receptional analysis reveals that medieval audiences understood the text as belonging to the system of preaching aids and that it was generically aligned to the genre of *exempla*-collection . . ."

[11] These themes are discussed above and at length, see chapter 1, pp. 22–30.

[12] Albert Soler, "Ramon Llull and Peter of Limoges," *Traditio* XLVIII (1993), p. 99.

and suffering nightmares of divine torture for their transgressions, clearly point to the perceived difficulties of balancing prayer and study. Preachers need to be educated if they hope to speak well and to move their audiences, but when does study become vain curiosity? Peter is well aware of these concerns.[13] Both a scholar and a preacher, his book quite often reads like a warning to those tempted to transform study into its own reward. Unbridled curiosity is a sin and too often, when people look upwards, their intentions are entirely towards the earth. Perhaps God is everywhere, but when we direct our eyes towards the concave mirror of the heavens, we see everything but Him.

Of course if God is everywhere, hidden but no less present, then He is present even in the phenomena of vision, the structure of the eye, the curious properties of mirrors, the science of perspective. Accordingly, on every page of the *Tractatus*, Peter himself must perform a careful balancing act between study and prayer, between curiosity and devotion, as he repeatedly moves from the science of perspective to its spiritual implications and hidden lessons. And like that other eye, the one displaced from the centre of the concave spherical mirror and blind to the truth that everywhere surrounds it, the lessons Peter draws are lessons that point to the essential inadequacy and permanent displacement of our spiritual vision. Perhaps this should come as no surprise. As the theologians liked to put it, *in this life* (*in statu isto*) we are alienated from God, displaced wayfarers, wanderers far from our spiritual home.[14] Peter, however, finds this displacement replicated in the very sorts of religious practices that sought to overcome and rectify it, in preaching and confession. These practices are both literally and metaphorically concerned with vision, practices whose success depends upon our seeing things as they really are and whose very structures forever defer and deny fulfilment of that vision. Not only does our vision fail us when we look towards the heavens, but even when we look around us, at each other and within ourselves.

---

[13] For example, Peter, *Tractatus*, IX.1, condemns the eye's insatiable curioisity, "Quam damnosa sit curiositas oculorum testificantur non solum diuinarum testimonia scripturarum, ymo eciam fabule poetarum." Structurally, the sin of curiosity is identical to the sin of scrupulosity, a sin that arises when a penitent engages in too detailed an examination of conscience. In both cases, investigation becomes an end in itself as the scholar or penitent fails to order his investigation towards God. On the sin of curiosity, see Hans Blumenberg, *The Legitimacy of the Modern Age*, pp. 309–60, Richard Newhauser, "Towards a History of Human Curiosity: A Prolegomenon to its Medieval Phase," *Deutsche Vierteljahrsschrift für Literaturwissenschaft und Geistesgeschichte*, 56.4 (1982), 559–75, and Edward Peters, "*Libertas inquirendi* and the *vitium curiositatis* in Medieval Thought," in George Makdisi, Dominique Sourdel and Janine Sourdel-Thomine (eds.), *La Notion de liberté au moyen age. Islam, Byzance, Occident* (Paris: Les Belles Lettres, 1985), pp. 89–98.

[14] Gerhart B. Ladner, "*Homo viator*: Mediaeval Ideas on Alienation and Order," in his *Images and Ideas in the Middle Ages: Selected Studies in History and Art*, vol. 2 (Rome: Edizioni di Storia e Letteratura, 1983), pp. 937–74

If it only makes sense that Peter would look to the science of perspective for clues to explain the displacement and failure of our spiritual vision, it remains for all that an interesting and telling strategy. Perspectivist optics does not share Peter's pessimistic belief that human vision is essentially flawed. Roger Bacon and his successors were certainly interested in cases of visual deception. Although the visual illusions associated with reflection and refraction fascinated them, at their core the perspectivists assumed the adequacy of vision and its object, of our ability to see things as they really are. Peter's manual, accordingly, walks an interesting and anything but straight line between vision and its metaphoric failure. Situating the ever-increasing religious preoccupation with seeing and being seen within the framework of the most advanced medieval theory of vision, Peter makes explicit a number of the epistemological and ontological assumptions at work within the practice of medieval religious life. At the same time, these same experiences, now explicitly articulated as analogies of visual experiences, cannot help but reconfigure the theoretical framework in which they have been placed and expressed. Peter's spiritual interpretations of the science of perspective, in other words, challenge the theoretical apparatus of that very science, reveal its hidden tensions and ultimate shortcomings. Spiritual metaphors and analogies quite suddenly become realities, demands to reconsider the nature of vision itself.

In a sense, this chapter will follow the trajectory of Peter's manual, if only to extend it – from the science of vision to its spiritual analogue, I will, in the end, return to the science itself. While I will primarily explore Peter's translation of moral and religious problems into visual problems, I also hope to demonstrate the ways in which Peter's spiritual interpretations of perspectivist optics foreshadow fourteenth-century debates concerning the nature of vision and the distinction between what appears and what exists. While it is unlikely that Peter's manual itself influenced the theologians and scholars that I will examine in the next chapter, Peter's effort to articulate moral and spiritual experience in visual terms, as visual failures, bears a remarkable likeness to the ways in which Peter Aureol and Nicholas of Autrecourt will come to describe our basic cognitive and visual orientation to the world. First, however, it will be necessary to examine the science of perspective itself. Introduced to Europe during the early thirteenth century, it provided Christian scholars with a fully developed account of vision, one they readily adopted and adapted. And it is precisely through these adaptations, through the myriad of unexpected ways in which European thinkers utilized perspectivist concepts, that we can trace the late medieval experience of vision and of a religious life that more and more came to frame its most basic problems in terms of seeing and being seen, and with an ever growing recognition of the fallibility of our spiritual vision.

### ALHACEN AND THE GEOMETRY OF INTROMISSION

Although we generally think of perspective as something pertaining primarily to Renaissance art, as a technique or collection of techniques associated with names like Alberti or Brunelleschi, the medieval science of perspective had nothing to do with art. *Perspectiva*, as it was called, constituted a fully developed and integrated account of light, visual perception and cognition. It combined elements of Galenic medical theory and Aristotelian natural philosophy with Euclidean and Ptolemaic geometrical analysis. Much of this synthesis arrived in Europe early in the thirteenth century, prepackaged in the form of an Arabic text most often translated into Latin with the title *De aspectibus*. Written by the Islamic natural philosopher Alhacen (Ibn al-Haytham) sometime around 1030, *De aspectibus* (or *Kitab al-Manazir*, as it was originally titled in Arabic) marks the crowning achievement of the Greco-Arabic optical tradition. Curiously enough and for no identifiable reason, the work remained largely unknown in the Islamic world until the 1320s.[15] European thinkers like Roger Bacon, John Pecham and Witelo, on the other hand, seized upon Alhacen's treatise almost as soon as it appeared in Europe, where it quickly became the single most influential optical text until Kepler's *Ad Vitellionem paralipomena* of 1604.

Nevertheless, European thinkers did not adopt Alhacen's theories wholesale. Or, it might be better to say, in adopting Alhacen's ideas, they simultaneously adapted them to cohere more fully with their own pre-existing theological and philosophical frameworks. These adaptations were, no doubt, all the easier to make because they were, to some extent, made unknowingly. Alhacen's treatise, as it turns out, was never fully translated into Latin. The first three chapters of *De aspectibus* never made it into any Latin translation, including Friedrich Risner's *Opticae thesaurus* of 1572.[16] As a result, the Latin versions uniformly failed to include Alhacen's explicit discussion of the nature and propagation of light. European thinkers, and Roger Bacon in particular, were completely free to place

---

[15] Ibn Al-Haytham (Alhacen), *The Optics of Ibn Al-Haytham: Books I–III, On Direct Vision*, ed. and trans. A. I. Sabra, 2 vols. (London: The Warburg Institute, 1989). On the reception and transmission of Alhacen's work in the Islamic world see Sabra's introductory comments, vol. II, pp. lxiv–lxxiii, and for its reception in Europe, pp. lxxiii–lxxvi.

[16] *Opticae thesaurus: Alhazeni arabis libri septem, nuncprimum editi. Eiusdem tractatus de crepusculis et nubium ascensionibus. Item Vitellonis Thuringopoloni libri x*, ed. Friedrich Risner (Basel, 1572), reprinted with an introduction by David Lindberg (New York: Johnson Reprint Corp., 1972).

Alhacen's optical theories within the context of their own ideas concerning light.[17]

Central to Alhacen's theory is the belief that vision does not occur through the emission or "extramission" of rays that somehow extend from the eye to the perceived object. Plato had argued for a version of this extramission theory, as had the Stoics and, in various places, Augustine. In the second century, Claudius Ptolemy developed the most sophisticated version of this theory when he combined Euclid's geometrical account of vision with existing Galenic physiological theories and Aristotelian psychology. Whereas Aristotle and Galen provided him with theories concerning the nature of light and cognition, as well as an anatomical account of the eye and brain, Euclid's geometry gave Ptolemy the ability to describe how the visual flux behaved as it moved from the eye to the object. Ptolemy's work remained unknown in Europe until the end of the twelfth century.[18] Throughout that century, William of Conches and Adelard of Bath continued to defend less sophisticated forms of the theory and, in the thirteenth century, Robert Grosseteste did the same. The extramission theory did have its opponents. The ancient atomists had already proposed an alternative theory of perception, an "intromission" theory. According to Leucippus, for example, perception occurred when "effluences" or "images" emanated from the object to the eye.[19] And even though Aristotle had presented devastating critiques of the atomists' theories, he and his followers continued to defend a different version of the intromission theory.

Surveying these seemingly irreconcilable theories, Alhacen admits that the opinions of the "natural scientists," that is, the Aristotelian-influenced defenders of the intromission theory, certainly seem to contradict the opinions of the "mathematicians," that is, the extramissionist followers

[17] Sabra, "Introduction," in *The Optics of Ibn al-Haytham*, vol. II, pp. lxxvi–lxxvii. Sabra writes, p. lxxvi, "The result of this choice was a hybrid theory combining heterogeneous elements that ill-suited one another, and the Latin medieval 'synthesis' was thus fated to bring about a serious weakening of the empirical logic rigorously adhered to in I.H.'s *Optics*." He does not, however, point to any specific aspects of Alhacen's theory so weakened. On Alhacen's experimental methodology see Sabra, "The Astronomical Origin of Ibn al-Haytham's Concept of Experiment," in *Actes du XIIe Congrès International d'Histoire des Sciences*, tome 3a (Paris: Albert Blanchard, 1968), pp. 133–6. Compare with Peter Dear, *Discipline and Experience: The Mathematical Way in the Scientific Revolution* (Chicago: The University of Chicago Press, 1995), pp. 51–53, for a more moderate assessment of Alhacen's accomplishment.

[18] For a translation and discussion of Ptolemy's *Optics*, see A. Mark Smith, *Ptolemy's Theory of Visual Perception: An English translation of the Optics with Introduction and Commentary*, Transactions of the American Philosophical Society, vol. 86, part 2 (Philadelphia: The American Philosophical Society, 1996). Also, A. Mark Smith, "The Psychology of Visual Perception in Ptolemy's *Optics*," *Isis* 79 (1988), 189–207, Gérard Simon, *Le regard, l'être et l'apparence dans l'optique de l'antiquité* (Paris: Editions du Seuil, 1988), pp. 83–186 and Lindberg, *Theories of Vision*, pp. 11–17.

[19] Kirk and Raven (eds.), *The Presocratic Philosophers*, pp. 428–9.

of Euclid and Ptolemy. Nevertheless, Alhacen contends that these differences are more apparent than real, the result of incomplete inquiries and weak methodologies.[20] Alhacen's great achievement was to fuse Ptolemy's mathematical and geometrical analysis of visual perception to an intromissionist program of vision. Alhacen imagines that every visible object consists of a discrete collection of tiny points. When the object is illuminated, forms of light and colour reflect or radiate from each of these points in all directions. Vision occurs when these forms reach the eye. Of course, it couldn't be quite this simple. As Alhacen was quick to recognize, this omnidirectional radiation of light and colour from all points on the surface of the visible object could easily lead to absolute perceptual chaos. If light and colour from every point of the visible object really do radiate in every possible direction, then it would seem to follow that light from each and every part of the object will land on each and every part of the eye's surface. To put it another way, it seems as if any given point on the eye will be bombarded with light from the entire object. The eye, it seems, would see a blur of colour, a mixture that in no way corresponds to the actual objects of vision.[21]

Be that as it may, we do not see a perceptual Babel. Barring injuries or illness, our visual field does, in fact, present us with clearly defined objects and colours. Accordingly, Alhacen reasons, the eye must somehow be capable of sorting through this barrage of light and colour, of selecting and perceiving only one of the multitude of forms of light and colour that reach each point of its surface.[22] And here, Alhacen called upon the tradition of Galenic ocular anatomy which held that sensation does not actually occur at the surface of the eye, but within the eye, on the anterior glacial humour or crystalline lens.[23] If sensation does not occur

---

[20] Alhacen, *The Optics*, I.1, paragraphs 3–6, pp. 4–6. Whenever possible, I shall work from and cite Risner's Latin edition of Alhacen's *Optics*. For those early sections not included in Risner's edition, as is the case here, I shall use Sabra's translation from the Arabic sources.

[21] Alhacen, *Opticae* (Risner, I.14, p. 7; Sabra, I.6, paragraphs 7–8, p. 65): "Peruenient ergo ad totam superficiem uisus multa lumina diuersa, & multi colores diuersi, & quilibet illorum implet superficiem uisus: perueniet ergo in superficiem uisus forma admixta ex coloribus diuersis, & luminibus diuersis. Si ergo senserit uisus illam formam admixtam, sentiet colorem diuersum à colore cuiuslibet illarum rerum, & non distinguentur ab eo uisibilia. Et si senserit unam illarum rerum uisibilium, & non senserit residuas: comprehendet unam rem uisibilem, & non alias: sed ipse comprehendit omnia illa uisibilia in eodem tempore, & comprehendit ipsa distincta. Et si non senserit unam illarum formarum, nihil sentiet ex ipsis, uel ex alijs visibilibus oppositis illi: sed ipse sentit omnia."

[22] Alhacen, *Opticae* (Risner, I.15, p. 8; Sabra, I.6 para. 13, p. 66): "Et si senserit formam uenientem ex uno puncto superficiei rei uisae ad totam superficiem uisus, ex uno puncto tantum superficiei ipsius uisus, & non senserit formam illius puncti tota eius superficie: ordinabuntur ab eo partes rei uisae, & distinguentur omnia uisibilia opposita."

[23] Alhacen, *Opticae* (Risner, I.16, p. 8; Sabra, I.6 para. 14, pp. 66): "Modo ergo consideremus utrum hoc fit conueniens, & possibile ad esse. Et dicamus prius, quod uisio non est nisi per glacialem,

on the eye's surface, Alhacen reasoned, then the surface must act as a refracting medium. When light from one medium (say air) passes through a denser medium (say the eye's outer coat, the cornea), two things can happen. If the ray penetrates the denser medium at a right angle, that is, perpendicularly, it will continue on its same course. If it penetrates the denser medium at some oblique angle, its course will be refracted, its direction will change.[24]

Where does this moderately complicated story of ocular-anatomical geometry get Alhacen? Of all the countless rays that land on each and every point of the crystalline lens, only one arrives at a right angle. Only this ray maintains its original course from a point on the surface of the visible object, through the eye's surface, to a corresponding point on the crystalline lens. Every other ray, by contrast, having reached the eye's surface at an oblique angle, finds its course refracted and altered, and reaches the lens at a similarly oblique angle.[25] Alhacen realized that if the lens could distinguish these two types of rays, that is, distinguish those rays that arrive at right angles from all the others, he could account for our clear vision of objects. When taken together, the sum total of these unrefracted rays effectively recreates the surface of the visible object, point for point, on the much smaller surface of the lens. For this reason, Alhacen suggests that the lens must possess a "selective sensitivity" that allows it to perceive the unrefracted rays, while ignoring the rest.[26] In other words, Alhacen does not provide a purely geometrical or physical account of

siue fiat uisio per formas uenientes ex re uisa ad uisum, siue secundum alium modum." As proof for this idea, Galen noted that vision is impaired when cataracts develop between the cornea and the crystalline lens. See Lindberg, *Theories of Vision*, p. 11.

[24] Alhacen, *Opticae* (Risner, I.17, p. 9; Sabra, I.6 para. 18, p. 68): "Et si fuerint quaedam lineae super quas uenit lux in primo corpore, perpendiculares super superficiem secundi corporis, & quaedam declinantes: extendetur lux, quae erat super lineas perpendiculares in secundo corpore secundum rectitudinem, & que erat super lineas declinantes, obliquabitur apud superficiem secundi corporis secundum lineas declinantes, & extendetur in eo secundum rectitudinem illarum linearum declinantium, super quas obliquabatur."

[25] Alhacen, *Opticae* (Risner, I.18, p. 10; Sabra, I.6 para. 23, p. 70): "Forma ergo, quae uenit super perpendicularem, distinguitur ab aliis formis duabus dispositionibus quarum altera est, quod ipsa extenditur à superficie rei uise ad punctum glacialis super lineam rectam, & residuae ueniunt super lineas refractas: altera autem est, quod ipsa perpendicularis erecta super superficiem uisus, est etiam perpendicularis super superficiem glacialis: & lineae residuae, super quas ueniunt formae residuae refractae, sunt declinantes super superficiem uisus."

[26] See, Sabra, *Commentary*, vol. 2, pp. 69–70, and A. Mark Smith, "Getting the Big Picture in Perspectivist Optics," *Isis* 72 (1981), 579–80. Alhacen, *Opticae* (Risner, I.18, p. 10; Sabra, I.6 para. 24, p. 70), argues that one reason the lens can make these discriminations is that rays are weakened when refracted: "Et operatio lucis uenientis super perpendiculares, est fortior operatione lucis uenientis super lineas inclinatas. Dignius ergo est, ut glacialis non sentiat ex quolibet puncto, nisi formam uenientem ad ipsum punctum super rectitudinem perpendicularis tantum, & non sentiat ex illo puncto illud, quod uenit ad illud punctum uerticationes refractas." Lindberg, *Theories of Vision*, pp. 71–80, provides a nice summary of Alhacen's intromission scheme and discusses some of its shortcomings.

image formation within the eye. Although he calls upon the geometry of refraction to differentiate between oblique and perpendicular rays, he also needs to posit a cognitive process within the crystalline lens that discriminates between types of rays. Even at this stage of visual perception, there is no clear distinction between the geometrical properties of the eye and cognitive activities of the sensible soul expressed through the lens' selective sensitivity.

### ROGER BACON AND THE MULTIPLICATION OF SPECIES

Despite its emphasis on geometrical analysis, Alhacen's optics and, more generally, the tradition of medieval optics Alhacen influenced, consists of much more than a mere reduction of vision to the demands of geometry. It is, ultimately, a theory of perception and visual cognition.[27] All the medieval perspectivists believed that optics provided a comprehensive account of how we first come to know the world, beginning with the radiation of light and colour from objects through the air to the eyes and, ultimately, the brain. For his part, Roger Bacon described this radiation as a "multiplication of species." The immediate source for this idea was, no doubt, Robert Grosseteste, who had been deeply influenced by Neo-Platonic notions of emanation and, more specifically, by the writings of the Islamic philosopher, al-Kindi.[28] For Grosseteste, the manner in which light diffused itself in all possible directions provided a model for all forms of natural causation. In *De lineis, angulis, et figuris*, he argued that all natural causation could be explained in terms of a multiplication of power along straight lines and in all possible directions from the agent to the recipient. "A natural agent," he wrote, "multiplies its power from itself to the recipient, whether it acts on sense or on matter. This power is sometimes called species, sometimes likeness, and it is the same thing whatever it may be called."[29] It was precisely this notion of species, as the

---

[27] Smith, "Getting the Big Picture," 568–9, emphasizes that *Perspectiva* was "the science not of visual perception alone, but of visual cognition." Simon, *Le regard*, makes a similar point concerning the entire optical tradition from antiquity through the Middle Ages. See David C. Lindberg, "Roger Bacon and the Origins of *Perspectiva* in the West," in Edward Grant and John E. Murdoch (eds.), *Mathematics and its Applications to Science and Natural Philosophy in the Middle Ages: Essays in Honor of Marshall Clagett* (Cambridge: Cambridge University Press, 1991), p. 252, n. 14, for a slightly moderating opinion.

[28] David C. Lindberg, "The Genesis of Kepler's Theory of Light: Light Metaphysics from Plotinus to Kepler," *Osiris*, 2nd series, 2 (1986), 12–23, charts al-Kindi's influence on medieval theories of light and the multiplication of species. Also, Vasco Ronchi, *The Nature of Light: An Historical Survey*, trans. V. Barocas (London: Heineman Educational Books, Ltd., 1970), pp. 43–5.

[29] Robert Grosseteste, *De lineis, angulis, et figuris*, trans. David C. Lindberg, in Grant (ed.), *A Sourcebook*, p. 385.

source of all natural causation, including the source of our sensory and intellectual awareness of the world, that Bacon placed at the very centre of his optical theories of perception and cognition.

Bacon contends that visual cognition occurs when species of light and colour reach the eye. Like Alhacen's forms of light and colour, Bacon's species multiply themselves in every possible direction. And again, just like Alhacen, Bacon will argue that only those species that land perpendicularly upon the eye's surface are actually perceived.[30] Bacon, however, is careful to specify the precise relation between an agent and its species. A species must not be thought of as if it were a part of the agent, like a little bit of stone chipped from a huge boulder.[31] Rather, it is an agent's first effect and is similar to that agent "in nature, definition, specific essence and operation."[32] Through its species, an agent reproduces itself in the surrounding medium or, perhaps more accurately, it assimilates the medium to itself. The medium becomes more like the agent.[33] For example, a flame generates species of fire in the surrounding air. These species heat the surrounding air and, therefore, assimilate the air to the nature of fire which is hot. Nevertheless, the fire is not completely present in the air. The air does not become fire. Accordingly, Bacon notes, species possess "a most incomplete being, one which is incapable of completion."[34] Through its species, the agent is present in its specific nature and essence, but not in its full reality. For this reason, Bacon notes, natural philosophers sometimes call a species an "intention . . . because of the weakness

---

[30] Bacon, *Perspectiva*, part 1, distinction 6, chapter 2, p. 74 (lines 86–92): "Et ideo cum corpus oculi sit densius aere, oportet secundum leges fractionis superius determinatas quod omnes ille declinantes frangantur in superficie cornee. Et quia casus ad angulos inequales debilitat speciem, et similiter fractio, et perpendicularis incessus est fortis, ideo species perpendicularis occultat omnes declinantes, sicut lux maior et fortior occultat multas luces debiles, ut lux solis luces stellarum infinitas occultat."

[31] Bacon, *De multiplicatione specierum*, part I, chapter 3, David C. Lindberg (ed. and trans.), *Roger Bacon's Philosophy of Nature: A Critical Edition, with English Translation, Introduction, and Notes, of "De multiplicatione specierum" and "De speculis comburentibus"* (Oxford: Clarendon Press, 1983), p. 44 (lines 4–7): "Et habet tres conclusiones, quarum prima est quod non potest species exire nec emitti ab ipso agente, quia accidens non permittat subiectum nec pars substantialis sine corruptione substantie totius."

[32] Bacon, *De multiplicatione specierum*, part 1, chapter 1, p. 6 (lines 80–5): "Et ideo nulli dubium est quin species sit primus effectus. Quod vero iste primus effectus cuiuslibet agentis naturaliter similis sit ei in essentia specifica et natura et operatione manifestum est ex dicendis, quia agens intendit assimilare sibi patiens, eo quod patiens, ut vult Aristoteles *Libro de generatione*, universaliter est in potentia tale quale est agens in actu, sicut ibidem dicit."

[33] Bacon, *De multiplicatione specierum*, part 1, chapter 3, p. 46 (lines 50–2): "Cum igitur nullo predictorum modorum fiat generatio speciei, manifestum est quod quinto modo oportet fieri, scilicet per veram immutationem et eductionem de potentia activa materie patientis . . ."

[34] Bacon, *De multiplicatione specierum*, part 1, chapter 1, p. 16 (lines 253–4): ". . . licet secundum esse incompletissimum, quod etiam impossibile est compleri . . ."

of its being with respect to the thing, claiming that it is not truly the thing, but rather the intention of the thing, that is, a similitude."[35]

The manner in which the recipient assimilates itself to the natural agent depends in large part on the nature of the recipient itself. While air, for example can be warmed, it cannot become fire. On the other hand, wood has the ability, the active potential, to become warm and, if warmed enough, to be transformed into fire. Likewise, the sense of touch has the capacity to feel and know warmth and the eyes, for their part, have the capacity to see and know the flame's light and colour. Nevertheless, Bacon argues, the natural agent does not generate a variety of species, with one type of species responsible for generating heat in the surrounding air, another for generating fire in wood and other types of species responsible for our various sensory cognitions. Rather, every natural agent acts in only one way, generates only one type of species. Different effects arise as these species gradually assimilate different sorts of recipients to the nature and essence of the agent, when they assimilate air, wood or the eyes.[36]

Now much, if not all, of this is really just standard Aristotelian natural philosophy and boils down to the notion that "whatever is received is received according to the mode of the receiver." It is an idea that appears in numerous guises and in numerous contexts throughout the works of Bacon's Dominican contemporary, Thomas Aquinas. Bacon himself employs the axiom, which he claims to derive from Boethius' *Consolation*, to explain that species are always assimilated to the recipient's mode of existence. All the same, it is worth emphasizing that for Bacon and the perspectivists in general, the same causal processes at work in the world are also at work within the senses, the brain, and even within the sensible

---

[35] Bacon, *De multiplicatione specierum*, part 1, chapter 1, p. 4 (lines 54–6): "Intentio vocatur in usu vulgi naturalium propter debilitatem sui esse respectu rei, dicentis quod non est vere res sed magis intentio rei, id est similitudo." Actually, Bacon contends that the virtue or power that he will primarily designate "species" goes by quite a few names: part 1, chapter 1, p. 2 (lines 23–6): "Et hec virtus secunda habet multa nomina, vocatur enim similitudo agentis et ymago et species et ydolum et simulacrum et fantasma et forma et intentio et passio et impressio et umbra philosophorum apud auctores de aspectibus." Tachau, *Vision and Certitude*, pp. 11–16, discusses some of the ambiguities in Bacon's identification of species with "intentions" and its roots in Avicenna, Alhacen and Averroes. See Robert Pasnau, *Theories of Cognition in the Later Middle Ages* (Cambridge: Cambridge University Press, 1997), pp. 63–85, and Katherine Tachau, "Some Aspects of the Notion of Intentional Existence at Paris, 1250–1320," in Sten Ebbesen and Russel L. Friedman (eds.), *Medieval Analyses in Language and Cognition* (Copenhagen: The Royal Danish Academy of Sciences and Letters, 1999), pp. 333–53, for overviews of later medieval ideas about intentions.

[36] Bacon, *De multiplicatione speciarum*, part 1, chapter 1, p. 18 (lines 296–300): "Et quia sic est quod agens naturale agit a parte sua uno modo, et omne agens quod est agens naturaliter et per modum nature, ideo cum calidum diversas operationes facit in frigidum et in tactum, hoc erit propter diversitatem recipientium, sicut sol per eandem virtutem dissolvit ceram et constringit lutum."

soul.[37] The multiplication of species establishes a real continuity between the agent, the medium and the senses, a continuity through which the visible object is, in some sense, immediately present to the senses. As species reproduce themselves within the eye on the crystalline lens, they assimilate the eye to the very nature of the visible object. But unlike the surrounding air, the eye has the capacity to assimilate itself to the visible object as seen and as cognized. In some sense, the eye becomes what it sees even as it sees what it sees.

### THE ANATOMY OF VISUAL COGNITION

Vision begins within the eye, with the eye's initial assimilation to the visible object. From Alhacen, the perspectivists had learned that the eye's anatomical geometry contributes to an organized reception of light and colour. The eye's spherical shape and the transparency of its outer coat or tunic allows perpendicular rays to pass through unharmed and unaffected. Incidental rays, on the other hand, are refracted and, in the process of being refracted, become too weak to be perceived. Be that as it may, the perspectivists, like Alhacen before them, did not simply treat the eye in terms of its refractive properties. The eye is more than a mere instrument in the cognitive process. Visual cognition actually begins within the eye, on the anterior glacial humour or, as it was also known, the crystalline lens.[38] The eye itself, Bacon argues, is sentient, animated by the visual power that flows to it from the ultimate sensory organ.[39] As a result, the eye has the active potential to assimilate itself to the visible object as

---

[37] Bacon, *Perspectiva*, part 1, distinction 6, chapter 4, p. 86 (lines 245–8): "Item est in medio corporali et materiali, et omne quod recipitur in alio est per modum recipientis, ut dicitur in *Libro de causis* et Boetius dicit in quinto *De consolatione*." Bacon silently acknowledges this continuity between causal processes in the world and within the soul with his reference here to Boethius, who, at this point in the *Consolation*, is actually discussing the relation between the knower and what is known. According to Boethius, *De consolatione philosophiae*, V.4, ed. Adrianus Scuto (London: Burns Oates & Washbourne, Ltd., 1925), p. 150 (lines 71–3): "Omne enim quod cognoscitur non secundum sui uim sed secundum cognoscentium potius comprehenditur facultatem." On Thomas' use of the axiom, John F. Wippel, "Thomas Aquinas and the Axiom 'What is Received is Received According to the Mode of the Receiver'," in Ruth Link-Salinger (ed.), *A Straight Path: Studies in Medieval Philosophy and Culture* (Washington: The Catholic University of America Press, 1988), pp. 279–89.

[38] Bacon, *Perspectiva*, part 1, distinction 4, chapter 2, p. 50 (lines 41–2): "Anterior autem glacialis habet multas proprietates. Nam prima et principalis est quod virtus visiva est tantum in eo, secundum Alhacen et ceteros." Also, Pecham, *Perspectiva communis*, part 1, proposition 36, p. 120.

[39] Bacon, *Perspectiva*, part 1, distinction 5, chapter 3, p. 66 (lines 120–7): "[S]ed incipitur iudicium in eis, et completur per ultimum sentiens, quod est virtus visiva fontalis in nervo communi. Et similiter patet quod oculi sentiunt, et non solum nervus communis. Sed quoniam oculi ordinantur ad virtutem radicalem et ab illa fluunt virtutes ad oculos, et continuatur virtus sensitiva per totum nervum a nervo communi ad oculos, ut dicit Alhacen, ideo una est operatio visiva et indivisa, que perficitur per oculos et nervum communem." Witelo, *Opticae*, book 3, proposition 4, p. 108.

sensed and as cognized.[40] Admittedly, at this stage the judgment is fairly basic. Although sight alone cannot discriminate between colours, when the eye looks at something (under the appropriate conditions), sight at least can judge "without error that light and colour are present."[41]

Visual cognition is not completed in the eye. The process of assimilation continues as species multiply themselves to the common nerve where the optic nerves from each eye come together and the species from each eye unite into a single form. The ultimate sentient organ, the source of all visual power, is located within the common nerve and, presented with one unified and coherently organized collection of species, it judges that one object is present to vision.[42] The assimilative process that began within eyes now deepens as the species proceed to multiply themselves within the brain which, Bacon notes (and here he follows Galen by way of Avicenna) consists of three chambers or cells, each of which possesses different assimilative powers and, therefore, perceives different characteristics of the object.[43] Behind every act of perceptual cognition, there lies a series of cognitive acts and judgments that begins with The eye's initial awareness of light and colour and unfolds throughout the brain's various

[40] One indication of the eye's inherently sentient nature is that it *feels* pain when struck by excessvely bright lights. See, for example, Pecham, *Perspectiva communis*, part 1, proposition 43, p. 126. Alhacen, *Optics* (Risner, I.26, pp. 15–16; Sabra, I.6, para. 67, p. 84), contends that the eye endures some degree of pain, even if at an insensibly low level, whenever it perceives. This pain is the clearest indication that the crystalline lens senses light and color. A. I. Sabra, "Sensation and Inference in Alhazen's Theory of Visual Perception," in Peter K. Machamer and Robert G. Turnbull (eds.), *Studies in Perception: Interrelations in the History of Philosophy and Science* (Columbus: Ohio State University Press, 1978), pp. 15–66, and Smith, "Getting the Big Picture," pp. 581–2, stress the intentional nature of the eye's sentience. Gary C. Hatfield and William Epstein, "The Sensory Core and the Medieval Foundations of Early Modern Perceptual Theory," *Isis* 70 (1979), 370, note that there is no clear distinction in medieval psychology between mental events and physiological events. The ordered reception of light on the crystalline lens depends on both the anatomical structure of the eye and the lens' ability to distinguish and perceive only the perpendicular rays.

[41] Bacon, *Perspectiva*, part 1, distinction 10, chapter 3, p. 154 (lines 145–8): "Est igitur prima cognitio solo sensu sine aliqua virtute anime; et sic cognoscuntur lux et color in universali. Nam visus potest iudicare quod sit color vel lux sine errore quando aspicit rem . . ."

[42] Bacon, *Perspectiva*, part 1, distinction 5, chapter 2, p. 64 (lines 70–3): "Naturaliter enim miscentur due forme eiusdem speciei in eadem materia et loco, et ideo non distinguuntur sed fit una postquam ad unum locum veniunt. Et tunc, quia virtus iudicans est una et species una, fit unum iudicium a re una." Although Bacon clearly distinguishes the ultimate sensory organ from the common sense, Alhacen and Witelo conflated and located them in the common sense. See Smith, "Getting the Big Picture," p. 584, n. 51.

[43] Bacon, *Perspectiva*, part 1, distinction 1, chapter 2, p. 6 (lines 71–2): "Et habet tres distinctiones, que vocantur thalami et cellule et partes et divisiones." Bacon's account of the senses, the brain, their parts and functions belongs to a long-standing tradition that located the various Aristotelian psychological faculties, such as the imagination and memory, within the brain's various chambers and conduits as described by Galen. See Harry Austryn Wolfson, "The Internal Senses in Latin, Arabic, and Hebrew Philosophical Texts," *Harvard Theological Review* 28 (1935), 69–133; Smith, "Getting the Big Picture," pp. 571–5; and, Tachau, *Vision and Certitude*, pp. 9–11.

faculties. Features of objects are seen and perceived as they are judged to be present and they are judged to be present as the object's species assimilate the brain, animated by the sensible soul, to object's nature and essence. The visible object comes to be more fully realized in the sensible soul and the soul more fully assimilated to the visible object through these cognitive acts. At every stage vision involves cognition and without these cognitive acts nothing would be seen.

### PRESENCE, RESEMBLANCE, CORRESPONDENCE

"But now I must tell you something about the nature of the senses in general, the more easily to explain that of sight in particular," writes René Descartes in his *Optics* of 1637. "We already know sufficiently well that it is the mind which senses, not the body."[44] Descartes here distinguishes something he calls the "body" from something he calls the "mind" and locates sensory awareness entirely in the mind. "It is the mind which sees," he will write a few pages later, "not the eye."[45] The eyes consist of nothing but a complex system of lenses capable of focusing and ordering light from external objects and transmitting this information in the form of quantifiable impulses along the optic nerves to the brain. Descartes' stark dualistic mind/body ontology reduces this entire physiological process to strictly mechanistic terms. There is no sensation, no sentient awareness or cognition within the eyes, the nerves or even the brain. Sensation only occurs within the mind's self-enclosed interiority as it receives, reads and interprets these impulses.

Descartes believed he had solved one of the central problems of seventeenth-century optics when he explained the transmission of optical information in terms of a series of mechanistic impulses. Earlier in the century, in 1604, Johannes Kepler had re-imagined the manner in which the eye received, refracted and organized light. "I say that vision occurs," he wrote in the *Paralimpomena ad Vitellionem*, "when the image of the whole hemisphere of the world that is before the eye and even a little more is formed on the white concave surface of the retina."[46] Kepler rejected the traditional perspectivist notion that the crystalline lens is sentient, that it possesses a selective sensitivity that allows it to distinguish and perceive only perpendicular rays. Instead, he conceived the crystalline lens to be just that, a lens capable of focusing all rays, oblique and perpendicular alike, onto the inner surface of the retina. The retinal image was not an *ens rationale*, a being whose existence required the

---

44 René Descartes, *Discourse on Method, Optics, Geometry, and Meteorology,* trans. Paul J. Olscamp (Indianapolis: The Bobbs-Merrill Company, Inc., 1965), p. 87.
45 Descartes, *Discourse,* p. 108.     46 Cited and translated in Lindberg, *Theories of Vision,* p. 203.

presence of a sensible soul that animated the eye and whose cognitive acts selected the rays it would perceive. It was a picture that existed solely because of the eye's geometrical anatomy.[47] As Descartes would point out thirty-three years later, the retinal image could actually be seen in the carefully dissected eye of a recently dead man, "or, for want of that, of an ox or some other large animal."[48]

In effect, Kepler clearly distinguished the physical formation of the retinal image from the soul's perception of that picture. Kepler never did explain how the soul ever saw this picture. Descartes, for his part, resolved the problem by rejecting it. He denied that the retinal image itself was conveyed to the brain, "as if there were eyes in our brain with which we could apprehend it."[49] Mere prejudice, Descartes claimed, had compelled philosophers to assume that the mind must be stimulated to thought through pictures that resemble objects. If Kepler mechanized the process of image-formation within the eye, Descartes mechanized the transmission of the retinal image along the nerves and within the brain to the soul. Rejecting wholesale the idea that objects generate species in all directions, Descartes contended that light is nothing but an impulse transmitted from objects through the air to the eye. The retinal image is simply the organized and focused reception of these various impulses within the eye, impulses that stimulate further impulses along the optic nerves and into the brain where they are communicated to the soul which interprets, perceives and understands them. Depending upon the precise properties of these impulses, the mind sees various intensities of light and various types of colour. Nevertheless, light and colour do not exist outside the mind. They have only a phenomenal or mental existence. The mind interprets and experiences these impulses as colours, and while each intensity of light and each colour *corresponds* to specific (and Descartes believed specifiable) types of impulses, they do not *resemble* anything outside the mind.[50]

---

[47] Sabra, *Commentary*, p. 70, contrasts Alhacen's concept of image formation with Kepler's theory of the retinal image and includes this distinction from Kepler's *Paralipomena*, "Definitio, Cum hactenus Imago fuerit Ens rationale, iam figurae rerum vere in papyro existentes, seu alio pariete, picturae dicantur." See Lindberg, *Theories of Vision*, pp. 193–202, for a summary discussion of Kepler's theory of the retinal image. Lindberg, pp. 205–7, views Kepler as the culminating figure of the medieval perspectivist tradition, who "presented a new solution (but not a new kind of solution) to a medieval problem." The real transformation in optics, he contends, occurred during the seventeenth century as various thinkers, such as Descartes, realized the implications of Kepler's ideas. Simon, *Le regard*, pp. 11–18, and *Sciences et savoirs aux XVIe et XVIIe siècles* (Paris: Presses Universitaires du Septentrion, 1996), pp. 17–21, emphasizes the revolutionary aspect of Kepler's retinal image, insofar as it provided a purely physical explanation of image formation within the eye.

[48] Descartes, *Discourse*, p. 91.    [49] Descartes, *Discourse*, p. 101.

[50] Descartes, *Discourse*, p. 101. In fact, Descartes, *Discourse*, pp. 67–8, compares visual awareness to a blind man feeling his way a with a stick. Although the blind man can learn all sorts of

Now all of this has taken us quite a distance from Roger Bacon, the perspectivists and the thirteenth century, but it is a useful detour. To imagine the eye as a purely physical instrument and sensation as an event enclosed within the soul is to imagine something that would have appeared quite strange, even incoherent, to Roger Bacon and to any of his thirteenth-century followers. The distinction between physical events and psychological events is not nearly so distinct for medieval writers as it would be for Descartes and the tradition that arose in his wake. While it is undeniable that the eye's anatomical structure plays a central role in making vision possible, for the perspectivists, the eye could never have been a mere physical instrument. The coherent reception of light and colour not only requires that oblique rays are refracted and weakened, but that the crystalline lens discriminate between oblique and direct rays, that it rejects the former while selecting the latter. And this, quite clearly, is no longer a strictly physical process. Bacon stresses this when he writes, "Although Alhacen says that the eye is the instrument of the ultimate sentient power and the intermediary between it and the visible object, nevertheless, the eye [itself] necessarily makes judgments and has the power of sight, though incompletely."[51] The

things about his surroundings through the motions communicated to him as he pokes his stick here and prods it there, these motions (Descartes tells us) bear no resemblance to the sensations and ideas he derives from them. Descartes was certainly not the first person to compare visual perception to a man exploring his surroundings with a stick. Diogenes Laertius, *Lives of Eminent Philosophers*, trans. R. D. Hicks, 2 vols. (Cambridge: Harvard University Press, 1950), vol. 1, p. 261, reports that Chrysippus and Apollodorus, two Stoic philosophers, believed that "the thing seen is reported to us by the medium of the air stretching out towards it, as if by a stick." In these ancient accounts, imagining the air as a stick had one distinct advantage. It explained how a distant visible object could, in some sense, be immediately before the eye (thus overcoming problems about mediation and action-at-a-distance). Nevertheless, these accounts were criticized precisely because they reduced vision to a form of touch and because visual perception, one would think, is quite different from tactile perception. See, for example, Galen, *On the Doctrines of Hippocrates and Plato*, ed. and trans. Phillip De Lacy, Corpus medicorum graecorum, vol. 5, part 4, no. 1, section 1–2 (Berlin: Akademie-Verlag, 1980), pp. 473–5. In other words, the primary problem with these accounts for antique philosophers became, for Descartes, their greatest virtue. See, Gérard Simon, "La théorie cartésienne de la vision, réponse à kepler et rupture avec la problématique médiévale," in Joël Biard and Roshdi Rashed (eds.), *Descartes et le Moyen Age* (Paris: J. Vrin, 1997), pp. 107–17, for a summary discussion of Descartes' shift from resemblance to correspondence and some of its epistemological consequences.

51 Bacon, *Perspectiva*, part 1, distinction 5, chapter 3, p. 66 (lines 127–30): "Et licet dicat [Alhacen] quod oculus est instrumentum ultimi sentientis et medium inter ipsum et visibile, tamen oculus necessario habet iudicium et virtutem videndi, licet incompletum." I suspect Alhacen would have agreed with Bacon on this point. None of the medieval perspectivists believed a picture of the world appeared on the crystalline lens (as Kepler argued appeared on the retina). If vision and cognition are intimately joined, then what appears or exists on the crystalline lens can only be those aspects of the species which the lens itself has the active potential to abstract or assimilate. Since the eyes themselves can only judge that colour and light are present, but not which specific colours, it must be that specific colours and light are not actually present on the lens. Rather, they are virtually present, present in the sense that some other power (the common sense, for

eye does not stand between the soul and the world. Rather, the eye, with its initial cognition and judgment, marks the sensitive soul's literal extension into the world and the world's immediate presence to the soul.

Just as sentient processes combine with physiological processes within the eye, in an odd way, they even combine within the medium itself. Vision, Bacon will contend, does not only occur through the eye's passive reception of species, but in necessary conjunction with the extramission of species from the eye to the visible object. "Just as inanimate things produce inanimate species," he writes, "so an animate thing produces species that partake some measure of the power of the soul."[52] These species ennoble the intervening medium "so that it is wholly conformable to and commensurate with the nobility of the animated body, the eye."[53] It is as if the animated sensory organ reaches out to the visible object and establishes a sort of preliminary contact with it. As a result, the medium no longer stands between the eye and its object. Transformed into an extension of the eye itself, assisting the visible object's species as they multiply themselves to the eye, the medium actually unites the eye with its object. In this sense, Bacon's perspectivism still shares certain affinities with classical extramission theories, with the Stoics, for example, who held that vision occurs through the emission of a visual pneuma so that, as Cicero put it in the *De natura deorum*, "the air itself sees with us."[54] Physical and psychological processes unite to form something like

---

example) with a different active potential could assimilate itself to them. In other words, there is no picture of the world imprinted on the crystalline lens. This is why it makes no sense to argue, as does Biernoff, *Sight and Embodiment*, p. 102, for "two very different reproductive paradigms" in Bacon's optics, one of which is a mathematico-geometric paradigm of "pictorial reproduction" (that foreshadows early modern notions of a disembodied soul that uses the body as its picture-taking device) and provides a foundation for experimental science. There simply is no such model present in Bacon's (or any other medieval writer's) work.

52 Bacon, *Perspectiva*, part 1, distinction 7, chapter 2, p. 100 (lines 82–8): "Unde sicut res inanimata facit suam speciem inanimatam, sic res animata facit speciem que habet quodammodo virtutem anime; nam sicut se habet res inanimata ad suam speciem, que similis est ei, sic se habet animata res ad speciem ei similem. Non tamen propter hoc medium quod est inanimatum erit animatum; sed assimilabitur animato per suam similitudinem iam receptam." Also, *De multiplicatione specierum*, part 1, chapter 2, p. 32. As evidence for this claim Bacon notes that when we look in a mirror we can see our own eyes, effectively conflating the species by which our eyes are seen and those species that enable our own vision. Pecham, *Perspectiva communis*, I.45, p. 128, denies that extramitted rays alone could suffice for vision, but quickly adds, I.46, p. 128, that the eyes must emit some sort of "natural light to alter visible species and make them commensurate with the visual power." Witelo, *Opticae*, III.5, p. 87, flatly denies that an extramission of species plays any part in visual awareness.

53 Bacon, *Perspectiva*, part 1, distinction 7, chapter 4, p. 104 (lines 147–9): "Et sic preparat incessum speciei ipsius rei visibilis, et insuper eam nobilitat, ut omnino sit conformis et proportionalis nobilitati corporis animati, quod est oculus."

54 Cited and translated in S. Sambursky, *Physics of the Stoics* (London: Routledge and Kegan Paul, 1959), p. 28.

a continuous and uninterrupted "optical medium" between the one who sees and what is seen.[55]

This emphasis on the continuity between physical, physiological and psychological processes, between the visible object, the medium, the eye and the soul is absolutely central to perspectivist theories of visual cognition, and appears again in the role assigned to the visible species. Just as Bacon makes it clear that the eye is not to be reduced to the level of a mere physical instrument and that the medium actually unites us with the visible object, he is also quite clear that the species themselves must not be thought of as some sort of third party or entity standing between us and the visible object. This is why Bacon stresses the multiplication of species across a quasi-animated medium. It is the visible object in its very nature and essence that arrives within the eye, that reproduces itself within the eye. As a result of the eye's assimilation to the nature of the visible object, Bacon tells us, we see the visible object, not its species, nor any sort of image.[56] John Pecham is even more explicit when he writes, "A species produced by a visible object has the essential property of manifesting the object whose similitude it is and since the species has no permanent being in itself, it necessarily leads into another whose [being] is [permanent]."[57] Species do not imprint pictures of the visible object within the eye. In conjunction with the eye's active potential, with its selective sensitivity, they manifest the object as immediately present to the soul.

Bacon, in other words, does not argue for a mere correspondence, not even for a resemblance, between the visible object and what is perceived.

[55] The expression "optical medium" comes from Lindberg, *Theories of Vision*, p. 9. Lindberg suggests that ancient extramission and intromission theories were united at a deeper level by the belief that vision requires an immediate connection between eye and object, hence the need to transform the medium into an "optical medium." Also, Simon, *Le regard*, pp. 30–6. I think Bacon is still under the sway of this tradition, and his odd mixture of intromission and extramission theories at this point is not so much an example of his desire to reconcile all authorities, but rather his way of reinforcing the immediate connection between eye and object. Compare this with Lindberg's introductory comments to the *Perspectiva*, p. lxxxvi. Similar desires are evident in fourteenth-century theologians like Peter Aureol, who argue that what appears to the senses is both the thing itself and a purely mental entity, it is the thing-as-seen. See below, chapter 4, pp. 129–32.

[56] Bacon, *De multiplicatione specierum*, Part II, chapter 5, p. 134 (lines 104–7): "Et ideo sicut res est terminus super linee recte per quam fit visus rectus, et dicitur sola videri, et non aliqua forma vel ymago, sic terminus linee reflexe erit ipsa res, et illa sola per eam videbitur, et nulla ymago in speculo nec in aere."

[57] Pecham, *Perspectiva communis*, II.5, p. 160 (lines 56–8): "Quod patet quoniam species genita a re visibili essentiali habet rem ostendere cuius similitudo, quoniam in se esse fixum non habens necessario ducit in alterum cuius est." Peter Aureol will make a similar observation in the early fourteenth century. He will distinguish appearances that *reveal* things to us as present and as existing, from pictures that merely *denominate* objects. In other words, when we look at something, we experience it as real and as really before us. Any perceptual theory that makes use of mediating pictures would be unable to account for this experience of the real object as present. Peter's distinction can be traced back to these sorts of optical theories. For more on Peter's theory see below, chapter 4, pp. 130–1.

Rather, he argues for their identity. To put it even more baldly, the science of perspective did not argue for a representational theory of knowledge. We do not see species, we see the object whose species they are. Species are the means by which the visible object reveals and manifests itself to the sensible soul. Whereas Kepler argued that visual perception occurred through the mediation of the retinal image, of a picture that represents the world, the perspectivists contend that visual cognition begins when the crystalline lens conforms itself to the visible object, when and insofar as it can, it becomes the visible object. And here it is not a question of a picture that correctly resembles the world, but of an animated sensory organ that has the capacity to become what it perceives, to be immediately united with its object through this assimilation to the object's very nature and essence.[58]

## FROM VISION TO VISUAL ERROR

Visual errors fascinated the perspectivists and they devoted a great deal of attention to them. Why does a stick appear broken when partially submerged in water? Why does the moon appear larger when it is near the horizon? Nevertheless, the perspectivists did not think that the experience of perceptual error revealed a radical distinction between what appears and what exists. If vision occurs through the eye's assimilation to the object, through the object's immediate presence to the eye, then visual errors arise when something interferes with this process. The object must still be present to the eye, otherwise it would not be perceived at all, but it is only partially present, incompletely assimilated to the eye. In other words, the perspectivists did not organize their discussions of vision around experiences of error and they did not think that the existence of perceptual error posed a fundamental threat to the stability of their theories. Perspectivist thought begins with the assumption that successful visual cognition, that is, truthful and accurate cognition, constitutes the norm through which and within which all varieties of visual cognition can be understood and explained, even cases of deceptive vision.[59]

---

[58] Bacon's position on the identity beween knower and known is even stronger than I present here. In a move that aligns his ideas with later developments in Franciscan theology, Bacon, *De multiplicatione specierum*, Part I, chapter 2, p. 40 (lines 350–3), argues that even singularity is a formal property of entities. In other words, the eye is not simply assimilated to a thing's general traits, but even to its very unique singular essence.

[59] Along these general lines, Simon, *Sciences et savoirs*, p. 83, notes that the topical organization of optical treatises before the seventeenth century progressed from descriptions of direct and accurate perception to discussions of reflected and refracted perception, that is, to cases of *deceptio visus*. While the perspectivist decision to organize their theories around successful visual cognitions has a certain common sense plausibility to it, it is a plausibility that failed to appear to several fourteenth-century theologians. In different ways, both Peter Aureol and Nicholas of Autrecourt,

The perspectivists invariably distinguish direct vision from cases of reflected and refracted vision. Direct vision occurs along straight lines, when the object is placed opposite the eye and species from the object multiply themselves in perfectly straight lines from the visible object to the eye. Reflected and refracted vision name two general sorts of circumstances in which the object's species are impeded and deflected off course, when they reach the eye along broken lines. For example, the object's species might only reach the eye after having been reflected off a mirror or after having been refracted as they passed through media of different densities (e.g., from water into the air). In any event, the perspectivists never questioned that, all things being equal, direct vision was more truthful than either reflected or refracted vision and, for that very reason, that it should provide the model through which all visual cognition could be understood. As Bacon notes almost as soon as he begins his discussion of reflection, "[S]uch vision is not as perfect as when the eye sees by a straight line, since reflection weakens a species."[60] It is this very principle that Alhacen and all his followers employed to account for the coherent reception of light and colour on the crystalline lens. The eye's outer tunics refract oblique rays. As a result these rays are weakened and become less perceptible, while perpendicular or straight rays pass through unimpeded and at full strength.

In addition to the distinction between direct, reflected and refracted vision, the perspectivists contend that there are a number of other conditions that determine the extent to which the visible object is present to the senses. Among other things there needs to be sufficient light and a

---

whom I will analyze in the following two chapters, while undeniably influenced by perspectivist thought, chose to organize their cognitive theories around cases of perceptual error.

[60] Bacon, *Perspectiva*, part 3, distinction 1, chapter 1, p. 252 (lines 28–30): "[V]erumptamen non ita perfecta sicut quando oculus videt per lineam rectam, quia reflexio debilitat speciem . . ." According to Witelo, *Opticae*, V.3, p. 191, reflected species are weaker because (1) their path has been broken and (2) they travel farther to reach the eye, "Lux uero reflexa ab aliquo polito corpore plus debilitatur, tum propter elongationem a loco reflexionis & disgregationem, tum propter ipsam reflexionem." Simon, *Sciences et savoirs*, p. 83, argues that, with Kepler, refracted rays suddenly become normative for understanding truthful vision. According to Kepler, the crystalline lens refracts rays in order to create a coherent retinal image. The eye, in other words, was transformed into an optical device that manipulated rays in order to assist vision. He writes, "Et c'est seulement après lui que des miroirs, les lentilles, les dispositifs optiques divers, cessent d'appartenir au domaine de la *magie naturelle* (comme chez Porta) et de ses curiosités trompeuses ou miraculeuse pour devenir les *instruments physiques* fiables d'une vision améliorée. Ainsi ce n'est pas comme on l'a dit trop souvent la défiance à l'égard des objects techniques, mais une théorie fausse de la vision, qui est à l'origine du piétinement médiéval dans l'utilisation des lentilles. La découverte du processus de la vision en 1604 est donc bel et bien une coupure épistémologique dans l'histoire de l'optique." Hans Blumenberg, *The Genesis of the Copernican World*, trans. Robert M. Wallace (Cambridge: The MIT Press, 1987), p. 642, attributes seventeenth-century receptiveness to optical devices (like telescopes and microscopes) to a growing sense of rupture "between the world and man's organs; the congruence between reality and visibility."

sufficiently rare medium through which the object can be seen. Likewise, the object must be both sufficiently dense or opaque, of a sensible magnitude, and at an appropriate distance from the eye.[61] As the perspectivists were fond of pointing out, an object placed immediately on the surface of the eye cannot be seen. Needless to say, these conditions do not define absolute standards. Alhacen notes that the amount of light required to see something will depend upon the object's size and its distance from the eye.[62] Although some objects are simply too small to be seen no matter how close they are to the eye, there are others which can be seen as long as they are within a certain distance. Small objects that can be seen up close become insensible when moved too far away, while a larger object at that same distance can be seen with ease and with accuracy. Accurate visual cognition takes place when these conditions are proportionate to one another – when, for example, *this* amount of light is adequate to see an object of *this* size at *this* distance.

Direct vision with a properly proportioned set of attendant conditions defines both the normal and the optimal circumstances in which to view an object. When these conditions obtain, sight operates perfectly and we see the object as well as we can given the nature of human visual cognition. When any of these conditions lose their due proportion to the others, sight becomes less accurate. The object reveals itself less fully. In such cases, "the form of the visible thing is not verified as it really is in the thing,"[63] and the perspectivists devoted no little effort to categorizing, analyzing and explaining precisely how these discrepancies came about. They were particularly interested in the sorts of discrepancies induced through the derivative modes of refraction and reflection. Of the ten books that make up his massive treatise, Witelo devotes six of them to reflection and refraction. Depending upon the specific combination of circumstances, refracted species might reveal the visible object to be larger or smaller than it really is. When we look at an object in a clear pool of

---

[61] Bacon, *Perspectiva*, part 1, distinction 8, chapter 1, p. 108 (lines 6–7), claims there are eight conditions, in addition to the presence of visible species: light, colour, moderate distance, the object must be opposite the eye, it must be large enough, it must be dense enough, the medium must be sufficiently transparent, time and a healthy eye. For similar lists see, Alhacen, *Optics*, I.2 para. 21, p. 11, Pecham, *Perspectiva communis*, I.47–54, pp. 130–4, and Witelo, *Opticae*, III.13–15, pp. 120–1.

[62] Alhacen, *Optics*, I.2 para. 15, p. 10.

[63] Witelo, *Opticae*, IV.1, p. 118: "Ex his, quae declarata sunt in libro tertio, patet octo esse necessaria ad perfectam operationem uisus, quae sunt: lux . . . distantia uisibilis à uisu . . . situs oppositionis ipsius uisus . . . magnitudo corporis . . . soliditas corporis uidendi . . . diaphanitas aeris . . . tempus conueniens intuitioni faciende . . . Quodlibet autem istorum latitudinem habet proportionatam ad rem uisam . . . Vniuersaliter ergo quilibet istorum modorum, in quo non uerificatur forma rei uisae, sicut est in rei ueritate, est egressus à temperantia ad rem illam uidendam proportionata: & hec omnia se alterutrum respiciunt secundum conuenientes adinuicem proportiones: & quodlibet ipsorum ad alia octo conuenientem oportet quòd habeat dispositionem, quorum pertractionem relinquimus considerationi animae res propinquius intuentis."

water, for example, it will look larger than it really is.[64] Likewise, species reflected off mirrors will manifest the object in a different place than it really is. The object might, for example, appear to be somewhere behind the mirror. In either case, this interference in the visual chain weakens the species and, therefore, weakens the species' ability to fully assimilate the senses to the object's nature and essence.

According to Pecham, when visual cognition occurs through the assimilation of weakened species, we see an "idol" or "image" of the thing. What is an image? Pecham adds, "I say that it is merely the appearance of an object outside its place." An image does not constitute an intermediary suddenly inserted between the eye and its object. To see an image does not mark the juncture at which perception as identity gives way to mere resemblance, at which the actual presence of the object gives way to some more or less accurate representation. When we see an image, we still see the object itself, only we see it under some sort of deforming condition. In the case of reflected species, "it is the object that is really seen in a mirror, although it is misapprehended in position and sometimes in number."[65] The multiplication of species guarantees that vision always occurs through the object's immediate presence to the senses, even if that presence is somehow weakened and debilitated.

Bacon is even more explicit about this. When he discusses the status of images seen in mirrors, he considers the possibility that what we see is some sort of form or picture of the object impressed in the mirror. There are obvious problems with such an explanation. Suppose I stand in front of a mirror and look at my reflection. If this reflection arises due to an image impressed in the mirror, then it would seem to follow that the image should remain in the mirror even if I move off to the side. Clearly this does not happen.[66] Experimental falsifications aside, what is more significant is Bacon's epistemological critique. "Such an impression," he writes, "would more impede vision, because it would be like a stain in

---

[64] Bacon, *Perspectiva*, part 3, distinction 2, chapter 2, p. 294 (lines 75–80): "Si vero oculus in perspicuo subtiliori, et inter oculum et rem visam sit medium densius, ut aqua plane superficiei vel cristallus vel vitrum et huiusmodi alia perspicua, tunc res apparet longe maior quam sit; nam videtur sub maiori angulo et satis propinquius quam si medium esset uniforme."

[65] Pecham, *Perspectiva communis*, II.19, p. 170 (lines 199–203): "Quid est igitur ydolum? Dico sola apparitio rei extra locum suum. Verbi gratia aliquando oculus ut supra patuit de uno iudicat duo esse, quia res apparet non solum in loco suo sed extra locum suum. Ita est in proposito quo ad hoc quia res in speculo secundum veritatem videtur sed in situ erratur et aliquando in numero . . ."

[66] Bacon, *De multiplicatione specierum*, Part II, chapter 5, p. 132 (lines 55–62): "Atque oportet sciri quarto quod determinant auctores perspective quod reflexio non est intelligenda ut forma seu species veniat a re et figatur in corpore polito et faciat suam speciem ulterius in sensum; quoniam tunc si sentiens primo videns illam formam in parte speculi prima, propter hoc quod forma ibi fixa est, incipiat moveri a situ illius partis adhuc videret se in parte illa speculi, quia forma eius fixa est, sicut quando sic movetur, videt rem quamcunque fixam in suo loco. Sed nunc non est ita . . ."

the mirror." We would only see the impressed image, not the visible object itself. "If the image of Hercules should be depicted in the stain," Bacon adds by way of example, "however much it resembles him, we would not see him . . . but only his image; by similar argument, in the present case, only the impressed image would be seen and not the thing of which it is the image." And again, this is clearly not acceptable because "we know and affirm that we see the thing itself through a reflected species . . .we see nothing but the thing."[67] Vision, all vision, operates on the assumption that sight sees the thing, not any sort of intermediary. As a result and in a rather curious manner, even cases of aberrant and deceptive vision go to confirm this basic assumption. Breaks or impediments in the line of direct vision do not reveal moments during which vision of the thing is somehow usurped, led astray into the order of resemblances and similitudes. They merely testify to the continued identity between object, image and species. Although weakened by impediments, species still manifest the visible object immediately to vision, but not fully and not with full accuracy. Or to repeat Pecham's point, when we see along reflected lines, we still see the object, we simply misapprehend its position.

## *MODO CONSIMILI*: THE VISUAL LIFE OF SIN

Occasionally in the *Tractatus moralis de oculo* Peter of Limoges will signal the shift from perspectivist theory to spiritual analogy with some sort of transitional expression. Having expounded on some selected bit of the science, he might, for example, alert his readers to the coming analogy with words like "similarly" (*modo consimili*) or "morally" (*moraliter*). Just as often, the transition is accomplished fairly abruptly. He might begin the spiritual analogy with some terse expression like "thus" (*sic*) or with no warning at all. In any event, the recitation of perspectivist theory is always distinguished and distinct from its spiritual analogy. Once the spiritual analogy is complete, Peter never returns to the perspectivist doctrine that inspired the analogy. While he uses perspectivist theory to reflect on the experience of spiritual life, he never returns the favour, never uses those experiences to reflect on perspectivist theory itself. This

---

[67] Bacon, *De multiplicatione specierum*, Part II, chapter 5, p. 134 (lines 94–106): "Ceterum magis impederit hec impressio, quia esset sicut macula in speculo. Et ideo si esset bene fortis et sensibilis, sentiretur et non ipsa res per eam, sicut nec aliquid videmus per maculam in speculo quantumcunque esset ei aliquid simile, sed ipsam solam maculam; quoniam si ymago Hercules esset ibi depicta, quantumcunque similis, non videretur Hercules iuxta positus, sed solum ymago; quare similiter hic sola ymago impressa videretur et non res cuius esset ymago. Cum tamen dicimus et scimus nos videre ipsam rem per ymaginem suam mediate speculo, et ideo nichil aliud videmus nisi ipsam rem per speciem reflexam, sicut nichil nisi rem videmus per speciem venientem super lineam rectam super speculo."

one way traffic from the better known (and easier to know) facts of human vision to the hidden secrets of scripture effectively conceals the manner in which Peter's spiritual analogies constantly upset and displace central tenets of perspectivist doctrine. Perhaps none of this would have interested Peter. As he warns his readers throughout the *Tractatus*, earthly knowledge must never become an end in itself. To reconsider the science of vision in light of its spiritual analogy might well have seemed like lowering one's eyes from God to the world and to do that would be to commit the sin of curiosity. It remains, nonetheless, that Peter's spiritual analogies are curious as he consistently develops them in ways that subvert their foundations in perspectivist optics.

"It is proved in the science of perspective," writes Peter, "that a thing appears larger than it really is when the eye is in a rarer medium and the opposite occurs when the eye is placed in a denser medium." By way of example, Peter considers the fairly standard case of an object placed in water. "This is why," he continues, "an object in water necessarily appears larger to an eye in the air and smaller when the eye has been placed in water and the object positioned in the air." None of this is surprising, nor inaccurate. When we see through refracted species, what we see will, depending upon the specific circumstances, appear larger or smaller than it really is. Peter's purpose, however, is not simply to repeat perspectivist doctrines, but to show their moral or spiritual implications. "In a similar way," he writes, "it often happens that when a poor man living in barren poverty sees someone rich in worldly wealth, he judges him to be great. But his sight is deceived in this judgment. And this is why a certain philosopher says, 'None of those who have been given the name sublime are, for this reason, really great: but they seem great to you because you judge them on their pedestal'."[68] Just like our bodily eyes, so too can our spiritual eyes see along refracted lines that distort the manner in which the object presents itself.

Of course, the problem of spiritual misperception and misapprehension does not only plague the poor. Perhaps it is true that when a poor man sees a rich man, sees the clothes he wears and society he keeps, the poor man's spiritual vision is refracted so that he judges the rich man to be great. But by the same token, Peter points out, the rich all too

---

[68] Peter of Limoges, *Tractatus*, VI.12: "Probatur insuper in scienciam perspectivam quod res visa maior quam sit secundum veritatem apparet oculo existente in medio rariore converso contigit oculo posito in medio densiore. Unde oculo existente in aere rem visam existentem in aqua maiorem necesse est apparere, minorem autem oculo in aqua defixo et re visa in aere collocata. Modo consimili plerumque contingit quod pauper aliquis existens in arido paupertatis cum videt aliquem mundanis opulentiis affluentem ipsum iudicabit esse magnum . . . Sed fallitur in iudicio visus eius. Unde dicit quidam philosophus, 'Nemo eorum quos nomen sublimes facit propter hoc magni sunt, sed tibi magni videntur quod metiris eos cum basi sua.'"

summarily dismiss the poor as weak and worthless. And if the poor are wrong in their estimations, the rich are no less wrong. "When a man who is immersed in the transitory riches of this world, sees a poor man far removed from the world of riches, he judges him to be practically nothing, although that same man is revered before the divine eye contemplating his poverty with an unerring judgment."[69] Or, Peter adds as he returns to this theme much later in his treatise, the rich, blinded by the light of prosperity do not even see those unfortunates trapped in the gloom of adversity.[70]

These are far from isolated examples of moral perceptual failure in the *Tractatus*. More often than not, when Peter chooses to allegorize perspectivist discussions of perception, he chooses precisely those discussions that focus on breakdowns in the perceptual process, those moments that emphasize discrepancies between what appears to the senses and what actually exists. All too often, to hear Peter tell it, our spiritual vision is placed in circumstances in which it is unable to properly see and judge its object. And even though Peter devotes quite a bit of attention to the sorts of misperceptions that befall the rich and the poor, priests and scholars, it is a problem that afflicts everyone. He devotes the eighth chapter of his treatise to a lengthy exploration of the many ways in which the seven vices distort our spiritual vision. Pride is like a spiritual blindness that prevents us from seeing our lowly origins.[71] Avarice brings temporal riches closer to the eyes of the heart causing us to imagine that such vile things are actually precious.[72]

---

[69] Peter of Limoges, *Tractatus*, VI.12: "Et Bernhardus ad Eugenium, 'Nunquid quia summus pontifex ideo summus. Econtrario qui transitoriis huius mundi diuitiis est immersus cum videt pauperem a mundanis diuitiis elongatum reputat eum modicum cum revera sit magnus apud diuinum oculum in pauperem respicientem et in iudicio non errantem.'"

[70] Peter of Limoges, *Tractatus*, XIII.2: "Oculus enim qui est in lumine non videt eum qui est in tenebris. Sic et diues qui est in luce prosperitatis non videt pauperem qui est in caligine aduersitatis."

[71] Peter of Limoges, *Tractatus*, VIII.1: "Et vere superbus cecus est cum seipsum esse hominem non cognoscat. Homo enim ab humo dicitur, si autem de humo se esse cognosceret instar terre que elementorum est infima nouissimum locum tenere contenderet et se humiliando infimum reputaret." Peter titles this chapter, "De septem differentiis oculorum iuxta differentiam septem capitalium viciorum." Admittedly, Peter's explicit references to true perspectivist doctrines grow a bit thin during the course of this exposé. He begins his discussion of envy by simply asserting that it is symbolized by the cross-eyed. I might add that this is also the chapter that contains Peter's moderately infamous bit of medieval misogyny at VIII.7, "Septima differenci de luxuria: quod oculi mulieris sint tela impudicicie quibus multi vulnerantur," in which and among other things, we learn that a libidinous vapour emanates from a woman's heart and is carried along with her extramitted visual species. These fumes enter the a man's eyes and infect his heart. Proof for this theory comes from the manner in which a dog's bite enables rabies to spread through the victim's body. See, Clark, "Optics for Preachers," pp. 341–3.

[72] Peter of Limoges, *Tractatus*, VIII.5: "Oculi autem rem clare et plene videre non potest nisi res ab eo proporcionabiliter distet et ideo quod cupidi temporales diuitias super oculos cordis ponunt, peruersum de diuitiis iudicium ferunt ut que sunt vilia reputent preciosa."

The problem of spiritual misperception extends not only to how we see others, but to how we are seen by others and to how we see ourselves. Peter warns his readers to worry about their self-presentation, about the example they give to others. A stick, when partially submerged in water, will appear broken due to the refraction that occurs as species multiply themselves from water to air. Likewise, a normally upright man who, due to the "necessary recreation of the body," partially submerges himself in a moment of delight, will appear morally broken to his neighbours.[73] Similarly, a sinner only perceives his sins through the refracting medium of his lusts. As a result, he does not see the malice in his acts, but only the improperly magnified delight his sin provides him.[74] Or again, just as we are unable to see a thick cloud of fog that surrounds us, so too the sinner is unable to see the clouds of sin in which he dwells.[75]

To a certain extent Peter's interest in and emphasis on experiences of perceptual error mirrors the obvious interest that the perspectivists had in those same phenomena. But there is one key difference. The perspectivists explained perceptual errors as temporary aberrations or interruptions in the visual process. They occurred when, to use Peter's own term, a "deformation" arose in one or more of the eight conditions that define accurate vision. For his part, Peter deploys experiences of perceptual error to quite different ends. Although he repeatedly urges his readers to look at themselves and at others through straight and direct lines, he constantly suggests and, at moments explicitly states, that the conditions for such spiritual vision rarely obtain in this world. Deformations to our spiritual vision are not temporary aberrations. Early on in his treatise, for example, Peter recalls the perspectivist notion that there are three modes of vision:

[73] Peter of Limoges, *Tractatus*, VI.4: "Experitur autem in dicta scientia quod baculus cuius una pars est in aqua et reliqua super aquam prominet oculo existente in aere fractus apparebit. Cuius causa redditur, nam ibidem probatur quod res quam in aqua conspicimus propinquior apparet oculo quam sit secundum veram distanciam sui situs et immo pars baculi existens in aqua non apparet visui in continuum et directum partis alterius, sed ipsi oculo apparet propinquior et ideo videtur esse fractus. Sic contingit interdum quod aliquis qui est secundum veritatem vir rectus et timens deum si fortassis ob causam aliquam aliquando vtatur deliciis huius mundi quo mundanorum oculis sunt propinqua quamuis non totaliter se immergat fluxui deliciarum huiusmodi sed solum ex parte, quia fortassis hoc non facit propter mentis petulanciam, sed propter corporis recreationem necessariam nichilominus quandoque scandalizat plurimos hoc videntes, et vulgo iudicatur spiritualiter esse fractus et a morum rectitudine obliquisse."

[74] Peter of Limoges, *Tractatus*, VI.11: "Peccator autem quando peccatum committit iam culpam non directe vel quasi per fractam lineam respicit seu obliquam vel oblique. Non ne aspicit ad ipsam peccati deformitatem siue maliciam, sed pocius ad delectationem annexam."

[75] Peter of Limoges, *Tractatus*, VI.1: "Probatum est in sciencia perspectiva et hoc docet per experienciam quod oculus in aere nebuloso locatus non videt nec percipit vaporem et nubila quibus est circumseptus cum autem recedens exierit huius modi aerem vaporosum, si tunc retro spiciat videt ipsam quem prius in ipso positus non videbat. Per hunc modum et peccator quamdiu est in peccato peccati sui tenebras non aduertit sed extra peccatum positus et lumine diuine gracie illustratus, tunc primo peccati magnitudinem et caliginem in qua fuit recognoscit."

direct, refracted and reflected. Similarly, he notes, there are three sorts of spiritual vision. One is perfect and will be had "in the state of glory after the final resurrection." This vision is direct or, as Paul writes in his first letter to the Corinthians, "face to face." The second is the refracted vision of the soul separated from the body and reposing in heaven as it awaits the final resurrection. The third mode of vision, the one had in this life, "is the weakest of all and it is characterized by this, that it is made through reflection, just as that vision by which something is seen in a mirror."[76] In this life we see "as through a mirror darkly." Or, as the thirteenth-century Franciscan theologian Bonaventure wrote, in this state of wretchedness we see through "a mirror darkened with the sin of the first man."[77]

Interpreted spiritually, the perspectivist paradigm of direct and accurate vision finds itself reversed. The weakest mode of vision constitutes the norm within which our spiritual vision must be understood. Distortions and deformations are not introduced from without, but constitute the very essence of spiritual vision in this life. Roger Bacon himself had already suggested as much. In the concluding section of the *Perspectiva*, as he extolled the religious value of the optical sciences, Bacon gave a variety of spiritual interpretations to the three modes of vision. For example, God's vision is direct, angelic vision refracted and human vision reflected. "For as a mirror is suited to assist vision by offering species the occasion for multiplying themselves to produce vision," he wrote, "so the body [for human beings], animated by the sensitive soul . . . assists the intellective soul in its cognition."[78] Likewise, human vision itself is threefold, and here, like Peter of Limoges, Bacon notes that in heaven we will possess perfect vision and will see with full rectitude. In this life, however, our vision is reflected and, as a result, departs significantly from rectitude, is significantly weakened. But even here in this life, according

[76] Peter of Limoges, *Tractatus*, III.1: "Doctores perspectiue distinguunt triplicem oculi visionem. Prima est per lineas rectas, secunda per lineas fractas, tercia per reflexas. Quarum prima perfectior est aliis, secunda certior quam tercia, et tercia minus certa. Modo consimili spiritualiter loquendo possumus in homine visionem triplicem designare. Unam perfectam que erit in statu glorie post resurrectionem vltimam. Alia est in anima seperata [*sic*] a corpore vsque ad resurrectionem in celo empireo, diuinam essenciam contemplante et hec visio debilior est quam prima. Tercia est in hac vita que est omnium debilissima et habet hec fieri per reflexionem sicut et visio qua aliquid videtur in speculo, habet fieri mediantibus reflexis lineis."

[77] Bonaventure, *Sententiarum*, Book 2, distinction 23, article 2, question 3, p. 543: "In statu vero *miseriae* videtur per speculum *obscuratum* per peccatum primi hominis; et ideo nunc videtur *per speculum et in aenigmate*. 'Aenigma enim, sicut Augustinus, decimo quinto de Trinitate, est similitudo obscura'."

[78] Bacon, *Perspectiva*, part 3, distinction 3, chapter 2, p. 328 (lines 109–27). Aside from its perspectivist coloring, this general use of I *Corinthians* 13:12, was fairly common. See, for example, Thomas Aquinas, *In Epistolam I ad Corinthios*, chapter 13, pp. 264–5.

to Bacon, the threefold division of vision plays itself out once more. After all, vision is said to be "direct in those who are perfect, refracted in those who are imperfect, and reflected in evildoers and those who ignore God's commandments."[79]

Bacon does not say anything more about his spiritual interpretations and, as far as they go, I suspect Peter of Limoges would not have disagreed with them. Some people possess a better or more accurate moral vision than others. Puffed up with pride, the vain are unable to discern truths accessible to the humble.[80] Certainly, Peter would have his readers count Master Alanus (most likely, Alan of Lille) among the humble. When one of his disciples asked him why he remained "in absurd poverty" while many of his students had become great men, one an abbot, another a bishop and still another an archbishop, Alan replied, "You don't know the lofty gait of perfect dignity and the true greatness of man. It is not to be a great bishop, but a good cleric."[81] Perhaps Peter's perspectivist explanation for Alan's good judgment will be obvious at this point. Whereas the disciple's spiritual eye is immersed in the dense and obscuring medium of worldly riches, Alan's exists in the more subtle and transparent medium of holy poverty.[82] Such examples, no doubt, remain as models to which we ought to aspire. But, given Peter's subversion of the perspectivist paradigm of direct vision, that is precisely the point. Direct moral vision cannot be assumed and the deformations that lead to deceptive vision can no longer be treated as peripheral concerns, as mere interruptions and potential annoyances. Rather, with reflection established as the normative model of spiritual vision, errors and deformations must be assumed as ever present. Accurate perception now stands

---

[79] Bacon, *Perspectiva*, part 3, distinction 3, chapter 2, pp. 328–30 (lines 128–42).

[80] Peter of Limoges, *Tractatus*, XI:i: "Debitam autem dispositionem oculi auferunt ista tria tumor puluis et humor. Sic spiritualiater [*sic*] tumor seu prominentia superbie, puluis auaricie: humor concretus luxurie. Propter primum dicit philosophus, xix, *De animalibus*, quod oculus eminens est visus debilis, profundus est visus boni et fortis. Modo consimili est de homine humili. Nam sicut oculos habentes profundos melius vident de longe distancia et eciam subtilia et minuta, quam habentes oculos tumidos vel prominentes, qui eciam de facili leduntur ab obiecto sensibili, sic et humiles clarius vident subtilia quam superbias."

[81] Peter of Limoges, *Tractatus*, VI.12: "Nota cum magistrum Alanum doctorem egregium et adhuc pauperem quidam quondam eius discipulus et iam factus episcopus ad prandium inuitasset cuius cernes inopiam miror inquit magister non modicum, quia scolares vestri iam facti sunt magni viri, unus est abbas, alter episcopus, alter archiepiscopus, et vos estis in paupertatis ridiculo derelictus. Alanus autem aliter sentiens tanquam habens verum et rectum iudicum tale fertur dedisse responsum. Nescicis inquit quid sit dignitatis perfectissime celsitudo et vera hominis magnitudo. Non est enim magnum esse episcopum, sed bonum clericum."

[82] Peter of Limoges, *Tractatus*, VI.12: "Iste siquidem episcopus cuius oculus erat tanquam in densiori medio diuiciarum immersus, Alanum vere magnum modicum reputabat quem in paupertatis medio subtiliori cernebat."

as something that can only be achieved through the identification and elimination of those deformations.

## THE EYE OF REASON IN THE HOUSE OF CONSCIENCE

In this life our spiritual vision is weakened, its objects deformed and distorted as they reflect against the flawed mirror of our sinful nature. What sorts of visual distortions do mirrors introduce? To someone looking in a mirror, surfaces appear reversed. "The eye," Peter writes, "should not judge something seen in a mirror because the right appears on the left and vice versa and what is high seems low and what is down is up." The moral lesson? We see something spiritually worthless and think it is of real value, while something valuable appears worthless. But if reflection names the conditions under which our spiritual vision finds itself hampered, Peter imagines another sort of reflection that works to undo the first, that allows us to see things as they are. The "eye of consideration" should judge things as they appear in the "mirror of sacred doctrine," only then will "those things that seem to be on the left, that is, what we call adversities, appear to be on the right, that is, prosperities; and vice versa, and so we ought to attend to the usefulness of adversity and the danger of prosperity."[83]

The eye of consideration names the moment in the spiritual-perceptual process when the errors and deformations inherent to that process can be corrected. Needless to say, there is no precise analogue for this moment in standard perspectivist theory. Although visual errors are possible, are perhaps even more common than we might ordinarily think, they are never the necessary outcome of an inherently flawed process. Still, there is a moment when, according to the perspectivists, the "benevolence of the creator" has constructed the visual system in such a way as to prevent potential errors.[84] Peter introduces this perspectivist notion early in his manual when he notes that vision is not completed in the eyes. Paraphrasing Bacon's *Perspectiva* at this point, Peter explains that if vision were completed in the eyes, whenever we look at one thing, we would necessarily see two things because each eye receives its own set of species from the visible object. This, obviously, does not normally occur. Accordingly, there must be another sense where vision is completed and this sense is

---

[83] Peter of Limoges, *Tractatus*, VI.10: "Oculo respicientis in speculo facies apparent prepostere et altitudines videntur euerse. Iudicat non oculus dum res in speculo cernit quod dextrus est esse sinistrus est sinistrus et econuerso et quod est superius esse inferius et quod deorsum esse sursum. Sic et si considerationis nostre oculus secundum doctrine sacre speculum de rebus iudicet, ea que videntur esse sinistra id est aduersa dicit esse dextra id est prospera: et econtrario, vtilitatem aduersitatis et prosperitatis periculum attendendo."

[84] Pecham, *Perspectiva communis*, I.32, pp. 116–18 (lines 697–707).

the "common nerve" or the *ultimum sentiens*, where the optic nerves from each eye meet and the different species from each eye unite into a single form.

In a sense, in this specific sense, Bacon does admit that the eyes are the instruments of the *ultimum sentiens*. By this he means only that they are the means by which different sets of species are able to multiply themselves to that point where the optic nerves meet. It remains, nonetheless, that the eyes are not mere instruments, as Bacon goes on to elaborate in the *Perspectiva*, and certainly not flawed instruments. Accurate visual cognition actually begins within the eyes, animated and brought to life as they are by the sensitive soul. The *ultimum sentiens* does not correct this initial cognition, it deepens it as it sees more of the object.[85] For his part, Peter neglects to mention this more nuanced aspect of perspectivist visual theory, asserting simply that the eyes are the instruments of this other hidden sense. "And since," he writes, "vision is not completed in exterior ocular appearances, but in the common nerve, which is hidden within, we are informed morally that we should avoid rash judgment so that we do not judge things as they first appear, but should recur through recourse to an inner judgment."[86] If all moral perception initially occurs under conditions of a deforming reflection, the second stage of moral perception must work to counteract that deformation, correct it so that our spiritual senses can assimilate themselves to their object's true nature and essence.

Peter addresses the idea of a corrective inner judgment in a variety of ways throughout the *Tractatus*. While his suggestion that we have recourse to such a judgment is obviously a warning not to equate beautiful appearances with moral worth, it also a warning that we must sometimes judge our inner selves, that we must close up our exterior senses and enter the house of our own conscience. We must correct ourselves, correct how we see ourselves. Involvement in the world must be followed by

[85] Peter of Limoges, *Tractatus*, V.1: "Sicut in sciencia perspectiua docetur visio in oculis non completur. Nam eiusdem rei due species diuerse ad vtrumque veniunt oculum et cum diversitas speciei diuersificet iudicium si visio completur in oculis, propter apprehensionem speciei gemine vna res iudicabitur esse due. Oportet igitur vt ponatur aliud senciens propter oculos in quo visio completur. Cuius sunt instrumenta oculi que reddunt ei speciem rei visibilis et hic est communis neruus in superficie cerebri situatus, vbi concurrunt duo nerui a duabus partibus anterioris cerebri, qui post concursum in duos iterum diuiduntur, et sic in oculos extenduntur. In illo ergo neruo communi virtus visiua fontaliter radicatur. Et quia tunc virtus fontalis est vna ad quam continuantur virtutes oculorum, ideo potest vna res apparere vna quamuis videatur a duobus oculis." Compare with, Bacon, *Perspectiva*, part 1, distinction 5, chapter 2, pp. 62–4.

[86] Peter of Limoges, *Tractatus*, V.1: "In hoc autem quod visio in oculis exterius apparentibus non completur, sed in neruo communi qui interius occultatur moraliter informamur vt temerarium iudicum declinemus, nec de rebus vt apparent prima facie iudicemus, sed per deliberationem ad internum iudicium recurramus."

self-examination if one hopes ever "to rest lovingly in God."[87] Although Peter suggests that this advice applies to everyone, clearly he thinks it is especially pertinent to priests. We have already seen Humbert of Romans suggest something similar. As soon as he returns from his travels, Humbert urges the Dominican preacher "to return to himself" and to look for any stains, any spiritual blemishes he may have incurred while standing before his audience.[88] Perhaps he took too much delight in the crowd's gaze or whipped them into a religious frenzy, not for their salvation, but merely to advance his own reputation. In any event, Humbert's text is witness to a fairly general concern that the preacher not be deceived by his own self-presentation, that the outer appearance of sanctity must always reveal a true inner sanctity. "Therefore, the priest, who is assigned to the body of the church through the eye," Peter writes, "as soon as he has fulfilled his external duties to the people assigned to him, ought to return inside to himself."[89]

From seeing and being seen to seeing oneself, the call for self-examination marks what seems to be a shift from an optics of exteriority to an optics of interiority. "There are all too many people," Peter adds, "whose eye wanders forever without and never wishes to return to its own conscience, like a house forsaken of its spiritual gifts." These people are like the actor who is always visiting someone else's house. Just as the hearth in the actor's house remains cold and his plates sit unwashed, so too in the hearts of those who waste their time on thoroughly useless things, "there is no fire of devotion, nor have their plates been washed by tears of compunction."[90] To see the contents of one's conscience is to rediscover those forgotten spiritual gifts, to rekindle a poorly tended devotion. In fact, with the shift in setting, it seems as if the analogies between corporal vision and spiritual vision break down. Peter suggests that the deformations that so often plague our spiritual vision vanish when we look within ourselves. The eye of the flesh cannot know itself

---

[87] Peter of Limoges, *Tractatus*, VII.12: "In quo oculi natura nos instruit quod cum homo circa administrationem exteriorum intenderit, expedit ei vt ad interiora redeat et sic somno spirituali dormire valeat et in deo delectabiliter requiescat."

[88] See above, chapter 1, p. 38. Humbert explicitly ties this self-examination to the institutionalized practice of personal confession.

[89] Peter of Limoges, *Tractatus*, VII.12: "Et ideo prelatus qui est corpori ecclesie pro oculo deputatus postquam vacauit exterius circa commissum sibi populum debet redire interius ad seipsum."

[90] Peter of Limoges, *Tractatus*, VII.12: "Sed multi sunt quorum oculus semper vagatur exterius, nec volunt unquam redire ad suam conscienciam vtpote domum cunctis donis spiritualibus destitutam. Et in hoc similes sunt histrioni qui inuitus inhabitat domum suam et libentius frequentat alienam. Sicut enim domo hystrionis focus est frigidus eo quod hystrio semper moratur exterius, nec est ibi vas ad ignem nec scutella lota, sic in corde hominis qui quotidie vagatur per inutilia nec est ignis deuotionis, nec scutella lota lacrimis compunctionis et ideo peccator non libenter intrat conscienciam suam quod nec ibi inueniret nisi maliciam suam."

and in this, Peter writes, it "differs from the eye of the mind." While our bodily eyes can see others, but never themselves, he explains, "the eyes of the heart can judge infallibly only about themselves."[91]

Unfortunately, the deformations that skew our vision and judgment when we look at others reappear even when we examine ourselves. The optimism that initially characterizes Peter's account of the powers of self-examination quickly fades as he develops the disanalogy, solely to demonstrate the foolishness of judging others before judging ourselves and the impossibility of ever seeing ourselves outside the distorting conditions of our sinfulness. Wise men might well follow scripture and place eyes above their hearts, but this does not guarantee that they see all their sins, nor that they see them as they really are.[92] Peter recalls a story from the *Vitae patrum* concerning the holy hermit Moses, who, having been requested to judge concerning a brother's guilt, arrived carrying a very old, very full basket. When asked about this, Moses responded, "My sins follow after me and I do not see them, yet today I come to judge another."[93] Distinctions between looking out and looking within blur as the very spiritual deformations that skew our moral judgments of others reappear to skew the judgments we make of ourselves. Moses cannot see the sins that he knows envelop him. If he cannot judge himself, how can he possibly judge someone else? Not surprisingly, Peter looks to the science of perspective to explain this spiritual blindness. When the eye is placed in foggy air, Peter writes somewhat earlier in the *Tractatus*, it cannot see the vapours that surround it. Likewise, "as long as a sinner inhabits his sins, he does not notice the shadows of sin [that surround him]."[94] When we look at ourselves, when we enter the house of our conscience, what we see will always come to us along refracted and reflected lines, through the dank unseen fog of sin and the obscuring opacity of lust.

---

91  Peter of Limoges, *Tractatus*, VII.8: "Octavo oculus corporalis est non sui sed alterius cognitiuus. Et in hoc differt oculus carnis ab oculo mentis. Nam oculi corporis semetipsos videre nequeunt sed alia conspiciunt econtrario oculi cordis de se non de aliis infallibiter iudicare possunt. Unde qui alios iudicant et seipsos non, hii oculos mentales conuertunt in corporales."

92  Peter of Limoges, *Tractatus*, VII.8: "Sancti ergo viri non temere iudicant alios, sed solicite norunt iudicare seipsos, scientes quod scriptum est *Ecclesiasticus* XVII, 'Posuit oculi ipsorum super corda ipsorum'."

93  Peter of Limoges, *Tractatus*, VII.8: "Legitur eciam in vitas patrum de sancto moyse heremita qui inuitatus erat in sicilia ad iudicandum ibi fratrem culpabilem, sportam vetustissimam plenam arena portabat. Interrogatus quid hoc esset respondit, 'Peccata mea sunt post me sequentia et non video ea, et hodie venio iudicare aliena'."

94  Peter of Limoges, *Tractatus*, VI.1: "Probatum est in sciencia perspectiva et hoc docet per experiencia quod oculus in aere nebuloso locatus non videt nec percipit vaporem et nubila quibus est circumseptus cum autem recedens exierit huius modi aerem vaporosum. Si tunc retrospiciat videt ipsum quem prius in ipso positus non videbat. Per hunc modum et peccator quamdiu est in peccato peccati sui tenebras non aduertit sed extra peccatum positus et lumine diuine gracie illustratus tunc primo peccati magnitudinem et caliginem in qua fuit recognoscit."

Incapable of stepping outside the circumstances that deform his spiritual vision, the sinner discovers that seeing oneself is little different than seeing another, that he sees himself as if he were another, through a deforming spiritual condition that makes him a stranger to himself. Peter's move to an optics of interiority, in other words, does not mark the shift to a new visual paradigm in which a new relation between (spiritual) eye and object obtains. Rather, it is more like a turn of the head. Instead of looking in *that* direction, now we look in *this* one. The model of external vision prevails and, as a result, even our efforts at self-examination require correction. It is within the context of the inherent failure of all our spiritual perceptions that Peter urges his readers to turn to a correcting vision, to an internal judgment. Here Peter's expression resonates with another metaphor, a metaphor employed to describe the practice of private confession. As early as the twelfth, but especially during and after the thirteenth century, theologians developed a contrast between the inner and outer fora. The outer or external forum was simply the court of law. The internal forum was the court of penance, the court of the soul and the court of conscience. In this court, as the Dominican archbishop of Florence, Antoninus, would explain, the penitent presents himself as both the accuser and the accused to his confessor who acts as the judge.[95] The literal and metaphorical interplay of seeing and being seen re-emerges within the house of conscience itself as the sinner opens himself up to the confessor's correcting eye of reason. According to perspectivist doctrine, Peter notes, a thing's quantity can never be accurately judged along refracted lines, but only along direct lines. "In a similar way," he continues, "sin can be apprehended with certainty according to its proper degree of quantity by him who can see sin directly with the eye of reason." And here, the "eye of reason" names nothing but the ability to interrogate penitents, that is, to hear and judge confessions, "a knowledge that is especially necessary to priests."[96]

For Peter, however, the visibility of preachers to their audience and of penitents to their confessors are simply special cases of the total visibility

---

[95] See above, chapter 2, pp. 70–1.

[96] Peter of Limoges, *Tractatus*, VI.11: "Probatum enim in sepedicta sciencia quod rei uise fractis radiis certificari non potest quantitas, potest autem si videatur per rectas lineas vicem de re aliqua quod nunc videtur in aere nunc in aqua. Modo consimili potest peccatum certitudinaliter apprehendi secundum gradum proprie quantitatis ab eo qui peccatum directe respicit oculo rationis. Hoc autem modo doctor aliquis vel quicunque alius studiosus peccatum respicit qui veritatem in singulis speculando de peccatorum gradibus agnoscendis considerat et inquirit. Et hec quidem notitia potissime prelatis est necessaria qui tenentur habere scrutandem discernendi inter lepram et lepram . . ." Clark, "Optics for Preachers," 337–41, who misses the broader connections between Peter's text and the practice (and problems) of confession, plausibly argues that Peter is also concerned in some of these passages with the strengthening of one's "inner censor." Biernoff, *Sight and Embodiment*, pp. 122–5, depends entirely on Clark's analysis of the *Tractatus*.

that defines us all. Near the very end of the *Tractatus*, Peter will return to the theme of God's ubiquity and omnivoyance with a story borrowed from the eleventh-century Benedictine reformer, Peter Damian. The story concerns a very kind and charitable man who steals a pig. As Peter of Limoges tells it, Jesus, who never neglects the charitable, immediately appears in the guise of a pauper and requests a haircut. The man agrees and, as he cuts the crypto-Christ's hair, discovers two hidden eyes. Terrified, the man asks for an explanation. "I am called Jesus," the pauper says, "who sees all things at all times. With these eyes, I saw the pig you have locked up in the pen." Jesus then vanishes and the man, with great contrition, returns the pig. Two centuries earlier, Peter Damian had told the story a bit differently. Despite its striking ocular imagery, Damian had originally seen in the tale an example of God's forgiveness and grace. His crime revealed, the man quickly recognizes within himself the divine clemency. Peter of Limoges, on the other hand, never says anything about pardon. For Peter, the story is, quite simply, a story about vision, about how everything is visible to God and how that is something we should always remember. Even when we do things in private, behind closed doors or concealed in the dark of night, God can still see these hidden acts with his own equally hidden eyes.[97]

Nevertheless, there are real differences between God's vision and human vision. In the practice of personal confession the ideal of a disembodied and ubiquitous divine surveillance necessarily gives way to the practical reality of the priest who listens, inspects and inquires. As the fourteenth-century Spanish curate Guido de Monte Rocherii would later note, "The priest cannot know [the penitent's sins] as God whose place he holds, unless they are spoken in confession."[98] What God sees

---

97  Peter of Limoges, *Tractatus*, XV.1: "Narrat Petrus Damascenus. Quod quidam homo suem furatus est alienam. Erat autem vir ille hospitalis valde, et quia beati misericordes quoniam ipsi misericordiam consequentur Dominus Ihesus qui nunquam obliuiscitur viros misericordie statim adest in pauperis effigie, et tanquam prolixo crine tonsuram rogauit ille protinus pauperi reuerenter assurgens assumptis forpicibus tondere eum cepit. Quod cum faceret in occipite eius, duos oculos latentes reperit. Quo uiso uehementer expauit, et quid hoc esset quesiuit, cui ihesus. Ego inquit Ihesus uocor qui vndique cunta contemplor. Et isti sunt oculi quibus vidi suem quam in cauea conclusisti, moxque disparuit, et ille uir compunctus suem restituit." According to Peter Damian, *Opuscula varia*, XLII.5, *PL* 145, col. 672, as soon as Jesus disappears, "Ille protinus ad cor rediens, et divinam circa se clementiam recognouit, et quod inique praesumpserat satisfactione purgauit." Newhauser, "Nature's Moral Eye," pp. 135–6, makes a similar point concerning Peter's reworking of this exemplum. The following section of Peter of Limoges' text reinforces this idea: XV.2, "Secundo oculorum diuinorum intuitus est timoris incussiuus ac per hoc a peccati perpetratore retractiuus. Fur ei non auderet furari si sciret a iudice se uideri."

98  Guido de Monte Rocherii, *Manipulus curatorum*, part 2, tractatus 2, chapter 5: "Quod autem teneatur confiteri peccata mortalia manifesta etiam confessori patet: quia ad hoc quod confessor absoluat peccatorem oportet quod sciat peccata ut deus cuius locum tenet, sed non potest scire ut deus cuius locum tenet nisi dicatur in confessione, ergo quantumcumque fit manifestum peccatum confessori debet sibi ipsum dicere in confessione."

immediately and intuitively, the priest must work to uncover as he assists the penitent's recollection and recitation of sins. The priestly eye of reason, accordingly, is in no way a disembodied eye that sees and is not seen. And it certainly cannot name (except as an unattainable ideal) a vantage from which the penitent's sins are fully and clearly revealed, impartially and objectively judged. Rather, it is fully embodied and fully situated in the institutionally orchestrated activity of hearing confessions itself, an activity in which confessions are not merely seen and heard, but produced and constructed. It is embodied in the very being of the confessor himself, in his virtues and in his flaws. Priests, after all, are sinners too and the *Tractatus* quite often reads like a condemnation of priests and scholars, caught up as they are in bodily lust, the desire for advancements, benefices, well-bound books and a sick curiosity for pagan philosophy. In the final analysis, even the confessor's direct gaze is not all that direct and if all spiritual vision operates under conditions of distortion and deformation, the confessor's gaze can be no exception.

To enter into the house of one's conscience, accordingly, is not to enter an essentially private and self-enclosed arena. It in no way, for example, conforms to the popular seventeenth-century visual metaphor of the camera obscura. Philosophers as diverse as Descartes and John Locke employed this metaphor to capture their beliefs concerning the absolute separation of mind and body and the representational nature of perception. The knowing subject, the mind, was like an individual placed and isolated within the dark room of the camera, only discovering the world through an image projected against one of the camera's interior walls.[99] To enter the house of one's conscience, by contrast, is to put oneself on display, to enter into the constructive exchange of gazes. None of the ocular metaphors that Peter deploys interchangeably throughout the *Tractatus*, metaphors like the eyes of the heart, the eyes of the mind, the eye of consideration and of reason, none of them point to the penitent's ability to look immediately and intuitively within himself. Rather, they allude to the increasing tendency among people during the thirteenth century to think about themselves and their spiritual lives in visual terms, in terms of a distinction between what appears and what exists. And as Peter repeatedly points out, as important as these

---

[99] Here is how John Locke, *An Essay Concerning Human Understanding*, book 2, chapter 11, section 17, ed. Peter H. Nidditch (Oxford: Clarendon Press, 1975), p. 163, used the metaphor of the camera, "For methinks the *Understanding* is not much unlike a Closet wholly shut from light, with only some little openings left, to let in external visible Resemblances or *Ideas* of things without; would the Pictures coming into such a dark Room but stay there, and lie so orderly as to be found upon occasion, it would very much resemble the Understanding of a Man in reference to all Objects of sight, and the *Ideas* of them."

distinctions are, they are distinctions that we all too often are unable to make.

## VISION AND CIRCUMSTANCE

Peter's manual assumes an ideal of direct and complete spiritual vision, only to render it unobtainable. The ideal remains in the image of the divine surveillance along with our failure to achieve it. Urging his readers to see themselves through God's eyes, to imagine their every act as utterly transparent, fully revealed and on public display, Peter simultaneously reminds them that what they see has always already been reflected or refracted and, in any case, weakened and distorted. At the risk of tumbling into what the art historian James Elkins refers to as the "maelstrom of metaphor," in which perspective becomes a metaphor for everything and nothing,[100] Peter's normalization of deformations within the moral-perceptual process is an acknowledgment that every perceptual act takes place from within a given perspective. Here, however, we can give a very precise content to this notion of perspective. Peter's spiritual interpretation of medieval optics reveals that every perceptual act is conditioned and potentially skewed by the unique circumstances in which it occurs. What manifests itself to the moral eye, to borrow John Pecham's expression, is an image, that is, the moral object itself, but incompletely, perhaps deceivingly, revealed. We see our sins, but misjudge their severity or number. We never see these moral objects directly, but obliquely. We see them from a given perspective, from a given set of circumstances, which in no case defines a privileged mode of vision, but can only mark our distance from rectitude. The deformations that attend and threaten to distort our every moral perception are not temporary aberrations. Rather, they constitute the very essence of our lives as sinners.

Peter could only draw this spiritual lesson from the science of perspective because the science of perspective itself had incorporated such conditions or circumstances into its very definition of vision. Successful and accurate visual cognition requires that a proper proportion exists between the various circumstances that accompany any visual experience. When these circumstances stand in due proportion to one another (when, for example, the object is of an appropriate size, at an appropriate distance, and so forth) we see the object for what it is and "vision is certified."[101] When these circumstances lose their due proportion, we

---

[100] Elkins, *The Poetics of Perspective*, pp. 15–19.
[101] Bacon, *Perspectiva*, part 1, distinction 10, chapter 1, p. 144 (lines 9–11).

see the object as an image of itself. Nothing in Peter's treatise indicates that he disagreed with any of this.

At the epistemological level, however, Peter's spiritual interpretations put in question our ability to distinguish different sets of circumstances. And here it is not simply a problem of always seeing ourselves and others through refracted or reflected lines. The real problem arises from our inability to recognize the presence of these visual distortions. The hermit Moses, to return to the exemplum mentioned above, does not merely complain that he is unworthy to judge another because his vision is distorted. He claims he is unworthy to judge because he cannot see his own sins. He cannot see and identify, and this means he cannot correct, the specific circumstances that skew his spiritual perceptions. He knows they must be present. For all his holiness, he remains forever on this earth a sinner. Nevertheless, to him they remain invisible. Moses is not an isolated case. All of Peter's examples of distorted spiritual vision reveal that the sinner fails to recognize that what he sees has been distorted. The sinner judges the morally worthless to be valuable because he does not perceive the opaque medium of his lusts. His vision is refracted, but he does not know it. As far as he can tell, he sees with a direct and true gaze. Although he sees the object partially, as an image of itself, he judges it to be the whole object.[102]

At every turn, the perspectivists emphasized the fully contextualized and fully embodied nature of visual cognition. The soul does not view a mechanistically formed retinal image (as Kepler would have it) nor does it read impulses from within the cordoned confines of its own transcendent self-enclosure (as Descartes would have it). For the perspectivists, there is no humanly accessible vantage point outside these circumstances. The soul is fully embodied within the brain and within the eyes. It works together with these organs to realize and to form the visual object as visually cognized. Bodies, for their part, are always specific bodies, existing in specific circumstances, in a fully determined here and now. These circumstances play a decisive role in determining how the object is cognized, how its species are able to reproduce the object within the eye and within the brain.

---

[102] There is a tendency throughout Peter's spiritual interpretations to reduce sin to a strictly episte-mological problem. We sin because we see things incorrectly. If we saw them for what they were, we would no longer sin. In other words, Peter does not account for sin in terms of a flawed will, a will that is so corrupted that it would knowingly seek to sin (think here of Augustine and the pear tree). We sin because we simply do not have the correct information to guide our moral choices. This is a clear case in which the perspectivist cognitive framework determines the shape of Peter's implied moral theory. In fact, the Franciscan spiritualist, Peter John Olivi, would reject perspectivist thought precisely because he believed it compromised human free will. See below, chapter 4, pp. 121–3.

Having thoroughly contextualized visual cognition, the perspectivists apparently failed to recognize that they had simultaneously undermined any ability to distinguish well-proportioned circumstances from deformed circumstances. After all, the perspectivists unanimously maintained that the success or failure of any given visual act depends upon whether certain conditions obtain or fail to obtain. But, as at least one master at the University of Paris would realize in the early fourteenth century, this sort of justification is circular. Any knowledge that the proper conditions obtain, itself presupposes an act of perception whose success already presupposes that those very conditions obtain.[103] Perhaps most perceptual acts are true and take place within a properly proportioned set of circumstances. Unfortunately, at least in the eyes of their critics, no perspectivist, perhaps no one, had any way of demonstrating this. And so it was that slowly, the specter of visual error moved to the very centre of medieval debates about knowledge.

[103] Nicholas of Autrecourt, *Exigit*, p. 228.

# Chapter 4

# NORMALIZING ERROR: PETER AUREOL
# ON THE IMPORTANCE OF APPEARANCES

## ON THE VALUE OF SEEING THINGS INCORRECTLY

When, in the course of his lectures on Lombard's *Sentences*, lectures he composed between 1316 and 1318, the Franciscan theologian Peter Aureol turns to the question of human knowledge, of how we are able to see and know the world around us, he does something that, for the time at least, was really quite novel. He begins his analysis by considering various experiences of perceptual error, experiences in which we fail to see things as they really are.[1] Borrowing from Augustine's *On the Trinity*, Aureol asks his reader to imagine what happens when they look directly at the sun for several seconds, maybe five, maybe ten, and then close their eyes. Even though they are no longer looking at the sun, Aureol points out that they will still see a ring of light, will still seem to see the sun, and this lingering vision only slowly fades away.[2] Later, in a related discussion, he repeats several of these experiences and adds a few more. For example, when a straight stick is partially submerged in water, it appears to be broken.[3] These are common experiences, even ordinary ones, and

---

[1] Portions of this chapter originally appeared in Dallas G. Denery II, "The Appearance of Reality: Peter Aureol and the Experience of Perceptual Error," *Franciscan Studies* 55 (1998), 27–52.

[2] Peter Aureol, *Scriptum super primum Sententiarum*, prooem., section 2, ed. Eligius Buytaert, 2 vols. (St. Bonaventure: Franciscan Institute Publications, 1953–6), vol. 1, p. 198 (lines 48–59): "Prima quidem in visionibus derelictis ex forti visibili, quam ponit Augustinus XI *De Trinitate* Cap. 2, qui ait quod 'plerumque cum diu solem attenderimus vel quaecumque luminaria, et deinde oculos clauserimus, quasi versantur in conspectu quidam colores lucidi varie sese commutantes et minus minusque fulgentes, donec omnino desistant, quos intelligendum est reliquias esse illius formae, quae facta erat in sensu;' et concludit quod 'erat etiam cum videremus et illa erat clarior et expressior, sed multum coniuncta cum specie rei eius quae cernebatur, ut discerni omnino non posset; et ipsa erat visio.' Haec Augustinus. Ex quo patet quod visio solis aut aliorum luminarium remanet in oculo, obiecto recedente, secundum eum et experientiam omnem." On dating Aureol's works, see Tachau, *Vision and Certitude*, p. 88. Stephen D. Dumont, "Theology as Science and Duns Scotus's Distinction between Intuitive and Abstractive Cognition," *Speculum* 64 (1989), 579–81, notes that, more often than not, fourteenth-century theologians raised these sorts of questions about the forms of human cognition, as Aureol does here, in the context of analyzing "the scientific character of theology."

[3] Aureol, *Scriptum*, distinction 3, section 14 (vol. 2, lines 697, p. 25–6): "*Tertia* experientia est de fractione baculi apparentis in aqua."

Aureol's peers and predecessors at the University of Paris had already cited and discussed many of them. What was unique, at least for the time, was what he thought these experiences could teach us. Aureol believed that these experiences of perceptual error held the key to understanding the nature of vision itself.

Aureol was hardly alone in thinking that experiences of perceptual error could play a significant role in epistemology. The ancient world had had its share of skeptics and skeptical schools of thought, and some three centuries after Aureol's death in 1322, René Descartes would find it necessary to utilize his procedure of methodic doubt as a defence against the ever present possibility of error in even the simplest and most seemingly evident perceptions. For all that, Aureol differs from both the ancient skeptics and from Descartes. Not only is Aureol no sceptic, he does not even believe these experiences of perceptual error pose any problem to the general enterprise of human knowledge. For Aureol, these experiences are valuable because they reveal essential aspects of perception and cognition that otherwise would have remained concealed.

What allowed, even compelled Aureol to employ experiences of error in this manner? What made him think that it was in our failure to see what really exists that the true mechanisms of human perception and knowing are revealed? It is certainly not the only possible approach and, what is more important, it had not been the approach of his peers and predecessors at Paris. In the 1270s, Thomas Aquinas, to take one prominent example, had taken a quite different tack. In Thomas' *Summa of Theology* error is a peripheral concern. The model for understanding cognition is drawn from successful experiences of knowing and perceiving. As a result, errors take on a secondary role. Thomas explains them in terms of aberrations and defects that have somehow been introduced into an otherwise properly functioning process.[4] As we saw in the last chapter, Thomas was hardly alone in this approach. Even the topical organization of Roger Bacon's, John Pecham's and Witelo's perspectivist treatises reveals affinities with the Dominican theologian's examination of perception and cognition. Like Thomas, these writers begin with descriptions of standard, direct visual experiences, experiences in which we see the object for what it is. Only then do they move on to more problematic cases in which the norm of direct vision is somehow upset through the introduction of various outside factors such as reflection or refraction. For both the proponents of perspectivist optics and Thomas, visual error

---

[4] For assessments of Thomas' "epistemological optimism," see Eleonore Stump, *Aquinas* (New York: Routledge, 2003), pp. 231–5, and Scott Macdonald, "Theory of Knowledge," in Norman Kretzman and Eleonore Stump (eds.), *The Cambridge Companion to Aquinas* (Cambridge: Cambridge University Press, 1993), pp. 185–9.

is understood entirely in terms of deviations from a norm of success-ful vision.[5] Though far from pessimistic about the existence of human knowledge, Aureol contends that the presence of perceptual error does not reveal aberrations in the cognitive process, it reveals the process itself.

Aureol's displacement of error from the periphery to the center of epistemology occupies a key position in the trajectory of later medieval intellectual life. The attention that later theologians and natural philoso-phers in both England and France would pay to Aureol's analysis should already suggest as much. Aureol's interest in specific cases of perceptual error, his emphasis on particular perceptual and cognitive experiences, is part and parcel of a more general transformation in theories of vision and knowledge that began during the mid-thirteenth and continued well into the fourteenth century. It is, in many ways, a transformation whose contours are best charted through its confrontation with error, a transfor-mation that suggests a radical reorientation in how people during these decades perceived and understood both the world and themselves.

While the medieval university provides the immediate institutional and intellectual context within which to make sense not only of Aureol's thought, but of fourteenth-century epistemological debates as a whole, there are other contexts, more diffuse but no less real, within which these controversies take on a greater cultural and religious significance. From the practices of public preaching and personal confession to Peter of Limoges' reflections on those practices, I have attempted to trace a growing interest in vision, visual relations and visual analogies, an interest arising from within the daily experience of later medieval religious life itself. Perhaps the ideal confession was one that uncovered every sin, that saw every nook and every corner of conscience for what it was, but the gap between what even the most conscientious of penitents could see when they looked within themselves and the full reality of their life as a sinner remained forever unbridgeable. This was a structural feature built into confession as an epistemological practice, a feature that Peter of Limoges articulated in explicitly visual terms, in visual analogies derived from perspectivist theory. When we look within ourselves, our vision is always obscured, refracted, reflected, weakened. While Aureol's decision to organize his analysis of human cognition around experiences of visual deception clearly has its place within the constellation of ideas circulating throughout the universities of England and France, expanding the frame of reference reveals it to be part of larger cultural and religious currents in which the (spiritual) experience of visual error had already come to occupy centre stage, had in some sense become the norm.

[5] See above, chapter 4, pp. 96–8.

It is less a question of pointing out direct lines of influence between religious practices and theological speculation, than it is of illuminating structural similarities and resonances between different fields of cultural experience, of using the vocabulary and experiences of one field to help give meaning to the other. If religious practice had brought the problem of visual error to the foreground, then fourteenth-century debates about the relation between appearance and reality, about how we come to know the world, can be seen as providing an analysis of that experience, of working out its implications. University scholars, for all their specialized training, were still members of their society, shaped by its expectations and participants in its practices, and for that very reason fourteenth-century debates concerning visual error provide us with a uniquely appropriate vocabulary and conceptual apparatus for understanding significant aspects of later medieval cultural and religious experience.[6] Peter Aureol's influential analysis of perceptual error gave rise to a very nuanced and subtle (not to mention problematic) distinction between what appears and what exists. For Aureol and for many of the thinkers who came after him, the discovery of the appearances marked the discovery of the world itself. As it turned out, it also marked the limits of what we could ever know about the world, perhaps even about ourselves.

## THE SCIENCE OF PERSPECTIVE AND ITS THEOLOGICAL OPPONENTS

Peter Aureol was hardly the first medieval thinker to focus on the role that appearances play in our perceptual, intellectual and moral lives. In a slightly different guise, the importance of appearances had already come to the fore with the thirteenth-century science of perspective. Drawing on a host of Greek and Islamic sources (particularly Alhacen's *Optics*), Roger Bacon, John Pecham and Witelo had investigated the structure of perception and the specific processes that determine how things are seen and cognized by viewers. Appealing, as we have seen, to a psycho-physiological causal framework in which the visible object assimilates the eye and sensible soul to its very nature and essence, the perspectivists claimed to have given an immediate, non-representational account of visual cognition. Three things need to be noted here. To begin with, recourse to the physical multiplication of species across the medium allowed the perspectivists to explain away cases of perceptual error in terms of such natural phenomena as, among other things, the refraction

---

[6] See Reiss, *Mirages*, pp. 51–4, for a recent defense of the deep relations between elite and popular cultures.

or reflection of species, the opacity of the medium or the distance of the object from the eye. At the same time, the perspectivists claimed that species were not mediating entities that stand between the eye and its object, entities that render direct access to the visible object forever occluded and blocked. Rather, the multiplication of species across the medium and into the eye establishes an identity between the eye and object. The eye, in some sense, is immediately joined with what it sees, becomes what it sees. As they constantly repeated, we see the visible object, not its species. Finally, Bacon emphasized this strict identity between knower and known when he placed the singular over the universal and claimed that species not only assimilate the eye to the visible object's formal properties, but even to its very singular nature.

While perspectivist thought influenced members of the arts and theology faculties at Paris and Oxford, the precise nature of that influence is somewhat difficult to chart. Predictably enough, the doctrine of the multiplication of species was at the centre of an extended controversy. Some theologians, such as Henry of Ghent, who played a supporting role in Bishop Tempier's condemnation of 219 suspect philosophical and theological propositions in 1277, agreed that visual cognition occurred through a multiplication of species. He also believed that the perspectivists had failed to give a particularly convincing account of how these species were ultimately multiplied from the sensible soul to the intellectual soul.[7] At the other extreme stood Peter Olivi, the controversial Franciscan spiritualist, who denied that a multiplication of species through the medium could accomplish the sorts of things the perspectivists had claimed for it. If each species really does generate the next species in this chain, Olivi argued, then the species that generates vision in the eye would most perfectly and immediately reveal the species that immediately preceded and generated it. The line of multiplied species could in no way account for our direct vision of things, but would insert itself as an infinite chain of mediating entities forever interfering with our direct access to the world.[8]

More telling than Olivi's arguments against the efficacy of species in generating a direct awareness of the perceptual object is the underlying

---

[7] The classic study on the controversy concerning species is Anneliese Maier, "Das Problem der 'Species in Medio' und die neue Naturphilosophie des 14. Jarhunderts," *Freiburger Zeitschrift für Philosophie und Theologie* 10 (1963), 3–32. Also, Katherine H. Tachau, "The Problem of the *Species in medio* at Oxford in the Generation after Ockham," *Mediaeval Studies* 44 (1982), 394–443.

[8] Peter John Olivi, *Quaestiones in secundum librum Sententiarum*, question 58, ed. Bernardus Jansen, 3 vols. (Florence: Quaracchi, 1922–6), vol. 2, p. 487: "Primo, quod illa species magis per se, immediatius et perfectius repraesentabit illam speciem quae est iuxta oculum a qua ipsa immediate gignitur quam possit repraesentare ipsum obiectum longe positum, quoniam omnis similitudo conformius et immediatius repraesentat suum efficiens a quo immediate gignitur quam illud a quo non nisi mediate, et hoc non per unum medium, sed per multa, sicut est in proposito." On Olivi's critique of perspectivist doctrines see Tachau, *Vision and Certitude*, pp. 39–54.

concern that motivates his critique. Olivi contends that perspectivist theory undermines human free will. As Olivi sees it, the perspectivists treated visual cognition as an essentially passive affair. Vision occurs when species, in the role of active agents, assimilate the eyes, in the role of passive recipients, to the nature of the visible object. Olivi feared that such cognitive passivity would necessarily entail a passivity of the human will, a position that not only contradicted common experience, but would undermine the nobility and dignity of our love for God.[9] Olivi's fears were confirmed, albeit implicitly, in the pastoral writings of his Parisian contemporary, Peter of Limoges.[10]

The need to maintain human free will compelled Olivi to posit a thoroughly active theory of cognition and perception. The visible object does not reproduce itself within the senses. Rather, Olivi contends, the cognitive faculties direct themselves towards the object. They apprehend the object through a "virtual attention" that somehow reaches out and conforms or configures itself to the object.[11] Only a direct, non-mediated grasp of the object's unique nature can guarantee that we cognize and perceive this particular individual, as opposed to some mediating entity.[12]

---

[9] Olivi, *Quaestiones*, question 74, vol. 3, p. 124: "Nam et principales rationes, quibus philoso-phantes conantur probare potentias cognitivas non esse activas sed passivas, non minus probant hoc de voluntate. Et tamen ex hoc sequitur destructio libertatis ac per consequens et omnis boni moralis . . ."

[10] See above, chapter 3, p. 114, note 102.

[11] Olivi, *Quaestiones*, question 72, vol. 3, p. 35: "Nam actus et aspectus cognitivus figitur in obiecto et intentionaliter habet ipsum intra se imbibitum; propter quod actus cognitivus vocatur apprehensio et apprehensiva tentio obiecti. In qua quidem tentione et imbibitione actus intime conformatur et configuratur obiecto; ipsum etiam obiectum se ipsum praesentat seu praesentialiter exhibet aspectui cognitivo et per actum sibi configuratum est quaedam repraesentatio eius." Olivi, *Quaestiones*, question 58, vol. 2, p. 407, is quite clear that an active theory of cognition thoroughly undermines perspectivist thought, "sed ponere quod visus sit potentia activa, ita quod eius actus non fiat per species ab obiectis venientes est destruere totam scientiam perspectivam aut maiorem eius partem."

[12] Olivi, *Quaestiones*, question 72, vol. 3, p. 37: "Rursus sciendum quod quia actus cognitivus obiecti individualis est terminatus in ipsum, in quantum est hoc individuum et non aliud: ideo de essentia talis actus est quod sit propria similitudo huius individui, in quantum huius, et quod non sit similitudo aliorum individuorum eiusdem speciei, pro quanto individualiter differunt ab isto. Quod igitur actus iste repraesentet individualem rationem et proprietatem sui obiecti . . ." Olivi is somewhat unclear as to how this virtual apprehension or grasp of the object occurs. He argues that it does not occur through any sort of physical emanation from the eye. Indeed, at *Quaestiones*, question 73, vol. 3, pp. 59–63, he explicitly rejects traditional extramission theories of perception. At *Quaestiones*, question 58, vol. 2, p. 490, he describes this virtual apprehension as a spiritual "extension" towards the object and he compares it with the sense of touch: "Qui radius non est aliud quam ipse aspectus sic virtualiter protensus, et pro quanto ipse aspectus quodam spirituali modo commetitur se pupillae ipsius oculi." Vital du Four would also invoke the metaphor of tactile sensation to describe our immediate visual awareness of objects, John E. Lynch, "The Knowledge of Singular Things according to Vital du Four," *Franciscan Studies* 29 (1969), 294. Late medieval appeals to touch as a means of describing vision are metaphorical appeals employed to stress vision's immediate apprehension of its object. Just as there is nothing between the hand and

Significantly, Olivi claims that both the senses and the intellect are capable of this direct apprehension of the visible object. Since cognition does not arise from the physical reception of species, but rather from the simple act of directing our attention towards the object, Olivi sees no reason why the intellect itself should be denied a direct apprehension of singular existing objects. Olivi admits that in this life the intellect cannot directly perceive objects. All visual cognition, as a matter of contingent fact, occurs through the senses. Nevertheless, he argues that it is bad reasoning to assume that what happens to be the case in this life is necessarily true of the intellect when it is considered in and of itself.[13]

With Olivi's claim that both the intellect and the senses can directly perceive the visible object, certain affinities begin to emerge between Olivi and the perspectivists (or at least between Olivi and Bacon). Bacon himself had already contended that the intellect, in principle at least, could have a direct grasp of the singular existing thing. The intellect, Bacon argued, receives both singular and universal species from the object and could, were it not for the intellect's "weakness in this life," immediately perceive the singular existing object.[14] In fact, Bacon contends that angels, whose intellects do not suffer from our peculiar debilities, do directly perceive singulars. While Olivi rejects the idea that cognition requires the reception of species, like Bacon, he grants the intellect the ability to cognize directly the individual existent. Through a rather circuitous route, Olivi rejects medieval perspectivist theory only to reaffirm one of its underlying assumptions: that the intellect possesses, in principle, if not in fact, a direct, non-mediated, non-representational awareness of the singular visible object.

Of course, we could approach this from the other direction and say that, in a rather surprising way, Bacon's treatment of the intellect works to undermine the very perspectivist methodology he so strongly promoted. The perspectivists had developed their theory of visual cognition by treating certain factual sorts of viewing circumstances as normative for understanding cognition as such. When conditions are normal, when we look directly at the object, we see it for what it is, and the soul's cognitive abilities are fully revealed. Bacon, however, posits singularity as a fundamental principle in objects, even though experience teaches

---

the object it touches, so there is nothing between the eye and what it sees. By contrast, early modern theorists like Descartes, seek to literally transform vision into a form of touch as a means of undermining the rule of visual semblance. See above, chapter 3, p. 92, note 50.

[13] See Pasnau, *Theories of Cognition*, pp. 171–2.

[14] Roger Bacon, *Libri primus communium naturalium fratris Rogeri*, in Robert Steele (ed.), *Opera hactenus inedita Rogeri Baconi*, Fasc. II (Oxford: Clarendon Press, 1909), pp. 104–5, para. 67. The passage is translated in Roger Bacon, *Three Treatments of Universals by Roger Bacon*, ed. and trans. Thomas Maloney (Binghamton: Medieval and Renaissance Texts and Studies, 1989), p. 100.

that we cannot cognize the singular as such. As soon as we try to speak about *this* particular object we necessarily lapse into a discussion of its shared properties (this is a red, soft, square . . .). In a bind, Bacon is practically compelled to posit an intellectual ability for which there is no evidence, an ability that finds itself muted in this life. In other words, for both Bacon and Olivi, this life no longer constitutes the paradigm within which human cognitive capacities can be fully understood. The only way to grasp the intellect's capacities is to abstract it from the concrete here and now and to consider it in and for itself, under ideal conditions. Around the turn of the century, yet another Franciscan theologian, Duns Scotus, would organize his entire theory of cognition around these sorts of ideal or limit cases and, in so doing, would fundamentally alter the way medieval intellectuals thought about cognition and the intellect.

## DUNS SCOTUS AND INTUITIVE COGNITION

"[Aristotle] frequently talks about an intellection of the quiddity," writes Duns Scotus in his commentary on Aristotle's *Metaphysics*, "but he seems to say nothing about intellectual vision."[15] It is not surprising that Aristotle should have said nothing about this. For Aristotle, only the senses perceive things. The intellect, on the other hand, knows essences or quiddities. It knows things in terms of their formal properties. The senses perceive a red rose. The intellect knows "redness." As any good Aristotelian would have put it, "The intellect traffics in universals, the senses in particulars" (*Intellectus est universalium, sensus particularium*). Scotus was certainly not the first medieval thinker to question this aspect of Aristotelian cognitive theory. Bacon had already rejected it and the metaphysical framework that supported it, when he argued that the intellect receives both singular and universal species from the visible object. In principle, if not in fact, the intellect, just like the senses, possesses an immediate awareness of the individual existing thing. Olivi too had argued for the intellect's ability to immediately apprehend the singular thing through an act of virtual attention. Scotus' great contribution to this developing line of thought was to distinguish an intellectual apprehension of a thing's singularity from an intellectual vision of its existence.[16] Scotus would refer to this second form of vision as an "intuitive cognition" and it was this particular form and understanding of intellectual vision that would demand the attention of several generations of scholars.

[15] Cited in Allan Wolter, "Duns Scotus on Intuition, Memory, and Our Knowledge of Individuals," in *The Philosophical Theology of John Duns Scotus* (Ithaca: Cornell University Press, 1990), p. 98.
[16] I take this way of framing Scotus' achievement from P. Isaac Miller, "Singularity in Medieval Minds," (PhD thesis, University of California, Berkeley, 1997), pp. 144–5.

According to Scotus, an intuitive cognition is an immediate grasp of a singular thing's presence and existence. He argued for the existence of this sort of cognition in a variety of contexts, generally contrasting it with another kind of cognition. An abstractive cognition, Scotus contends, is a cognition indifferent to a thing's existence or non-existence. Beginning with the simpler and more accessible case of sensory knowledge, Scotus argues that the senses can have both an intuitive and an abstractive cognition of an object. For example, the senses intuitively grasp or see a singular thing in its "actual existence" whenever they perceive some singular thing, a rose perhaps, as present and existing. Likewise, the senses (according to scholastic psychology) can abstractively grasp that same object when it is no longer present or no longer exists. We can, for example, imagine the rose when we close our eyes. Scotus, however, argued that the intellect was also capable of both intuitive and abstractive cognitions. No one denied that the intellect grasped objects abstractively. We experience intellectual abstractive cognitions whenever we think about "universals and the essences of things . . . whether they exist extramentally in some subject or not, or whether we have an instance of them actually present or not."[17] The intellect abstractively cognizes the redness of the rose when it contemplates redness as such, as a common nature or universal property. But Scotus claimed more. He also argued that the intellect, in principle, could cognize redness intuitively, as existing right here and right now in the singular thing placed before it or, more simply, that the intellect could intuitively cognize the singular thing as existing.[18]

This was a much more controversial claim and more difficult to prove. In this life at least, it certainly seems as if all awareness of external objects

---

[17] John Duns Scotus, quodlibet 6, article 1 in Wadding (ed.), *Opera omnia*, vol. 25 (Paris: 1891–5), p. 243–4: "Major probatur ex perfectione actus beatifici, qui ut melius capiatur, distinguitur de duplici actu intellectus, et hoc loquendo de simplici apprehensione sive intellectione objecti simplicis, unus indifferenter potest esse respectu objecti existentis, et non existentis, et indifferenter etiam respectu objecti, non realiter praesentis, sicut et realiter praesentis; istum actum frequenter experimur in nobis, quia universalia, sive quidditates rerum intelligimus aeque, sive habeant ex natura rei *esse* extra in aliquo supposito, sive non, et ita de praesentia et absentia . . . Alius autem actus intelligendi est, quem tamen non ita certitudinaliter experimur in nobis; possibilis tamen est talis, qui, scilicet praecise sit objecti praesentis ut praesentis, et existentis ut existentis." *God and Creatures: The Quodlibetal Questions*, trans. Felix Alluntis and Allan B. Wolter (Princeton: Princeton University Press, 1975), pp. 135–6.

[18] Scotus develops the contrast between sensory and intellectual cognition at *Lectura*, book 2, distinction 3, part 2, question 2, in *Ioannis Duns Scoti doctoris subtilis et mariani opera omnia*, eds. Carl Balic *et al.* (Vatican City: Typis Polyglottis Vaticanis, 1950–), vol. 18, p. 323: "Ista autem duplex cognitio potest apparere in cognitione sensitiva, nam aliter cognoscit imaginativa quam visiva: visus enim cognoscit rem in exsistentia sua dum praesens est, sed imaginativa imaginatur res dum absentes sunt sicut quando sunt praesentes; nunc autem quae sparsa sunt in inferioribus, unita sunt in superioribus; et ideo intellectus habet proportionaliter quasi vim sensitivam et imaginativam, nam intellectus quando cognoscit rem in exsistentia sua, tunc dicitur videre et esse visus, – sed quando cognoscit rem abstrahendo ab exsistentia, tunc dicitur cognoscere sicut imaginativa . . ."

is mediated through the senses. In his earlier writings, Scotus defended the existence of intellectual intuitive cognitions by considering the limit case of the beatific vision. In heaven, the beatified soul is promised a direct, face-to-face vision of God.[19] Like Olivi before him, Scotus was more than willing to treat such extraordinary cases as normative for his cognitive theory. And this should not be surprising. Theology differs from natural philosophy, and as a theologian Scotus would naturally look to the articles of faith as first principles around which to form his theories.[20] Given what faith teaches, the apparent absence of such cognitions in this life is no indication that our intellect inherently lacks them. Our embodied state may well suppress them, allowing us to utilize only our sensory powers of intuitive cognition here in this life.[21]

The distinction between intuitive and abstractive cognitions not only allowed Scotus to account for the beatific vision, it also responded to his metaphysical conception of singularity. For Scotus, what made a man *this* man, that is, *this* particular man and not *that* particular man, was a formal principle which he variously referred to as the *"differentia individualis"* or (more famously, if less frequently) *"haecceitas."*[22] Bacon's notion of a singular species certainly foreshadowed Scotus' emphasis on the real uniqueness of each individual thing. Most of Scotus' contemporaries were less concerned with the problem of uniqueness and more concerned with the problem of numerability. How could a universal form (the form of man, for example) be multiplied into a plurality of individual instances, into me and you and him and her? As a result, Scotus

---

[19] Scotus, *Lectura* I, distinction 3, n. 92, in Balic *et al.* (eds.), *Opera omnia*, vol. 16, p. 259: "Opinio, quae ponit quod quiditas rei materialis sit primum obiectum adaequatum ipsius intellectus, non est vera . . . Nullus catholicus potest hoc dicere, quia tunc esset alia potentia quando videret essentiam divinam in patria et alia immaterialia." Also, quodlibet 13, article 2, p. 521: "Hoc probatur primo, quia patet quod aliqua potest esse intellectio non existentis; aliqua etiam potest esse objecti existentis, ut existentis, quia talem habebit beatus de objecto beatifico, alioquin posset aliquis esse beatus in objecto, esto per impossibile, ipsum non esset existens, de quo dicitur habere claram visionem, sive facialem, propter hoc quod actus ejus cognoscendi tendit in illud, ut in se praesens in propria existentia actuali." On Scotus' gradual development and extension of intuitive cognition, see Alan Wolter, "Duns Scotus on Intuition," pp. 68–81.

[20] See M.-D. Chenu, *La Théologie comme science au XIIIe siècle* (Paris: Librairie Philosophique J. Vrin, 1957), pp. 71–2, for a general discussion contrasting and comparing first principles in medieval natural science and theology.

[21] Scotus, *Ordinatio* book 2, distinction 3, part 2, question 2, in Balic *et al.* (eds.), *Opera omnia*, vol. 7, p. 535: "Sed quod est impedimentum? – Respondeo: intellectus noster pro statu isto non est natus movere vel moveri immediate, nisi ab aliquo imaginabili vel 'sensibili extra' prius movetur."

[22] See the two essays by Allan B. Wolter, "John Duns Scotus (B. ca. 1265; D. 1308)," in Jorge Gracia (ed.), *Individuation in Scholasticism: The Later Middle Ages and the Counter-Reformation* (Albany: State University of New York Press, 1994), pp. 290–1, and "Scotus' Theory of Individuation," in *The Philosophical Theology of John Duns Scotus*, pp. 68–97. For an interesting survey of conceptions concerning the individual and individuation from Aristotle through Scotus and up to Fichte, see Heinz Heimsoeth, *The Six Great Themes of Western Metaphysics and the End of the Middle Ages*, Ramon J. Betanzos trans. (Detroit: Wayne State University Press, 1987), pp. 193–223.

contends, these theologians had defined individuality negatively, as an accidental property, as the by-product of a thing's existence, of its matter or, perhaps, of its quantity. Scotus found all such explanations deficient. None of these supposed causes accounted for the absolute uniqueness that defines any given singular thing as the very thing it is. Existence, for example, is a property common to all existing things and, therefore, cannot account for any given thing's absolute specificity. Only a positive and formal individuating principle could account for the essential diversity between individuals.

With the notion of *haecceitas*, Scotus effectively disentangled questions concerning individuation and singularity from questions concerning existence. A thing's singularity was no longer tied to its existence, to its instantiation in matter, for example. Rather, it resulted from a positive, formal, and intelligible individuating principle, and this resulted in a new kind of epistemological dilemma. How do we distinguish non-existing singular things from existing singular things? The contrast with Thomas Aquinas is helpful. Aquinas, in brief, had argued that matter individuated things into singulars. As a result, he had found it necessary to ask how God, who was immaterial, could know singulars. This was no longer a problem for Scotus. Singularity had nothing to do with materiality and existence. It was a formal and intelligible property of things and, therefore, in principle knowable to the intellect. Instead, Scotus was compelled to ask how God could know if any given singular thing existed.[23] Or, to put it another way, how could God or the angels or even human beings distinguish a real and existing singular thing from a merely possible or imagined singular thing?[24] It was at this juncture that Scotus found it necessary to extend the role of intuitive intellectual cognitions into this life, claiming that sensitive and intellective intuitive cognitions grasp the singular thing as existing, whereas abstractive cognitions abstract their object from existence or non-existence, from presence or absence. Simply put, intuitive cognitions allow us to make certain existential judgments about the objects of perception and intellection. Intuitive cognitions arise necessarily when a "real and actual relation" is established between the

---

[23] Amos Funkenstein, *Theology and the Scientific Imagination* (Princeton: Princeton University Press, 1983), pp. 138–9. Scotus denied that we, in this life, can grasp a thing's haecceity, *QQ in Met.* VII, question 15, n. 6, in Wadding (ed.), *Opera omnia*, vol. VII, p. 438a: "existentia, quae est alterius ab entitate quidditativa et individuali, quae tamen movet ad intellectionem, quae est visio, . . . omnis entitas actualis est ratio agendi immediate in intellectum, qui capax est, non cujuslibet actionis immediate, sed a tali entitate, sic intellectus Angeli a quacumque entitate, noster non, nunc ab entitate individuali. Quae ratio cum sit capax actionis ab existentia, quae magis videtur alterius rationis." See Miller, *Singularity*, p. 145, n. 40.

[24] John F. Boler, "Intuitive and Abstractive Cognition," in *The Cambridge History of Later Medieval Philosophy*, eds. Norman Kretzman *et al.* (Cambridge: Cambridge University Press, 1982), pp. 465–7.

knower and the object, when the present and existing object acts as the cognition's *per se* motive factor or efficient cause. Abstractive cognitions occur when the motive factor is something other than the object's actual existence, when it arises through some mediating entity, an intelligible species, for example, or some other representation.[25]

## PETER AUREOL, SENSORY ERROR AND APPEARING BEINGS

Scotus' distinction between intuitive and abstractive cognition proved both enormously inspiring and infuriating to subsequent theologians. Peter Aureol can certainly be numbered among those who were influenced by, if ultimately dissatisfied with, Scotus' theory. Summarizing Scotus' distinction, Aureol writes, "intuitive cognition concerns the presence and existence of the thing, and terminates at the thing in its existence." Abstractive cognition, by contrast, "abstracts from being and non-being, existence and non-existence, and from [the thing's] presence."[26] An intuitive cognition, according to Scotus, names a necessary relation between perceiver and perceived. It is impossible to have an intuitive cognition except in the presence of the intuited object. Needless to say, Aureol simply could not agree with Scotus' distinction.[27] As he saw it, both everyday experience and logic demonstrate that we can have

---

[25] Scotus, quodlibet 13, article 2, in Wadding (ed.), *Opera omnia*, vol. 25, p. 522: "Dicentur igitur cognitiones distinctae, et hoc secundum speciem propter rationes formales motivas hinc inde, quia cognitione intuitiva res in propria existentia est per se motiva objective; in cognitione autem abstractiva est per se motivum aliquid, in quo res habet *esse* cognoscibile, sive sit causa virtualiter continens rem, ut cognoscibile, sive ut effectus, puta species vel similitudo repraesentative continens ipsum, cujus est similitudo." Also, p. 525: "Ista distinctione actus cognoscendi supposita potest dici quod primus, scilicet, qui est rei existentis, in se necessario habet annexam relationem realem et actualem ad ipsum objectum; et ratio est, quia non potest esse talis cognitio, nisi cognoscens habeat actualiter ad objectum talem habitudinem, quae necessario requirit extrema in actu, et realiter distincta, et quae etiam naturam extremorum necessario consequitur."

[26] Aureol, *Scriptum*, prooem., section 2, vol. 1, p. 191 (lines 10–12): "Est enim intuitiva, quae concernit rei praesentialitatem et existentiam, et terminatur ad rem ut in se existentem. Abstractiva vero dicitur quae abstrahit ab esse et non esse, existere et non existere, et a praesentialitate." For a brief survey of the fourteenth-century debate concerning intuitive cognition see, Rega Wood, "Intuitive Cognition and Divine Omnipotence: Ockham in Fourteenth-Century Perspective," in Anne Hudson and Michael Wilks (eds.), *From Ockham to Wyclif* (London: Basil Blackwell, 1987), pp. 51–61.

[27] Despite Scotus' claim at quodlibet 13, article 2, in Alluntis and Wolter (trans.), *God and Creature*, p. 292, that "there can be no knowledge of this sort unless the knower has to the object an actual relationship that is such that the *relata* actually exist and are really distinct and given the nature of the relata the relationship necessarily arises," it is not at all clear that he would have characterized intuitive cognition as a merely relational cognition, as a cognition that can only arise when a relation to an existent object exists. When considering the limit case of beatific vision a little later at pp. 296–7, he suggests that the operation of intuitively knowing God is the true perfection of the act and "it is more perfect than anything accompanying it, including also that relationship which the union formally implies, for if I could have the operation without the relation, I would still be beatified." Philotheus Boehner, "*Notitia intuitiva* of Non-Existents

---

intuitive knowledge of objects even if they do not exist or are not actually present. It was at this juncture in his commentary on Lombard's *Sentences* that Aureol introduced his experiences of visual illusions. It was a fateful move, a move that situated the problem of perceptual error at the very centre of medieval theology and cognitive philosophy.

To make his case against Scotus, Aureol considers some relatively common experiences of sensory error. When a straight stick is partially submerged in water, it appears to be broken. When we stare at the sun for a while and then turn away, we continue to see little circles of light that only slowly fade into nothingness.[28] Moving from *a posteriori* arguments to *a priori* arguments, Aureol appeals to the logic of the divine omnipotence. A cognition does not become intuitive simply because it sits in a denominative and causal relation with a real object. God, who can do anything that does not imply a logical contradiction, could interfere in the causal chain. He could destroy the object while maintaining its effects. We could have a supernaturally induced intuitive cognition of a non-existent object.[29] Accordingly, Aureol rejects Scotus' attempt to distinguish intuitive from abstract cognitions in terms of the presence or absence of an existing and present object. A cognition is not intuitive because it stands in some sort of relation to something else. An intuitive cognition is an independent operation, something that can occur whether an existing object is present or not.[30]

Aureol's appeal to sensory error and to the possibility of divine deception are not merely critical elements in his epistemological arsenal. They are also his most basic constructive elements. They reveal not only the distinction, but also the fundamental link between what appears and what exists. In each experience, Aureol contends, what appears to the perceiver differs from what actually exists. He names the thing-as-sensed an apparent or appearing being (*esse apparens*) and contrasts it with the real

According to Peter Aureoli," *Franciscan Studies* 8 (1948), 391, and Rega Wood, "Adam Wodeham on Sensory Illusions with and Edition of *Lectura secunda, prologus, quaestio 3*," *Traditio* 38 (1982), 215, both suggest Aureol misinterpreted (knowingly or not) Scotus.

[28] Aureol, *Scriptum* book 1, prooem., section 2, vol. 1, pp. 198–9 (lines 40–85), presents six such experiences (the first of which is the case of after-images). He presents another eight at I *Scriptum*, distinction 3, section 14, vol. II, pp. 696–7 (lines 8–57); the stick that appears broken is the third.

[29] Aureol, *Scriptum* book 1, prooem., section 2, vol. 1, p. 202 (lines 177–82): "Praeterea, Deus potest omnem rem conservare absque omni alia re a qua non dependet, nisi effective. Potest enim suspendere effectivam causalitatem omnis creaturae, conservato eius effectu; sed absolutum intuitivae notitiae est quaedam res de praedicamento qualitatis secundum sic ponentes, et per consequens non dependet ab obiecto, nisi effective tantum."

[30] Aureol, *Scriptum* book 1, prooem., section 2, vol. 1, p. 203 (lines 1–10): ". . . non bene definitur abstractiva notitia, dicendo quod est illa, quae non terminatur ad rei existentiam et actualitatem praesentem, sed abstrahit ab eis . . . [A]ctualitas, praesentialitas et existentia rei possunt cognosci abstractive; et quod etiam non bene definitur intuitiva, dicendo quod sit illa, quae coexigit rei praesentialitatem . . ."

being (*esse reale*), that is, the thing considered apart from its existence as an object of cognition. Aureol contends that some such distinction must be posited. Among other things, it allows us to avoid falling into the error of those who claim that "everything that appears exists."[31] After all, the partially submerged stick really is straight. Its "brokenness" is only an appearance, possesses only apparent being. The real value of these experiences of sensory error, however, is that they reveal the mode through which all perception and all cognition occurs, including veridical perception.[32] Even when I see a broken stick as a broken stick, for example, appearing being is involved. We do not normally realize this, he argues, because in true vision, the appearing being and the real being coincide.[33]

Aureol's talk of a coincidence between real and appearing beings can be more than a little misleading. Aureol does not mean that the apparent being stands between the perceiver and the thing like an accurate or inaccurate picture or representation. He is aware of the sceptical consequences that arise when intermediaries are posited in the cognitive process. Unlike appearances, representations merely denominate their object. Looking at a picture of Caesar is quite different from meeting the man in the flesh. When Caesar actually appears, walks through the open doorway, we experience him as present before us.[34] Aureol similarly rejects any attempt to explain away his appearances as the result of species or sense-data impressing themselves on the eye.[35] Nor does he want to claim, as some of his critics thought, that we see both the real being and

---

[31] Aureol, *Scriptum* book 1, distinction 3, section 14, vol. 2, p. 697 (lines 57–9): "Et universaliter qui negat multa habere esse intentionale et apparens tantummodo, et omnia quae videntur putat esse extra in rerum natura, negat omnem ludificationem et incidet in errore dicentium quod omnia sunt quae apparent."

[32] Aureol defends his use of sensory error as a means for defining the nature of all cognition, true or false, at *Scriptum* book 1, prooem., section 2, vol. I, p. 200 (lines 99–115).

[33] Aureol, *Scriptum* book 1, distinction 2, section 10, vol. 2, p. 549 (lines 54–7): "Sed per huiusmodi apparentiam obiectivam ostenditur et capitur id quod est de re. Ergo talis apparentia proprie veritas et falsitas dici potest, secundum quod correspondet res vel non correspondet."

[34] Aureol, *Scriptum* book 1, distinction 3, section 14, vol. 2, p. 712 (lines 8–12) clearly distinguishes the formal properties of appearances from representations and pictures: "A priori quidem sic, quoniam impossibile est quin apparitioni formali aliquid appareat obiective. Sicut enim albedine aliquid albet et repraesentatione aliquid repraesentatur et pictura aliquid pingitur, sic apparitione aliquid apparet." He then goes on to develop the contrast between things that appear and things that denominate, vol. 2, p. 713 (lines 33–40): "Sed non potest dici quod denominari tantum, sic quod esse intellectum non sit nisi denominatio quaedam, sicut Caesar pictus denominatur a pictura; per hanc enim denominationem Caesar non est praesens picturae, nec sibi obicitur nec apparet. Ergo necesse est dicere quod per intellectionem tamquam rei simillimam res capiat quoddam esse, ita ut esse intellectum non sit denominatio sola, sed quoddam esse intentionale diminutum et apparens . . ."

[35] Aureol, *Scriptum* book 1, distinction 3, section 14, vol. 2, p. 698 (lines 86–8): "Non valet etiam si dicatur quod illae apparentiae proveniunt ex impressionibus factis in oculo vel dispositione medii, vel ex motibus spirituum vel ex quibuscumque aliis causis." Among other things, Aureol argues that if we perceive, imagine, or in any way think about things through their species, then each of

the apparent being. When I look at the partially submerged stick, I do not see two sticks, one real unbroken stick and another apparent and broken stick. All I experience is the cognition of a single broken stick. Like most every other scholastic thinker, Aureol assumed that our perceptual and intellectual access to the world was direct and unmediated. Appearances do nothing to hinder this access. They make it possible.

Aureol struggled to express this insight. Consider another of his sensory errors. When a candle is moved quickly in a circle in a dark room, the viewer sees a burning circle hovering in the air. Aureol asks two questions: "Where is that circle?" and "What is that circle?" The answer to the first question is that the circle is in the air. But, as he quickly notes, real burning circles do not simply hover in mid-air. This compels him to answer the second question by asserting that the circle is an intentional or apparent being. The circle "is *in the air* having intentional being, or apparent, judged and seen being." Despite this statement placing the circle in the air, Aureol consistently asserts that apparent being has no existence apart from and outside the soul. It is both in the air and in the soul.[36] Of course, there is another related question implicit here, namely, where did this coloured circle seen hovering in the air come from in the first place? Aureol's answer to this question explains why he feels compelled to place the appearance both in the mind and in the air, and why he feels that appearances are not intermediaries standing between the perceiver and perceived.

Aureol contends that these experiences of perceptual error not only reveal a distinction between what appears and what exists, they also teach us that perceptual cognition cannot be passive, cannot arise through the mere reception of species or sense data. Cognition is a productive activity, an activity that results in the creation of apparent beings. In fact, Aureol's position is even stronger. The senses, he tells us, "reach across" to the real being (*transire super rem*), interrogate it and fashion it into a certain

---

these cognitions would be about their respective species and not about the perceived, imagined or intellected thing itself. Needless to say, such a result fails to accord with experience.

[36] Aureol, *Scriptum* book 1, distinction 3, section 14, vol. 2, pp. 696–7 (lines 16–25): "*Secunda experientia est in motu subito baculi et circulari in aere. Apparet enim quidam circulus in aere fieri ex baculo sic moto. Quaeritur ergo quid sit ille circulus qui apparet videnti; aut enim est aliquid reale existens in baculo, quod esse non potest cum sit rectus; aut in aere, quod minus esse potest, nam circulus coloratus et terminatus in aere esse non potest; nec potest esse ipsa visio, quia tunc visio videretur, et iterum visio non est in aere ubi circulus ille apparet; nec alicubi intra oculum esse potest propter easdem rationes. Et ideo relinquitur quod sit in aere habens esse intentionale sive in esse apparenti iudicato et viso.*" Marilyn McCord Adams, *William Ockham* (Notre Dame: University of Notre Dame Press, 1987), pp. 95–6, suggests something similar to this interpretation. But she interprets Aureol through the lens of Ockham's critique and so fails to recognize Aureol's claim that the circle is the subject of a double predication – it is somehow both in the air and in the mind.

kind of being, that is, into an apparent and intentional being.[37] Similarly, in being seen, the real being grasps or accrues that same intentional, diminished and apparent being.[38] The productive interaction between the exterior senses and the thing results in the creation of an apparent being. The candle alone, for example, cannot be responsible for the coloured circle hovering in the air. Not only is the candle straight (and not circular), at any given moment it is in exactly and only one spot. The perceiver himself, in other words, must play some part in generating this appearance. Regardless, Aureol denies that the appearance is an absolute entity, numerically separable from the thing. "The appearance," he writes, "must not be understood as affixed to or superimposed on the thing (as is the case with other sorts of relations), but rather as entirely intrinsic to and indistinguishably joined to it."[39] And this despite the fact (as we have seen) that the thing is "out there" and appearances allegedly have no existence apart from the soul. There is no discrepancy here, Aureol believes, because the appearance does not denominate or represent its object. The appearance is the real being under the mode of being cognized or, even more simply, it is the thing-as-seen.[40] Since nothing is seen or thought unless it appears to the senses or to the intellect, all perception and all intellection are necessarily of appearing beings.[41] They are the terminus of every perceptual and intellectual act. We do not perceive the thing together with its appearance. We perceive the thing as it appears, as an appearing being.[42]

---

[37] Aureol, *Scriptum* book 1, distinction 3, section 14, vol. 2, p. 696 (lines 7–8): ". . . sed actus exterioris sensus ponit rem in esse intentionali, ut patet in multis experientis."

[38] Aureol, *Scriptum* book 1, distinction 3, section 14, vol. 2, p. 713 (lines 25–6): "Ergo relinquitur quod per eam res capiunt esse apparens," and vol. 2, p. 713 (lines 29–30) "Patet igitur a priori quod omnis intellectio, immo omnis cognitio est id quo res apparent et ponuntur in esse praesentiali."

[39] Aureol, *Commentarium in primum librum Sententiarum* book 1, distinction 27, article 1 (Romae, 1596), p. 621; "Claudit tamen aliquid respectivum, videlicet apparere, quod non debet intelligi ut affixam aut superpositum illi rei sicut ceterae relationes sed omnino intrinsecum et indistinguibiliter adunatum." This passage also provides a key for interpreting Aureol's puzzling use of the term "conformity" to define truth, see my "The Appearance of Reality," p. 44, note 54.

[40] At *Scriptum* book 1, distinction 3, section 14, vol. 2, pp. 698–9 (lines 95–117), for example, Aureol cites Augustine's discussion of self-knowledge in *De Trinitate* as the model for this identity between the *esse reale* and its *esse apparens*, that is, between a thing and its appearance. When the mind turns towards itself, it is, in effect, placed before itself in the mode of intentional or apparent being. This split does not divide the soul from itself. It marks the soul's immediate presence to itself. The soul is present to itself in and through its appearance.

[41] Aureol, *Scriptum* book 1, distinction 3, section 14, vol. 2, p. 696 (lines 4–8) argues that if the exterior senses can, and necessarily do, produce appearing beings, so must the interior senses and the intellect which are not less "formative." We fail to recognize this purely intellectual and immediate grasp of the thing because of the intellect's conjunction with the senses.

[42] Aureol, *Scriptum* book 1, distinction 2, section 10, vol. 2, p. 548 (lines 3–79). Wood, "Adam Wodeham." 217–18, n. 19, recognizes both aspects of Aureol's claim. She writes, "Aureol seems to want to claim that the *esse apparens* is both the same as and different from the object." Wood,

## SEEING NON-EXISTENT THINGS

Aureol's emphasis on experience will likewise organize his understanding of intuitive cognition, those cognitions that Scotus believed secured our existential knowledge of the world around us. Since all cognition is cognition of appearing beings, Aureol cannot distinguish intuitive from abstractive cognitions in terms of an immediate grasp of a thing's real being. Since we only cognize real beings through appearing beings, Aureol must distinguish intuitive and abstractive cognitions in terms of the formal traits of appearing beings themselves. These formal traits determine how the perceiver experiences or cognizes the thing. An intuitive cognition is one in which we experience the perceived thing directly, as existing right here and right now.[43] An abstractive cognition is one in which we perceive or cognize a thing in its absence, when, perhaps, we remember it. Aureol suggests that the inherited terms "abstractive" and "intuitive" are probably not the best terms to describe our perceptual and cognitive experience of the world. We occasionally perceive non-existent objects as present. If we perceive a non-existent broken stick, to repeat examples, the perception is false, but no less real. To better jibe with experience, Aureol suggests the term "abstractive" be replaced with "as if imaginary" and "intuitive" be replaced with "as if seen and as if intuitive."[44]

Aureol's shift in terminology is telling and speaks to the same sort of impasse that haunted Peter of Limoges' spiritual interpretations of optical theory some thirty-five years earlier. Employed as a model for articulating

however, ultimately stresses Aureol's claim that the *esse apparens* is a distinct or absolute entity. In a similar interpretive vein, see Julius Weinberg, "The Problem of Sensory Cognition," in *Ockham, Descartes and Hume* (Madison: The University of Wisconsin Press, 1977), pp. 33–49 and Tachau, *Vision and Certitude*, pp. 102–3, who interprets the *esse apparens* as a representation of the extramental thing. Pierre Alferi, *Guillaume d'Ockham: le singulier* (Paris: Les Editions de Minuit, 1989), pp. 219–20, contrasts the distinction between appearing and real beings with Kant's distinction between phenomena and noumena. The comparison with Kant is wrong because Aureol contends there is an identity between appearing and real being. They are the same thing under different modes of being. It seems incorrect, therefore, to reduce apparent being to a strictly subjective phenomenon. Appearing beings cross any subjective/objective or phenomena/noumena distinction. It is both what we perceive and the thing itself. It is worth noting that in England around 1330, Adam Wodeham, *Lectura secunda in librum primum Sententiarum*, prologue, question 4, section 4, eds. Gedeon Gál and Rega Wood (St. Bonaventure: Franciscan Institute Publications, 1990), recognized that Aureol did not want to posit the *esse apparens* as an absolute and, therefore, mediating and representational entity. Wodeham judged Aureol's claim to be incoherent.

43 Aureol, *Scriptum* book 1, prooem., section 2, vol. 1, pp. 204–5 (lines 19–56), contends that an appearance presents its object intuitively when it presents it to the perceiver as (1) immediately before us, (2) as present, (3) as actual and (4) as existing. See Boehner, "*Notitia intuitiva*," pp. 397–402 and Tachau, *Vision and Certitude*, p. 108.

44 Aureol, *Scriptum* book 1, prooem., section 2, vol. 1, p. 217 (lines 38–42): "Vocabulum autem 'abstractivae notitiae' non est multum proprium. Unde magis compenter dici potest 'quasi imaginaria', sicut et altera 'quasi visiva' et 'quasi intuitiva'; utrumque enim vocabulum a sensitiva notitia transfertur ad intellectum."

our religious and moral experience, medieval optical theory left the individual in the rather unenviable situation of never really being able to determine the directness and, therefore, the truth of his spiritual perceptions. The perspectivists posited direct vision as a standard and norm against which less accurate modes of vision could be read off as mere deviations. For the individual placed within such a cognitive and epistemological framework, these discriminations proved rather hard to make. What I referred to in the last chapter as the experience of perspective is precisely this recognition that every cognitive act is always already contextualized, quite possibly deformed. As Peter of Limoges' spiritual interpretations revealed, these deformations can be quite invisible and impossible to identify. We believe we see things correctly, but we do not. The experience of perspective is the experience of experience's own self-enclosure, its necessary self-referentiality, of the individual's inability to ever move outside of experience to determine its rectitude and conformity to the norm of direct vision.[45] What is the lesson learned from the practice of personal confession and from Peter's reflections on our moral and spiritual lives? We are as opaque to ourselves as we are to others. The quality of our moral acts, so clear at first glance, is reflected and refracted through countless intentions and hidden motives. These tears, this contrition, in the end they are nothing more than appearances, revealing as much as they conceal, forever foreclosing on the possibility that we could move beyond them to the whole truth. Aureol's distinction between intuitive and abstractive cognition, a distinction that no longer refers to an object outside experience, but solely to the phenomenological qualities of cognition itself, is a distinction that mirrors Peter of Limoges' spiritual analogies. If Peter of Limoges moved from the science of perspective to its spiritual analogy, Peter Aureol's theories seem to have incorporated the lessons of those spiritual analogies and reapplied them to cognitive philosophy and to epistemology.

Predictably enough, having incorporated those analogies, Aureol incorporates the dilemma that went along with them. Aureol's analysis of experience merely replaces one set of problems with another. Aureol rejects Scotus' attempt to define cognitions in terms of their relation to extramental objects. Intuitive cognitions, according to Scotus (according to Aureol), arise when a perceiver and an object stand in the correct causal relation to one another. The problem, as Aureol saw it, is that we can experience an object as present, even if it is absent. In other words, cognitions are absolute operations. A cognition is intuitive if it presents

---

[45] Compare this with what Karsten Harries, *The Infinity of Perspective* (Cambridge: The MIT Press, 2001), p. 43, refers to as the "principle of perspective," something he believes can be found in Nicholas of Cusa's fifteenth-century writings.

its object as present and existing, whether or not that object is present, even if it does not exist. The character of the cognition derives entirely from traits arising within the act or operation of cognition itself. Defining intuitive cognition as an absolute, self-contained operation had the potential advantage of explaining our immediate and veridical cognitive access to the world around us. Every cognition terminates in an appearing being and, at least in veridical perceptions, the appearance of a stick, let's say, is not a representation. It is the stick itself as it appears. But how to discriminate true from false intuitive cognitions? In principle, they are qualitatively identical. Indeed, how are we even to account for them?

The perspectivists, of course, could appeal to a physical explanation for perceptual errors. When species are refracted or reflected, when the medium is opaque, when the light is too bright or too dim, we see the object as an image of itself. They could also appeal to the physiology of the eye or brain. If the individual has cataracts or has suffered some trauma to the head, the sensible soul's anatomically-localized cognitive capacities might be hindered. Aureol can have no such recourse. Although he accepts the existence of species, sensitive and intellectual intuitive cognition occurs independently of them. Our cognitive powers reach out to their objects directly and without any mediating entities. Having posited a non-physical grasp of the visible object, Aureol can no longer appeal to physical excesses or defects in either the medium or the knower.[46] Which is to say, Aureol cannot explain away the possibility of deceptive appearances in terms of anything other than the appearances themselves. Error necessarily moves to the very centre of Aureol's epistemology, an epistemology that can no longer treat visual deceptions as a subsidiary phenomenon, but rather must treat them as its central organizing principle. After all, it is precisely those experiences that reveal the distinction between appearing beings and real beings, that indicate that an appearing being must serve as the terminative object for every cognitive act.

Error may well have become normative for Aureol's understanding of perception and cognition, but this does not mean he thought our every cognition was doomed to failure. Despite propounding a theory of cognition that made the intuitive cognition of non-existents not only a supernatural, but even a natural occurrence, Aureol will blithely announce that under the natural order, an intellectual intuitive cognition ceases immediately with the departure of its object. At Oxford, William Ockham, Walter Chatton and Adam Wodeham recognized the problem with this position and developed extensive objections to Aureol's

---

[46] At *Scriptum* book I, prooem, section 2, vol. I, pp. 208–9 (lines 46–66), for example, Aureol will borrow the full range of perspectivist requirements for direct material vision, transfer them to the mind, while simultaneously translating them into spiritualist, non-material terms.

appearances, arguing that they could only be understood as intermediaries standing between perceiver and perceived, forever endangering our immediate and certain grasp of things.[47] In the 1330s, in Paris, Nicholas of Autrecourt would raise a similar objection against a fellow theological student who held views that bear at least a passing resemblance to Aureol's. If you define an intuitive cognition solely in terms of how it appears to the viewer and then admit that what appears need not exist, it becomes quite impossible to know if any of the things we perceive actually exist. To what evidence could you ever appeal? More appearances? But then the question simply repeats itself, "On what basis do you trust these additional appearances?"

This evidential circle became something like a touchstone for later medieval conceptions of human perception and cognition, for defining the sort of certitude and knowledge that we could have about the world around us. Almost every theologian and natural philosopher had to address it at some point, most recognized it, accepted it, and then (like Aureol) sought to mitigate its implications. Nicholas of Autrecourt would do something different; confronting those implications head-on, he developed a cognitive philosophy that marks something like the limit beyond which medieval conceptions of vision, experience and the self could not move.

---

[47] For arguments against the existence of an *esse apparens* see William of Ockham, *Ordinatio* book 1, distinction 27, question 3, *Opera philosophica et theologica*, vol. 4, pp. 238–58; Walter Chatton, *Reportatio et lectura super Sententias*, prologue, question 2, article 2, ed. Joseph C. Wey (Toronto: Pontifical Institute of Mediaeval Studies, 1989), pp. 86–97; and Adam Wodeham, *Lectura secunda*, prologue, question 2. Chatton developed extensive objections to Ockham's refutation of Aureol, as did Wodeham to Chatton's. In one way or another, each of these theologians attempted to explain away Aureol's appearing beings in terms of errors in judgment. None of their solutions proved really satisfactory, and the same sorts of problems that plagued Aureol's theories reappeared in their own work.

# Chapter 5

# PROBABILITY AND PERSPECTIVE: NICHOLAS OF AUTRECOURT AND THE FRAGMENTATION OF VISION

Surveying the Parisian academic scene around 1330, Nicholas of Autre-court laments. He sees men who have studied Aristotle and Averroes for years, even decades, until their hair turns grey. And though they have achieved some kind of success, though they are esteemed great scholars, Nicholas sees that this success has been achieved at great cost. They have abandoned the study of scripture, the performing of good works and everything moral. They have surrendered themselves to petty jealousies, envy and the desire for empty praise as they ceaselessly argue about the correct interpretation of pagan writers. What is worse, they seem content with this immoral state of affairs. When someone, a friend of the truth, rose up, Nicholas writes, "sounding his trumpet to awaken those sleepers from their slumber, they heaved a sigh, and looking altogether upset, attacked him as if engaged in deadly combat."[1] Needless to say, Nicholas himself was this friend of the truth, this herald coming from without to awaken and save his peers and teachers from their scholastic slumber. And, as he suggests here, in the prologue to the *Exigit ordo*, his so called *Useful Treatise*, people were not as receptive as he might have hoped. Seventeen years later, seventeen years filled with controversy and

---

[1] Nicholas of Autrecourt, *Exigit ordo executionis*, p. 181 (lines 17–25): ". . . immo inter cetera de quo maxime dolendum, si verum sit, vidi, licet visione non plena, quod aliqui reverendi patres quorum capita jam albescunt canitie, ad quorum pedes in pulvere propter compositionem animi eorum in moribus rectam vix dicere ausus fuissem deliberato judicio dignum me sedere, sic proh dolor illum habitum qui secundum mores dicitur visi sunt sprevisse quod, cum insurrexit amicus veritatis et suam fecit sonare tubam ut dormientes a somno excitaret, emiserunt suspiria, omnino fecerunt signa tristiae, et resumpto spiritu quasi armati ad capitale proelium in eum irruerunt." The condition of Nicholas' text which survives in only one, error-ridden, and incomplete copy (MS Canon. Misc. 43, ff. 1ra–24va, at the Bodleian Library, Oxford) has come under much recent scrutiny. For a thorough examination and analysis of the state of the manuscript see Zénon Kaluza, *Nicholas d'Autrecourt: l'ami de la vérité*, Histoire Littéraire de la France, Tome 42, fasc. 1 (1995), pp. 148–85, and especially pp. 153–5 for the work's proper "title." The *Exigit* is translated as *The Universal Treatise of Nicholas* by Leonard Kennedy, Richard Arnold and Arthur Milward (Milwaukee: Marquette University Press, 1971). On possible problems with this translation see Tachau, *Vision and Certitude*, p. 340, note 75. Although I have made use of the Kennedy translation, I have altered it where necessary and ultimately depend upon the O'Donnell edition.

papal inquiries, people had grown even less receptive. In 1347, Nicholas of Autrecourt was compelled to recant sixty-six allegedly heretical propositions and watch the public burning of his works. He was stripped of his academic degrees. He lost the right to teach.[2]

Nicholas had accused his peers at the University of Paris of a sort of intellectual idolatry. They had substituted the study of Aristotle for the study of nature itself. They had taken the opinions of Aristotle to be a source of evident truths about nature. This would not have been so bad had Aristotle got everything right, but Nicholas rather doubted this was the case. In a surviving letter to a fellow theology student, a Franciscan named Bernard of Arezzo, Nicholas asserted that there was (most likely) not a single evident truth in all of Aristotle's natural philosophy and metaphysics.[3] In the *Exigit*, he made a similar claim. Although there are many difficult "quasi-conclusions" in Aristotle's writings, they are not evident. Opposing conclusions can be defended. Indeed, Nicholas believes he can propose contrary conclusions that can "be held as *probably* as the ones proposed" by Aristotle and his commentator Averroes. And this brings us to the heart of the matter. Nicholas' recourse to probability marks his response to a set of concerns that obsessed and motivated almost all of his peers and immediate predecessors. As he put it at another place in the prologue to the *Exigit*, "I saw that scarcely any certitude can be had about things through their natural appearances, and what can be had, will be had in a short time, if men would turn their minds immediately to things as they had turned them to the minds of other men."[4] It is not just that Aristotle is not a source of evident truth. Even the direct study of nature, of the natural appearances, is no real source of truth. Nicholas, however, does not invoke the notion of probability simply to undermine Aristotle's credibility before a medieval university that had enshrined the Philosopher at the very centre of its pedagogy. He invokes the

---

[2] For an attempted reconstruction of Nicholas' life, both before and after his condemnation, as well as a thorough examination of the problems with dating, reading and interpreting his surviving works, see Kaluza, *L'Ami de la verité*. For a briefer account of the trial and its consequences see William Courtenay, "Inquiry and Inquisition: Academic Freedom in Medieval Universities," *Church History* 58, no. 2 (1989), 168–81, who suggests that the effects of these condemnations should not be overestimated. In the wake of his condemnation, for example, Nicholas went on to serve as dean of the cathedral at Metz. Also, J. M. M. H. Thijssen, *Censure and Heresy at the University of Paris, 1200–1400* (Philadelphia: University of Pennsylvania Press, 1998), pp. 73–82.

[3] L. M. De Rijk (ed. and trans.), *Nicholas of Autrecourt: His Correspondence with Master Giles and Bernard of Arezzo* (New York: E. J. Brill, 1994), p. 72 (para. 23). Hereafter, I will refer to Nicholas' letters by number, page and paragraph.

[4] Nicholas, *Exigit*, p. 181 (lines 32–6): "Redeundo unde sermo primus cum sic vidi quod de rebus per apparentia naturalia quasi nulla certitudo potest metiri et quod brevi tempore illud, quod potest haberi, habebitur si homines sic immediate intellectum suum convertant ad res sicut fecerunt ad intellectum hominum Aristotelis et commentatoris Averrois."

notion of probability to account for the essential weakness and deficiency of human vision and visual evidence.

## CRITIQUE, SELF-ASSERTION AND THE INDIVIDUAL

In the various prologues to the *Exigit*, Nicholas imagines himself to be something of an outsider to the academic life at the University of Paris. This self-conception is far from an incidental element in his writings and is not merely due to the fact that he disagrees with so many of his contemporaries. It responds to assumptions operating at the heart of his philosophy, assumptions linked to his ideas about the natural appearances and probability, as well as to ideas concerning the nature of authority and individual self-assertion. One way to grasp the connections between these various ideas is to take seriously the multiple levels of critique that make up the *Exigit*. The *Exigit* is, all at once, a moral critique, a pedagogical critique and a logical critique. To hear Nicholas tell it, it is a moral critique because it is a pedagogical critique, because the Aristotelian-based curriculum at the University of Paris had led to a shocking decline in moral standards. It is a pedagogical critique because it is, most fundamentally, a logical critique, because the decision to base university training on the sayings and opinions of Aristotle did not respond to the demands and standards of logic, the only standard appropriate to speculative activity. It is at the level of logic and speculation that Nicholas seeks to support his decision to separate or distance himself from what he will variously call the "group," the "community," or the "mob."[5]

Nicholas argues that university officials did not adopt their Aristotelian-based curriculum because they thought Aristotle's writings were a source of evident truth. Their decision was based upon much more practical concerns. Speculation, Nicholas tells us, is difficult and few people if left to their own devices could struggle their way to "the knowledge of even one hidden thought." Fearing the majority of people would despair of learning anything and turn to physical delights, Nicholas contends that

---

[5] Surprisingly, with the exception of Christophe Grellard, "Amour de soi, amour du prochain. Nicholas d'Autrécourt, Jean Buridan et l'idée d'une morale laïque (autour de l'article condamné no. 66)," in Paul J. J. M. Bakker (ed.), *Chemins de la pensée médiévale: etudes offertes à Zénon Kaluza* (Turnhout: Brepols, 2002), pp. 215–51, none of Nicholas' modern commentators have attempted to place his epistemological critique within the context of the moral and pedagogical critiques. I suspect most have assumed Nicholas was not altogether sincere when he claimed that a decline in morals motivated his thought. It was, they assume, something of a dodge, a claim made after the fact in order to deflect certain sorts of criticisms. While it is clear from the prologues that Nicholas wrote them after significant portions of the main manuscript had already circulated and been criticized, I do not believe this in any way weakens their significance. As I hope to show, they are intimately related to his epistemological enterprise, giving that enterprise its real coherence.

the reverend fathers took a safer and less demanding course. They decided to impose such reverence for Aristotle's opinions that by studying him people might at least feel as if they were slowly acquiring a great and important science. "Now I see the thing has gone too far," Nicholas writes, "for very few turn themselves towards the nature of things and the majority turn only to the opinions of men." In order to correct this deplorable situation, Nicholas hopes to show "the true way for inquiring into difficult things," that is, he hopes to show how one obeys the standards appropriate to speculative activity.[6]

Nicholas knew it would be an uphill battle. Accepted opinion and the entire institutional setting in which he worked were against him. Having distanced himself from the university community, he had lost whatever authority came from affiliation with that society. It is at precisely this juncture that the problem of presumption or presumptuousness seems to arise. In making these claims, Nicholas might well seem to have an unwarranted opinion of his own abilities. What basis could he possibly have for teaching "conclusions contradictory to those long approved by men of every level of understanding"?[7] Isn't the judgment of the whole human community "sounder than that of two or three members of that community"?[8] It necessarily becomes a moral dilemma for two reasons, because he is fighting against a community which has suffered a staggering moral collapse (to hear him tell it) and because his own motives might be questioned. The two points are related. The standards that justify Nicholas' critique are the same standards that the university community has failed to uphold. These are the standards that apply to speculative matters "where the only aim is proof" and any other standard (such as community assent, tradition or mere utility) is unworthy, even morally and ethically reprehensible.[9]

---

[6] Nicholas, *Exigit*, p. 185 (lines 12–16): "Nunc video quod res est nimis in extremo; nam pauciores satis quam expediret convertunt se ad naturam rei et plures convertunt se ad intellectum hominum. Ergo ut res reducatur ad medium satis volo ostendere quis sit verus modus occulta inquirendi."

[7] Nicholas, *Exigit*, p. 182 (lines 28–30): "[I]tem ultra quam natura rei se habeat, dicens videtur existimare de se ipso quae sunt contradictoriae conclusionibus approbatis in communitate longo tempore ab hominibus qualiscumque intellectus fuerint."

[8] Nicholas, *Exigit*, p. 183 (lines 16–20): "Cum ista considerant et vident quod illi de opposita conclusione sunt valde pauci, tunc accidit quasi quoddam bellum in eis et arguit intellectum eorum quod illud quod facto approbat communitas est faciendum arguendo sic: illi sunt imitandi qui sunt rectioris judicii; nunc est verisimile quod tota communitas hominum sunt rectioris judicii quam duo vel tres illius communitatis."

[9] Nicholas, *Exigit*, p. 184 (lines 32–46): "Nunc in speculativis non quaerimus nisi ipsum scire ut res veniat in apparentia apud animam. Non est sicut in observantiis legalibus ubi quaeritur non cognitio sed opus; et ideo ibi talibus argumentis utitur legislator ut homines inducat ad assensum; nam scit quod assensu posito sequetur opus. Sed hic non quaerimus nisi evidentiam, et ideo non videtur quod dignum sit uti talibus argumentis; sed quaeramus veritatem quaesitorum in propositionibus per se notis et in experimentis."

Nicholas' appeal to the standards appropriate to speculative activity is an appeal to the demands of logic. It is both an intellectual and an ethical appeal, because only through the logical analysis of concepts, of "self-evident propositions and experience," will men be able to free themselves from the errors in Aristotle's words and, ultimately, return to God. At the same time, Nicholas phrases this appeal to logic in markedly individualizing and interiorizing terms. The appeal to logical-speculative standards can be made independently of any institutional or communal authority. A man can confidently hold conclusions that go "beyond those set down by the whole group," that are "directly opposed to them," Nicholas writes, when he has derived them from concepts "that have come [to him], as though from within himself." These concepts might well be ones accepted by the community at large or they might be "other concepts as clear as the former, and clearer." Having developed them himself, the individual is in a better position to judge their truth, to make sure that only the standards of speculative proof were employed in their adoption. In so doing, "the individual seems to reach things themselves better and to bring them more intimately within himself." He rises above his peers becoming "another man in the grade of excellence."[10] The logical analysis of concepts allows the individual to become the source of his own authority, provides an alternative to an authority based solely on community consensus, tradition or university fiat. The appeal to the standards of speculation and logic is the very move that separates the thinker from the community, that positions him as an outside, even higher, authority.[11]

Nicholas' language of opposition and his effort to redefine the source of intellectual authority mark a conscious attempt to subvert the intellectual hegemony of the medieval university system. As Nicholas' critique of its Aristotelian-based pedagogy suggests, the very structure of scholastic academic practice prevented any wholesale rejection of Aristotle's ideas, practically guaranteeing that criticisms of Aristotle would always remain at the level of minor corrections, additions or extrapolations. Not only did Aristotle's works form the core curriculum for the arts faculty at Paris,

---

[10] Nicholas, *Exigit*, p. 183 (lines 2–10): "Cum igitur aliquis percipit et experitur quod super aliquibus quaesitis occurrunt sibi multi conceptus, et cum hoc scit ut certitudo potest in talibus contingere, quod omnes illos conceptus quos alii formant ipse format et multos alios per quos magis quasi subintrando attingit res, tunc videt quod est quasi tota illa multitudo in virtute quantum ad quaesita circa quae format tot conceptus ut tota multitudo; et ultra quantum ad alios conceptus est quasi alius homo in gradu excellenti, tunc cognoscit quod talis est apud quem notitia conclusionum ultra alios nata est pervenire."

[11] Grellard, "Amour de soi," pp. 242–3, describes Nicholas' claim as a "laïcisation d'un discours de type théologique" along the lines of Avicenna's prophet–philosopher or, more to the point, Anaxagoras' notion of the philosopher. See also, Kaluza, *Nicholas d'Autrecourt*, p. 168.

but the preferred mode of academic discourse was the commentary. As a result, Aristotle's ideas and topical organization dictated both the subject matter and the order in which it was investigated.[12] There was, moreover, a marked tendency among members of the arts faculties, derived from the practice of academic oral disputation, to decompose Aristotle's works into sequences of discrete questions. Analysis, not synthesis, was the order of the day and no radical reassessment of the Philosopher's views could ever really be undertaken. Corrections and additions to the foundational texts of medieval academic life, although common enough at the micro-level, were rarely integrated with one another and were almost never reordered into a form that challenged Aristotle's overall status and standing within the academic community.[13]

Nicholas himself was a part of the very scholastic academic community he criticized. He participated in formal quodlibetal debates and lectured on Lombard's *Sentences* and Aristotle's *Ethics*. None of these works have survived. In place of these standardized and standardizing forms of scholastic discourse, what has come down to us over the centuries are a few letters and the wildly speculative *Exigit*, works whose very form demonstrate Nicholas' attempt to step entirely outside the orbit of Aristotle's institutionally sanctioned authority. None of these works adopt the formalized methods of the scholastic commentary or question. Nicholas rarely cites any authorities, and when he does, he usually only employs them as elements in an argument *ad hominem*. At one point, for example, Nicholas asks his peers why they consider him to be a half-wit (*orbatum intellectum*) for contradicting Aristotle. How is it that they can think Aristotle's opinions are so clear and evident, when

---

[12] M. D. Chenu, *Toward Understanding Saint Thomas*, trans. A.-M. Landry and D. Hughes (Chicago: Henry Regnery Company, 1964), pp. 83–4, discusses the stagnation associated with the *quaestio* method and its use of authorities, as it evolved between the fourteenth and fifteenth centuries, in terms markedly similar to those Nicholas uses to describe his own early fourteenth-century contemporaries. Chenu writes, p. 83, "Instead of being the means to open the mind to a knowledge of objects, realities, the tendency was to consider [authorities] as the 'objects' of learning . . . Philosophical knowledge meant to learn Aristotle, instead of trying to discover the laws that govern the phenomena of nature . . . The commentator allowed himself to be taken in by his own game. Having lost little by little his power of discovery, he condemned in principle anyone so impudent as to find anything in contradiction to his book." Chenu concludes that Descartes contrasted his *Meditations* with the "disputations and questions" of philosophers, as the best means for discovering the truth of things.

[13] Edward Grant, *The Foundations of Modern Science in the Middle Ages: Their Religious, Institutional and Intellectual Contexts* (Cambridge: Cambridge University Press, 1996), pp. 127–31. The characterization of medieval academic practice as prone to analysis, not synthesis, is his. At pp. 166–7, Grant suggests that Aristotelian thought could never have been reformed or overthrown from within because its basic principles "such as potentiality–actuality, the four causes, matter and form, the four elements, the doctrine of natural place, were so broad and comprehensive that they were easily applied to rival theories and arguments." In essence, one could remain an Aristotelian even while refuting Aristotle.

Aristotle himself, whom they claim to follow so closely, admitted that they were extremely complex and open to dispute?[14] Rather than adopting these more typically scholastic forms of inquiry and authorization, Nicholas' surviving work takes the form of extended exercises in logical derivation as he draws out every conceivable implication from either his opponents' or his own assumptions. He constantly stresses that the process of logical analysis alone constitutes the true nature of philosophical inquiry. "Whoever posits an antecedent," he writes in one of his letters, "must posit the consequent that, by formal implication, is inferred from that antecedent."[15] In his letters, for example, Nicholas analyzes a few of Bernard's claims about the nature of cognition and then draws out implications that Bernard either had failed to draw or had inadequately attempted to forestall. He does something similar in the *Exigit*. After an extended series of prologues in which he explains his motivations, his ideas about probability and the assumptions that will guide his investigation, Nicholas proceeds to draw out the numerous (and occasionally contradictory) consequences of these assumptions as he argues for a radically non-Aristotelian atomistic cosmology.

All of which serves to highlight the broader contexts in which Nicholas will make his plea for the individual's right to speak out against what is commonly accepted. Nicholas is not merely interested in undermining Aristotle's authority, but any purely human authority. This applies as much to Nicholas' individual with his personal grasp of concepts, as it does to Aristotle and his institutionally sanctioned opinions. Accordingly, the transferral of intellectual authority from so-called "authorities" and institutions to logically-minded individuals is more than a bit ambiguous. Nicholas' self-authorizing individual falls well short of the sort of authority that, for example, Descartes' knowing subject comes to possess, and this in interesting and, as we shall see, telling ways. Behind Nicholas' moral, pedagogical and logical critiques of the medieval university, rests a

---

[14] Nicholas, *Exigit*, p. 197 (lines 22–5): "Nunc autem eorum magister Aristoteles quem ita de prope insequi volunt dixit quod haec quaestio est difficillima; unde eam enumerat inter quaestiones difficillimas in 3 *Meta.* suae prope principium."

[15] Nicholas, letter 1, p. 48 (para. 4): "Et ita, cum quicumque ponat antecedens habeat ponere consequens quod formali consequentia infertur ex illo antecedente . . ." Along these lines, Miller, "Singularity in Medieval Minds," p. 213, makes the extremely interesting observation that Nicholas, in abandoning the *lectio* and *quaestio* method, simultaneously abandons institutionalized forms of orality, of classroom textual commentary and public disputation. Nicholas' emphasis on an almost hyper-logical analysis of terms "practically requires an extended isolation with one's own thoughts behind closed doors." Also, Kaluza, *Nicholas d'Autrecourt*, pp. 167–72, who suggests the overtly personal nature of the *Exigit* derives, in part, from its unfinished status. It reads more like a set of exploratory notes, a private journal working towards a never completed work. On the general transformation of the *quaestio* from an oral to a written genre during the fourteenth century, see Daniel Hobbins, "The Schoolman as Public Intellectual: Jean Gerson and the Late Medieval Tract," *The American Historical Review*, 108.5 (2003), 1314.

more far-reaching and all-encompassing critique, a critique based upon the evidential value of the natural appearances themselves, a critique that undermines all human forms of authority.

### THE PROBLEM WITH CERTAINTY

Situating Nicholas' surviving writings within the varied intellectual movements and trajectories of fourteenth-century Paris is both surprisingly difficult and relatively easy. It is difficult because Nicholas, with few exceptions, never mentions his contemporaries, never explicitly indicates which of his peers, mentors or predecessors he borrows from, agrees with or opposes. For all that, it is easy because much of Nicholas's surviving work addresses problems that were widely discussed and debated during his time in Paris. When Nicholas analyses the nature of human vision, the distinction between intuitive and abstractive cognition or the distinction between appearance and reality, he clearly shows himself to be a product of his time and no matter how original his ideas are, they clearly have their place within the ebb and flow of later medieval intellectual life.

All of this is really a roundabout way of admitting that, barring the unexpected discovery of yet unknown manuscripts, situating Nicholas in his time is less a process of delineating precise genealogies than it is of establishing family relations, resonances and dissonances with the writings of his contemporaries. These lines of relationship can, of course, be drawn in various ways to reach various (though not, I believe, too various) results. That being said, there seems good reason to make sense of Nicholas' thought within the horizon's of Peter Aureol's theological writings.[16] Nicholas' writings manifest a deep sympathy with Aureol's emphasis on experience, with Aureol's belief that the reality and nature of cognition have nothing to do with its truthfulness. For all that, there are also real differences between the two thinkers, differences that give shape to and define Nicholas' real speculative creativity. As we saw in the last chapter,

---

[16] Here I follow the lead of Tachau, *Vision and Certitude*, pp. 340–4, who first asserted a connection between Aureol's and Nicholas' ideas. For most of this century, it had been assumed that Ockham was the immediate source behind many of Nicholas' propositions, see for example, O'Donnell's notes to his edition of the *Exigit*, p. 242, note 181, and Julius Weinberg, *Nicolas of Autrecourt* (New York: Greenwood Press, 1969), pp. 9–10. Thijssen, "The Quest for Certain Knowledge," in Juha Shivola (ed.), *Ancient Scepticism and the Sceptical Tradition* (Helsinki: The Philosophical Society of Finland, 2000), pp. 210–12, and Christophe Grellard, "*Sicut specula sine macula*: la perception et son objet chez Nicolas d'Autrecourt," in Anca Vasiliu (ed.), *Image et représentation dans la pensée médiévale* (Paris: Vrin, forthcoming), both suggest Aristotle's *Metaphysics* as another likely source for Nicholas' ideas.

despite his distinction between real and appearing being, Aureol believed that in normal, and this also means in most, cases the two completely coincide, an appearing being is the real being under the mode of being perceived. Appearing beings provide direct, non-representational visual awareness of the world around us. Nicholas has his doubts about this and his writings convey deep suspicions about any claim that we can move beyond appearances to knowledge of (or even an awareness of) real being.

Nicholas elaborated these suspicions most fully in a series of letters he wrote during the mid-1330s to Bernard of Arezzo and an otherwise unknown Giles (the only two contemporaries he cites by name), who had taken up Bernard's defence. Bernard had argued that a "clear intuitive cognition is that through which we judge a thing to be, whether it is or not." In other words, "an intuitive cognition does not require an existing thing."[17] While apparently admitting an absolute distinction between cognition and the existing thing, Bernard, like Aureol before him, did not believe that this distinction ultimately undermined our knowledge of contingent singular states of affairs, that is, of our knowledge of the world around us. Drawing on the common distinction between natural and supernatural causes, Bernard argues that it is possible for God to interfere in the normal causal chain and to generate in us false intuitive cognitions. Nevertheless, he contends that the existence of a seen object can be inferred when it has been generated naturally.[18]

The central issue for Nicholas, the issue that connects these letters to the *Exigit*, which he had written several years earlier, is whether Bernard's account of intuitive cognition allows for evident and, therefore, certain statements about contingent singular states of affairs. The short answer

---

[17] Nicholas, letter 1, p. 46 (para. 2): "Prima, que ponitur a vobis *Sententiarum*, dist. 3, q. 4, est ista: Notitia intuitiva clara est per quam iudicamus rem esse, sive sit sive non sit. Secunda propositio vestra, que ponitur *ubi supra*, est talis: 'Obiectum non est; igitur non videtur'; non valet consequentia; nec ista: 'hoc videtur; ergo hoc est.' Ymo utrobique est fallacia, sicut in hiis consequentiis: 'Cesar est in opinione; igitur Cesar est'; 'Cesar non est; igitur Cesar non est in opinione.' Tertia propositio, ibidem posita, est ista: Notitia intuitiva non requirit necessario rem existentem." We only know of Bernard's work through Nicholas' letters. None of his writings, if they still exist, have been discovered. For what is known about Bernard, see Kaluza, *L'Ami de la verité*, pp. 56–62. In his introduction to the recent French edition of Nicholas' letters, *Nicholas d'Autrecourt: correspondance, articles condamnés*, ed. L. M. de Rijk (Paris: Librairie Philosophique J. Vrin, 2001), pp. 12–16, Christophe Grellard notes the connections between Bernard's ideas and those of the English Franciscan Walter Chatton.

[18] Nicholas, letter 1, p. 48 (para. 5): "Sed forsan dicetis, prout, <ut> michi videtur, volebatis innuere in quadam disputatione apud Predicatores – quod, licet ex visione non possit inferri obiectum visum esse quando visio ponitur in esse a causa supernaturali vel conservatur ab ipsa, tamen quando posita est in esse a causis naturalibus precise, concurrente influentia generali Primi Agentis, tunc potest inferri."

is no. Nicholas bases this response on a rather stringent definition of truth. He equates certitude with indubitability and the logical principle of non-contradiction. According to this principle, Nicholas explains, "contradictories cannot be simultaneously true."[19] An inference is valid and satisfies the principle of non-contradiction when a total or partial identity obtains between the premises and the conclusion. Every valid syllogism, for example, satisfies this requirement because nothing appears in the conclusion that does not first appear in the premises.[20] On the other hand, the existence of one absolute thing cannot be inferred from the existence of another absolute thing because there need not be any identity whatsoever between the known entity (the antecedent) and the inferred entity (the consequent). Given the existence of the antecedent, no contradiction ensues whether the consequent exists or fails to exist.[21]

Bernard had, in fact, contended that intuitive cognitions were absolute operations. They did not require the actual presence and existence of an exterior object. A person could intuitively cognize an object as existing, whether it exists or fails to exist. Applying his logical standard of certitude to Bernard's theories, Nicholas draws out the obvious epistemological problem, namely, any inference from what is seen to what exists is fallacious. There need not even be a partial identity between the cognition of a thing and the thing itself. Since intuitive cognitions of non-existent objects are qualitatively identical to cognitions of existent objects, it becomes impossible to discriminate true from false cognitions.[22] What are the further consequences of Bernard's position? A rather gleeful Nicholas spells them out in surreal detail. If Bernard is to remain at all consistent to his own assumptions, he will have to admit that he cannot be sure whether the things around him exist, whether today's sky is the same as yesterday's, or whether the Chancellor or the Pope exist. Likewise, the entire structure of civil and political society will collapse, for if witnesses are called to testify, it will not follow that the things they testify to having seen actually happened. Extending this line

---

[19] Nicholas, letter 2, p. 58 (para. 2): "Et primum quod occurrit in ordine dicendorum, est istud principium: 'Contradictoria non possunt simul esse vera.'"

[20] Nicholas, letter 2, p. 62 (para. 9): "In omni consequentia immediate reducta in primum principium consequens et ipsum totum antecedens vel pars ipsius antecedentis sunt idem realiter."

[21] Nicholas, letter 2, p. 64 (para. 11): "Ex eo quod aliqua res est cognita esse, non potest evidenter, evidentia reducta in primum principium, vel in certitudinem primi principii, inferri quod alia res sit . . . In tali consequentia in qua ex una re inferretur alia, consequens non esset idem realiter cum antecedente, vel cum parte significati per antecedens. Igitur sequitur quod talis consequentia non esset evidenter nota evidentia primi principii descripta."

[22] Nicholas, letter 1, pp. 46–8 (para. 3): "Et unam aliam propositionem, que quinta est; et est talis: In lumine naturali non possumus esse certi quando apparentia nostra de existentia obiectorum extra sit vera vel falsa quia uniformiter, ut dicitis, representat rem esse, sive sit sive non sit."

of reasoning, it even follows that the Apostles cannot be sure that Christ suffered and died on the cross or that he rose from the dead.[23]

It is not clear whether Bernard would have accepted Nicholas' logical criterion as an appropriate one for judging the truth of our empirical knowledge about the world. Other criteria do exist. More likely than not both Duns Scotus and William Ockham would have rejected Nicholas' absolute standard. This is not to say that they were not interested in problems of certitude, only that they would have found such extreme demands unreasonable. Given God's ability to intervene in the causal order, to replace true intuitive cognitions with cognitions of non-existing objects, Nicholas' standard might in principle be impossible to meet. Rather than attempting to develop epistemologies to meet Nicholas' hyperbolic logical demands, they constructed theories to explain how we could achieve certainty according to a more realistic standard, that is, how we could come to possess cognitions that are free from "doubt and error."[24] Nicholas' senior contemporary at the University of Paris, John Buridan, seems to have taken a similar approach when he distinguished between the absolute certitude required by logic and a second, lesser sort of certitude that (Buridan believed) fully met the practical needs of the natural philosopher and scientist.[25] When Ockham's secretary, Adam Wodeham, considered the problem in his own *Sentence* commentary, he opted for an even more nuanced approach suggesting that evidence be stratified into three levels, ranging from the least to the most evident. The first two levels referred to the different sorts of evidence we can have in making judgments about contingent singulars. The highest level referred to self-evident propositions.[26] While this sort of categorization might not secure an infallible knowledge of the things around us, Wodeham hoped

---

[23] Nicholas, letter 1, p. 54 (para. 14).

[24] M. A. Adams, *William Ockham*, pp. 572–601 and, more generally, G. R. Evans, *Getting It Wrong: The Medieval Epistemology of Error* (Leiden: Brill, 1998), pp. 173–6.

[25] Jack Zupko, "On Certitude," in J. H. H. M. Thijssen and Jack Zupko (eds.), *The Metaphysics and Natural Philosophy of John Buridan* (Leiden: Brill, 2001), p. 175, quotes the following passage from Buridan's *Summulae de demonstrationibus*, "However, another sort of human certainty on the part of the proposition is that of a true proposition which cannot be falsified by any natural power and by any manner of natural operation, although it can be falsified by a supernatural power and in a miraculous way. And such certainty suffices for natural sciences. And this I truly know, by natural science, that the heavens are moved and that the sun is bright."

[26] Wodeham, *Lectura secunda*, prologue, question 6, section 12, p. 163 (lines 11–23): "Illam propositionem voco evidentem suo modo quae ex talibus componitur simplicibus apprehensionibus, et taliter quod ipsa informante animam non potest sibi non apparere sic esse in re sicut ipsa significat, sive ipsa sit vera sive falsa, licet per rationem vel experimentiam aliunde posset convinci non sic esse quandoque . . . Aut magis stricte: illa evidens propositio qua posita nec potest non apparere sic esse sicut ipsa significat nec non esse sicut apparere. Et ideo forte omnis propositio evidens isto secundo modo significans rem esse categorice est necessaria. – Tertio modo, adhuc strictius: illa evidens propositio quae habet duas istas condiciones; et ultra hoc, stant generali Dei influentia, nata est necessitare intellectum in quo est ad assentiendum sic esse sicut ipsa significat."

it might at least serve to clarify the different sorts of reasons we have when we evaluate evidence and propositions.

Needless to say, Nicholas would have rejected any attempt to redefine or lower the standard for what constitutes certain knowledge. In his letters to Bernard, for example, he argues that there can be "no certitude but that which is not founded on falsity." If any lower standard were accepted, if we were to accept as certain and true evidence that could be falsified, we would eventually find ourselves in the incoherent position of accepting something as certain and true which is actually false.[27] Since all certitude must be resolvable into the principle of non-contradiction, certitude cannot be stratified into levels or degrees. One piece of evidence cannot be more certain than another. Certitude is an absolute standard and it is a standard that Bernard's theory of cognition cannot meet. Perhaps no theory could successfully meet it. As late thirteenth- and fourteenth-century scholasticism played itself out, no one seemed particularly satisfied with anyone's account of cognition, regardless of what standards of evidence, certitude and truth they set for themselves.

For his part, Nicholas opted out of the contest. By defining truth and certitude in terms of the principle of non-contradiction, Nicholas was not setting himself up as the scholastic sceptic. He was not so much interested in denying the possibility of knowledge, as he was in forcing his peers to rethink the sort of knowledge that we can obtain about the world. Nicholas' strategy, when seen in this light, is to push commonly held assumptions to their logical, even absurd, extremes. His contemporaries seemed content to admit the possibility of false intuitive cognitions and then downplay or ignore their implications. Aureol and Bernard, for example, having defined cognition as an absolute, self-enclosed operation, as distinguishable solely in terms of how the individual experiences it, then ignore the real consequences of such a position. They simply assert a connection between certain sorts of cognitions and the world. Nicholas refuses such stopgap measures. If any intuitive cognition can be false, then that possibility must be incorporated as foundational to a coherent epistemology. Unlike his contemporaries, Nicholas did just that.

---

[27] Nicholas, letter 2, p. 62 (para. 7): "Tertium corelarium quod infero iuxta dicta, est quod: Excepta certitudine fidei, nulla est alia certitudo nisi certitudo primi principii, vel que in primum principium potest resolvi. Nam nulla est certitudo nisi illa cui non subest falsum, quia: Si esset aliqua cui posset subesse, sit ita quod ei subsit falsum. Tunc, cum remaneat, per te, ipsa certitudo, sequitur quod aliquis erit certus de eo cuius oppositum contradictorie est verum." Grellard, *Nicholas d'Autrecourt*, pp. 29–45, argues that Nicholas' logical principles as outlined in these letters not only serve the negative function of undermining contemporary fourteenth-century epistemologies, but also of establishing a new and innovative theory of consequences.

## METAPHYSICAL PROBABILITY

When Nicholas finally turns to the problem of appearances in the *Exigit*, he does so by way of two related questions. He tells us he is going to consider "whether everything which appears is, and whether everything which appears to be true is true." In other words, are there false appearances? Nicholas will defend what he considers to be the generally held belief that the external senses provide certain knowledge about the world, that what appears exists and that "everything which appears is true."[28] Later in the *Exigit*, and again in a letter to Bernard, he will assert that we possess certain knowledge of "sensible objects and the acts we experience in ourselves . . . and of principles known from their terms and the conclusions depending on them."[29] All of this despite the fact that he begins the *Exigit* with the assertion that little certainty can be derived from the natural appearances and later goes on to admit that, through experience alone, we can never even know if "the thing we call 'cognition' is a likeness of an object."[30]

To sort this muddle out, it is important to keep in mind that it is far from evident that everything that appears exists. Aureol's experiences of sensory error can be (and were) interpreted as demonstrating that a great many things appear that do not exist. Nicholas' decision to define certitude in terms of the principle of non-contradiction can be interpreted as an attempt to demonstrate that almost all of his peers and immediate predecessors had committed themselves to a number of problematic assumptions concerning the nature of cognition. These assumptions had entangled them in insoluble contradictions precisely because they had (in one form or another) distinguished what appears from what exists, while simultaneously asserting their identity. Bernard may have been Nicholas' particular whipping post for these arguments, but he was a representative whipping post nonetheless.

---

[28] Nicholas, *Exigit*, p. 228 (lines 5–12): "Consequenter tractandum est de hoc problemate an omne illud quod apparet sit; et omne illud quod apparet esse verum sit verum. Circa quod considerandum est quod dicens: omne quod apparet est verum, saltem loquendo de apparentia quae attenditur secundum sensus exteriores, sufficit satis quod sciat respondere ad contrarium; nam regula generaliter posita non debet modificari nec restringi nisi sit necessitas cogens ad modificandum, et ita sufficit quod sic dicens sustineat onus respondentis; sufficit enim quantum ad faciendum inclinari magis intellectum isti conclusioni quam oppositae."

[29] Nicholas, *Exigit*, p. 235 (lines 6–9): "Haec vero proprie sunt evidentia: objecta sensibilia, actus quos <experimur> in nobis, et hoc quantum ad incomplexa; quantum vero ad complexa principia nota ex terminis et conclusiones dependentes ex eis." letter 1, p. 56–7 (para. 15): "Et ideo, ad evitandum tales absurditates, sustinui in aula Sorbonne in disputationibus quod sum certus evidenter de obiectis quinque sensuum et de actibus meis."

[30] Nicholas, *Exigit*, p. 243 (lines. 3–4): "Et quod talis rem quam cognitionem appellamus sit similitudo objecti, hoc nescimus per viam experientiae."

Nicholas never denies any of this, never attempts to back off from his critiques. Rather, he responds to the dilemma of discriminating true from false appearances by shifting the entire frame of the debate. Or, perhaps more accurately, he attempts to pre-empt the debate, to stop it before it has a chance to begin. Scotus had sought to ground our existential awareness of things in a class of infallible cognitions, namely, intuitive cognitions. Although Aureol had demonstrated that intuitive cognitions could be inaccurate, he was willing to overlook such failings and assert the evidential value of intuitive cognitions given the normal course of events. What both Scotus and Aureol (and almost all of their peers) shared was a belief that the only acceptable epistemological foundation was a foundation grounded in certitude (however defined). The problem they then faced was that they could not coherently provide it. Nicholas will look for a different sort of foundation. Rather than ground his epistemology in some form of certitude, he will look to ground certitude itself in what is probable. As Nicholas puts it, "[I]f any certitude about things is to be found in us, it is probable that everything that appears exists and that everything that appears to be true is true."[31]

In the Aristotelian tradition, the distinction between certain knowledge and probable opinion was a distinction rooted in two different sorts of syllogisms. Demonstrative syllogisms were formally valid proofs that employed self-evident premises. Dialectical syllogisms, by contrast, employed less than certain premises, that is, merely probable ones.[32] How did a premise become probable? More often than not, we tend to think about probability in terms of mathematical or statistical frequency, in terms of a quantifiable accumulation of evidence. An opinion is probable if there is reasonable evidence to support it. It becomes more probable as more or different sorts of corroborating evidence is gathered. While medieval thinkers certainly recognized that an opinion's probability was tied to supporting evidence, medieval conceptions of evidence were tied up with the notion of authority, with who was fit to judge and assess evidence. As John of Salisbury noted in his twelfth-century *Metalogicon*, "A proposition is probable if it seems obvious to a person of judgment, and if it occurs thus in all instances and times, or is otherwise only in exceptional cases and on rare occasions."[33]

---

[31] Nicholas, *Exigit*, p. 228 (lines 18–20): "Dico igitur si aliqua certitudo nobis insit de rebus quod probabile est quod omne illud quod apparet esse sit, et quod omne illud quod apparet esse verum sit verum."

[32] Eileen Serene, "Demonstrative Science," in Kretzman, *et al.* (eds.), *Cambridge History*, pp. 496–7. Evans, *Getting It Wrong*, pp. 130–49, places the distinction between probable and necessary proof within the context of the rhetorical tradition of topics and places.

[33] John of Salisbury, *The Metalogicon: A Twelfth-century Defense of the Verbal and Logical Arts of the Trivium*, II.14, trans. Daniel D. McGarry (Berkeley: University of California Press, 1955), p. 106.

The connection between authority and probability is particularly clear in the procedures of Aristotelian natural philosophy. Whereas proper scientific demonstrations require necessary and universal premises, perceptual experience, by its very nature, is always of contingent, singular events. This is how Aristotle succinctly phrased the problem in the *Posterior Analytics*, "One necessarily perceives an individual at a place and at a time, and it is impossible to perceive what is universal and holds in every case." Individual perceptions generated scientific evidence only over time as they were repeated, remembered and formalized by common consent or "through the statements of a weighty authority."[34] Once authorized, additional perceptual "evidence" becomes more or less irrelevant. If the proper authorities already approve an opinion, it needs no additional support and could hardly become more probable. By the same token, any disconfirming instances, precisely because of their novelty, would not yet have risen to the level of probable scientific evidence and, therefore, could in no way really undermine generally approved opinion. For most medieval thinkers an opinion was worthy of approval, that is, probable, if the right sorts of people approved it, and if the right sorts of people approved it, it could be used as a premise in scientific demonstrations.[35]

Nicholas never denies the link between probability and authority. He will, however, radically redefine the source of authority. Whereas traditional notions of probability looked to community assent as the ground for their authority, an authority established across time and among the appropriate sorts of people, Nicholas suggests a different set of relations among authority, community, the individual and tradition. Neither tradition,

When, a short while later, John introduces the idea of degrees of probability, he again links it to the idea of authority, "A proposition's probability is increased in proportion as it is more easily and surely known by one who has judgment."

[34] Peter Dear, *Discipline and Experience*, p. 22, from whom I take the passage from Aristotle's *Posterior Analytics*. Mary Carruthers, *The Book of Memory: A Study of Memory in Medieval Culture* (Cambridge: Cambridge University Press, 1990), pp. 212–14, makes a similar point about medieval intellectual culture generally, when she notes that a treatise (in this case she happens to be discussing Anselm's *Proslogion* and Gaunilo's response) achieved "full authority not by closing debate but by accumulating it."

[35] Ian Hacking, *The Emergence of Probability* (Cambridge: Cambridge University Press, 1975), pp. 20–3, stresses the non-evidential character of medieval notions of the probable and the attendant emphasis on authority. Daniel Garber and Sandy Zabell, "On the Emergence of Probability," *Archive for the History of Exact Sciences* 21, no. 1 (1979), 33–53, contend that the connection between evidence and probability dates at least as far back as Cicero. I suspect both Hacking and Garber somewhat overstate their cases. While it is clear (*pace* Hacking) that medieval thinkers possessed a concept of evidence, it is also clear (*pace* Garber) that evidence required authorization. In the *Exigit*, Nicholas aims to demonstrate and undermine the ways in which the structure of scientific practice, particularly in the institutionalized form imposed on it within the medieval university, allows people to treat merely probable opinion as self-evident truth. For a different account of the rise of probability theory, see J. van Brakel, "Some Remarks on the Prehistory of the Concept of Statistical Probability," *Archive for the History of Exact Sciences* 16, no. 2 (1976), 119–36.

community assent, nor institutional fiat can render one opinion more probable than another, and it most certainly cannot transform the merely probable into the self-evident. Whether a proposition is true, probable or merely possible depends, first and foremost, on the relation between its terms, between antecedent and consequent. What the majority or the wise think has no effect on this relation, and the individual, accordingly, must look at the terms themselves to determine the nature of their relation. If the individual, after discussing "the matter with persons whose judgment he respects," Nicholas writes, "has remained confident for a long time because his views have appeared and still appear [clear] to him, he can and should . . . declare his own judgment honestly, and set down his views as true, yet so as to expose [his judgment] in those matters to examination."[36] Communal assent transforms into the individual's ability to maintain his position over and against the arguments of respected people, and tradition names the individual's ability to maintain that position over time. The individual becomes the ground for his own authority precisely to the extent that he can logically maintain his difference from others. In Nicholas' hands, probability no longer generates the shared assumptions of a homogenized intellectual community. In fact, it does something quite different. It creates the possibility for radical dissent and heterodoxy.

No doubt Nicholas imagines himself to be just such an individual, and he registers his dissent from scholastic Aristotelianism by claiming that his theories are not simply as probable as, but more probable than Aristotle's. Be that as it may, Nicholas cannot ascertain a proposition's degree of probability through an accumulation of perceptual experiences and supporting evidence. Putting aside the rather vexed question concerning the possibility of false appearances, what we perceive rarely, if ever, allows us to make formal inferences concerning the fundamental nature of things. In the *Exigit*, Nicholas contends that it is more probable to assert that all things are eternal than to argue, as Aristotle had, that things consist in generable and corruptible substances. By this Nicholas does not mean to deny that what appears to us now might fail to appear to us later or that we see things degenerate and rot away. He means that such appearances do not provide us with any real clues concerning their underlying causes. On the one hand, we could follow Aristotle and explain such appearances in terms of the generation and corruption of substances. On the other

---

[36] Nicholas, *Exigit*, p. 183 (lines 36–41): "Igitur ad me exonerandum pono aliam regulam civilem quae est ista: omnis homo cui super aliquibus quaesitis occurrunt aliqua contraria toti communitati et tractatu habito cum aliquibus quos existimat recti judicii, stetit longo tempore quod sibi apparuerunt et adhuc apparent, potest et debet praecipue in mere speculativis manifestare fideliter suum judicium et ponere ea ut vera, sed ut consideretur in eis . . ."

hand, we could explain them (as Nicholas does) through recourse to an atomistic cosmology.[37] Just because something no longer appears to us is no reason to assume it has ceased to exist. Its constituent atoms might simply have dispersed themselves into imperceptible units. While neither explanation is formally true, both are compatible with what appears. There is nothing in the appearances themselves to suggest which conclusion is true or even more probable. If evidence played an ambiguous role in traditional Aristotelian natural philosophy, it has almost no role to play in Nicholas' natural philosophy.[38]

Nicholas' responds to this evidential dilemma with a mode of argumentation that does not depend upon the appearances. Nicholas will utilize a conceptual or, as he terms it, "metaphysical" notion of probability, a notion based on the idea of final cause. Nicholas appeals to this metaphysical style of argument because the logic of appearances prevents any formal inferences from what appears to what really exists. If what appears can be explained in terms of a number of competing theories, then some other criteria must be employed to determine which of these competing theories is more probable than the others. In Nicholas' hands, metaphysical principles operate in just this fashion, as regulative ideals that guide and organize all natural inquiry. For example, Nicholas introduces the "Principle of the Good" as one such ideal.[39] We must assume that things are good and exist in the best possible manner. One theory will be more probable than another, if it more fully satisfies this criterion.[40] After all, there is "no end to evil or negation," and if we assume the universe to embody anything but the highest conceivable degree of goodness, it

---

[37] Nicholas, *Exigit*, pp. 198–9 (lines 31–4).

[38] Contrast this with Weinberg, *Nicolas of Autrecourt*, pp. 121–5, who suggests that a proposition's probability increases or decreases based upon current information. While this might be true from our perspective, I doubt it describes the situation as Nicholas saw it. Nicholas intentionally downplays the role of evidence because all perceptual evidence is necessarily equivocal with respect to its explanatory causes. As he demonstrates repeatedly throughout the *Exigit*, his preferred mode of argumentation is the thought experiment, a style of argument which pretty much avoids any reference to "evidence." Nicholas' use of thought experiments or experiments *secundum imaginationem* places him in the mainstream of fourteenth-century scientific practice, see Edward Grant, "Medieval Natural Philosophy: Empiricism without Observation," in Cees Leijenhorst, Christoph Lüthy and J. M. M. H. Thijssen (eds.), *The Dynamics of Aristotelian Natural Philosophy from Antiquity to the Seventeenth Century* (Leiden: Brill, 2002), pp. 165–8.

[39] Nicholas, *Exigit*, p. 185 (lines 21–5): "Unum principium est quod bonum est apud intellectum pro mensura in quantificando entia et universaliter in determinando dispositiones contingentes in eis ut accipiat quod entia universi sunt rectissime disposita et quod sic res sunt sicut bonum est eas esse et sic non sunt sicut malum esset eas esse." In total, Nicholas offers four preliminary metaphysical principles, pp. 185–6: (1) the principle of the good, (2) the interconnectedness of all beings, (3) the necessary importance of all beings, and (4) the universe's constant/unchanging degree of perfection. For a more detailed discussion of these principles, see Weinberg, *Nicolaus of Autrecourt*, pp. 127–39.

[40] Nicholas, *Exigit*, p. 204 (lines 5–9).

will forever elude us as to "why things are made in one way rather than another."[41]

The shift from formal to metaphysical explanations might seem to accomplish little more than to push the deeper epistemological problem back one step. Just as little certitude can be had about things according to their natural appearances, Nicholas also recognizes that we cannot be certain about these final causes, about the ends towards which nature tends. But then again, Nicholas does not assert these metaphysical principles as true. He introduces them with a nod to tradition and notes that they are the sorts of assumptions philosophers have traditionally made about the universe.[42] He is equally clear that he only asserts them as probable. They are suppositions we must make if our desire to know the universe is to be satisfied. They have little to do with how the universe really is and everything to do with our cognitive limitations in this life. If the universe is to be at all intelligible to us, we have no choice but to "*suppose* that the beings of the universe are disposed as would please a sound intellect more."[43] We certainly cannot know that this principle holds true. Nothing in the appearances warrants a certain conclusion one way or the other, but we must posit this principle as the condition of possibility for any inquiry.

When Nicholas turns to the twin problems of certitude and appearances, he will adopt a similar metaphysical argument. Nicholas will argue that if we hope to explain how certitude could be possible, the most probable hypothesis we can make is that everything that appears exists and everything that appears to be true is true. It is the hypothesis that most coherently satisfies the explanandum. To begin with he suggests

---

[41] Nicholas, *Exigit*, p. 185 (lines 42–6): "Et sic in aliis apparet propositio ex causa ut supra in rebus artis quia malum est infinitum et negatio boni: unde tunc non esset intelligibile quare magis fierent sub una dispositione quam sub alia, nec sciremus e quibus haberemus terminare quaesita naturaliter quae oriuntur in nobis super consideratione dispositionis circa entitatem rerum in quantitate et qualitate."

[42] Nicholas, *Exigit*, p. 186 (lines 18–26).

[43] Nicholas, *Exigit*, p. 185 (lines 46–9): "Sicut ergo artifex intendit dispositionem convenientissimam effectus et quae est sibi placentissima, sic existimandum quod entia universi sunt sub illa dispositione quae esset magis placens intellectui recto." Although Nicholas will exploit this particular conception of metaphysical probability more than others, he certainly was not the only medieval thinker to employ it. The English Franciscan William Ockham, who lectured on Lombard's *Sentences* a little over a decade before Nicholas composed the *Exigit*, employs the principle of parsimony (his famous razor) in precisely the same manner. When considering, for example, whether intellectual cognition requires the mediation of species, he notes at *Reportatio* II, questions 12–13, in *Opera philosophica et theologica*, vol. 7, p. 256, that the existence of such species cannot be "evidently disproved through natural reasons. Nevertheless," he continues, "it seems more probable . . . that the opposite position is true because a plurality of beings should not be posited without necessity." That is, an explanation of intellectual cognition that does without sensible species is more probable given the conceptual criteria of theoretical parsimony. Of course, it is another issue altogether whether the universe actually obeys this principle.

that as a general rule people have always accepted the veracity of our sense perceptions. The burden of proof, in other words, is on those who wish to undermine this rule or hypothesis, not so much because tradition is always correct (clearly a position Nicholas could not accept), but simply because some good reason must be presented to convince people to give up a position they have long held to be true.[44] Nicholas feels that no compelling reason exists to give up this faith in the senses. To give it up would prove disastrous. Any hypothesis that posits the possibility of a false appearance (or any sort of distinction between what appears and what exists) automatically undermines itself and renders certain knowledge about the world impossible. Any theory that argues that certain knowledge is possible so long as some antecedent condition is met (for example, that God has not interfered in the causal order) also undermines itself because those antecedent conditions themselves are, in principle, unverifiable. Nicholas simply side steps this whole morass. Just as he argued that we should accept the existence of eternal and indivisible atoms because such a hypothesis better accounts for the universe's perfection, now he will argue that we should assume that everything that appears exists because it best explains conditions under which certitude could exist. Whereas Bernard could offer no evidence that his antecedent conditions were met, at least Nicholas can present probable reasons for accepting his principle at all times, namely it better meets the regulative ideal of certainty.[45]

---

44 Nicholas, *Exigit*, p. 228 (lines 5–12): "Consequenter tractandum est de hoc problemate an omne illud quod apparet sit; et omne illud quod apparet esse verum sit verum. Circa quod considerandum est quod dicens: omne quod apparet est verum, saltem loquendo de apparentia quae attenditur secundum sensus exteriores, sufficit satis quod sciat respondere ad contrarium; nam regula generaliter posita non debet modificari nec restringi nisi sit necessitas cogens ad modificandum, et ita sufficit quod sic dicens sustineat onus respondentis; sufficit enim quantum ad faciendum inclinari magis intellectum isti conclusioni quam oppositae."

45 T. K. Scott, "Nicholas of Autrecourt, Buridan and Ockhamism," *Journal of the History of Philosophy*, 9.1 (1971), 26–7, is one of the few scholars to interpret the correspondence with Bernard of Arezzo in light of Nicholas' discussion of probability in the *Exigit*. Scott may in part have been motivated to do this because he incorrectly believed (following Weinberg) that the correspondence preceded the *Exigit* and that the *Exigit* therefore supposedly represented something like a refinement of earlier ideas; see p. 22, note 18. Recent commentators, perhaps because of the revised manuscript chronology, have not followed Scott's lead and have consistently separated Nicholas' theory of probability from the epistemology he articulates in the correspondence with Bernard; see for example, Zénon Kaluza, "Voir: la clarté de la connaissance," pp. 94–101 and J. M. M. H. Thijssen, "The Quest for Certain Knowledge," pp. 201–10. I have opted to read Nicholas' surviving writings as all of a piece because: (1) nothing Nicholas writes in the correspondence contradicts what he had earlier written in the *Exigit*; (2) there are no explicit indications in the correspondence that he intends them to replace or supersede the *Exigit*; and (3) when taken together his writings seem to form a more coherent and intellectually interesting whole. In particular, it saves him from committing Bernard's mistake, that is, from asserting that certain sorts of cognitions can be known as true and certain despite the ever-present possibility that they are false.

## EXTERNALIZING THE APPEARANCES

Nicholas' treatment of intuitive cognition is telling, more like an aside, a reference to a controversy worth noting, if already surpassed. Scotus had initially developed the idea of an intuitive cognition in order to account for our grasp of the singular thing as existing. Even Aureol, who had severed the link between intuitive cognition and real being, who had admitted that we could have intuitive cognitions of non-existent objects, had maintained this emphasis on existence. We cognize an object intuitively when we experience it as present, as before us right here and right now. Aureol (like Bernard after him) had attempted to forge a link between our experience of a thing's presence and its actual existence, its real being, when he argued that, given the common course of nature, intuitive cognitions coincided with real beings. And it is here, with this focus on existence, that Nicholas' approach to cognition separates itself from these earlier writers. If everything that appears exists, then the very distinction between intuitive and abstractive cognition becomes meaningless. Every cognition is a cognition of an existing being. Intuitive cognitions are simply clearer than abstractive cognitions. Compared to God's knowledge, which is the clearest possible, our intuitive cognitions seem less clear, seem like mere abstractive cognitions.[46]

Having relativized the distinction between types of cognition, Nicholas finds it necessary to distinguish every distinct cognitive object from every other cognitive object. To make his case, Nicholas generates a thought experiment. He asks whether the same thing could be seen both clearly and obscurely. Imagine two white patches, one bright, the other dim. "Since a [cognitive] act is a certain configuration of the object in the intellect," Nicholas asserts that the act of seeing the bright whiteness will be clearer than the act of seeing the dim whiteness. Now imagine that the bright whiteness is seen from further away or at dusk. What do we see? Nicholas argues that we do not now see the bright whiteness as dim. If we did, then what appears would not always exist. A bright whiteness might sometimes appear as a non-existent dim whiteness. Accordingly, Nicholas will argue that for every distinct cognitive act, there must be a distinct cognitive object or appearance appropriate to that act. Since this new cognitive act is an act of seeing a dim whiteness, its object must be a

---

[46] Nicholas, *Exigit*, p. 242 (lines 25–9): ". . . quaelibet cognitio est rei existentis, sed in hoc est differentia, quia intuitiva est rei existentis sub esse claro magis, et si Deus sic clarissime omnia cognoscat ut creditur, nostra intuitiva etiam posset dici abstractiva respectu cognitionis Dei quae intuitiva simpliciter diceretur." Also, p. 264 (lines 19–27).

patch of dim whiteness.[47] Simply put, each and every act of the exterior senses must have its own unique cognitive object."[48]

Not only is every cognitive object distinguished from every other cognitive object, Nicholas also distinguishes them from our acts of perceiving and knowing them. Although each faculty presupposes the existence of its appropriate object or appearance, "no faculty will produce it."[49] Aureol, of course, had held the opposite position. The senses and the intellect, according to Aureol, produce the *esse apparens* which serves as the terminus and object of every cognitive act. Aureol had good reasons for giving the senses this productive role. How else could we explain the intuitive cognition of non-existent entities (like the coloured circle seen hovering in mid air), real cognitions in which what appears fails to possess real being? Nicholas avoids this entire problematic by assuming from the outset that everything that appears exists. By definition there can be no such thing as an intuitive cognition of a non-existing thing. This might simply seem to beg the central question, "Then what object is seen and presupposed in cases of sensory error?" Nicholas' answer, in short, is to deny that there really is any such thing as sensory error.[50] Which is to

---

[47] Nicholas, *Exigit*, p. 238 (lines 25–38): "Est igitur conclusio prima quod cognitio clara et obscura numquam possunt esse respectu ejusdem rei. Et ad hoc ostendendum recipio duas albedines quarum una sit clara et alia obscura; prima dicatur *a*, secunda *b*. Nunc recipiatur actus videndi *a* et sit *c*, et actus videndi *b* et sit *d*; certum est quod *c* erit actus magis clarus quam *d* sicut *a* est albedo magis clara quam *b*, cum actus sit configuratio quaedam objecti in intellectu. Quando igitur a remotis videtur albedo *a*, vel videtur quasi in tenebris recedente lumine sicut circa noctem, certum est quod habet actum videndi obscurum *d*. Tunc arguitur sic: pro quocumque instanti est in visu actus videndi alicujus objecti videtur illud objectum; et pro quocumque instanti non est in potentia actus videndi alicujus objecti non videtur illud objectum; sed pro hoc instanti per positum est in visu actus videndi *b*, scilicet *d* et non actus videndi *a*; ergo videtur albedo *b* et non albedo *a*, vel si videtur, hoc non est nisi quia videtur albedo *b* quae est aliquo modo eadem sibi et quasi in ipsa continetur evidenter."

[48] Nicholas, *Exigit*, p. 239 (lines 14–18), will apply this line of thought to the faculties themselves, arguing that sight and intellect each have their own types of cognitive objects, "Sequitur quinta conclusio quod intellectus et visus vel aliqua quaecumque alia potentia sensitiva numquam sunt ejusdem objecti, vel duae potentiae quaecumque quia semper actus unius potentiae vel est disparatus vel est magis clarus respectu ejusdem objecti, et utroque modo sequitur distinctio ex parte rei."

[49] Nicholas, *Exigit*, p. 241 (lines 14–15): ". . . et ita erit verum quod quaelibet virtus praesupponet suum subjectum esse et nulla constituet ipsum. Unde ut sensibilia puta visibilia praecedunt et necessario habent praecedere visum, sic imaginabilia imaginationem."

[50] Nicholas contends that what are commonly referred to as "sensory errors" or cases of visual deception are really only errors of judgment. For example, *Exigit*, pp. 228 (lines 29–31) and 231 (lines 45–7), Nicholas considers the case of a feverish person who is given something sweet to eat, but tastes something bitter. The bitter taste is not false, rather it reflects or discloses something about the sick person's tongue, not the food. The error, in other words, consists in incorrectly identifying the appearance's origin, in misinterpreting what it is an appearance of. On the distinction between appearance and judgment in Nicholas' thought see Thijssen, "The Quest for Certain Knowledge," pp. 204–7 and Kaluza, "Voir: la clarté de la connaissance," pp. 100–2.

say, Nicholas totally externalizes the appearances and reads them back into the world. They are not products of cognitive acts. They are real aspects of the (or some) *res extra*. Every cognitive object that appears to the external senses, every *esse obiectivum*, image, concept, appearance, partial appearance, or natural appearance (as he will variously call them) reveals some real aspect of the (or in more complicated cases, of some) subjectively existing thing.[51]

As a methodological move, as a move made in response to the demands of his probabilistic epistemology, Nicholas' decision to sever cognitive objects from any sort of existential dependence on cognitive acts makes sense. It was precisely this dependence that had undermined Aureol's epistemology. Aureol had argued that appearing beings were produced by the soul's faculties as they interacted with real beings. An appearing being was the real being under the mode of being perceived. Unfortunately for Aureol, apparent beings could not carry the evidential burden he had assigned to them. The experiences of sensory error that revealed their existence, also demonstrated that they could exist in the absence of any real being. The mere experience of a thing as present could never actually guarantee its real presence. Nicholas retains Aureol's emphasis on experience. Our natural awareness of the world begins and ends with what appears to us. But if experience cannot guarantee or certify its own truth, then the only coherent move we can make, as Nicholas sees it, is to *assume* that every experience is true. Since valid inferences require an identity between terms, this requires that we posit a real identity between appearances and reality, an identity independent of, though presupposed by, every distinct cognitive act.

## APPEARANCE OF PERMANENCE AND THE PERMANENCE OF APPEARANCE

Appearances, consequently, come to play a double role in Nicholas' thought, roles that correspond to Nicholas' smaller and larger agendas,

---

[51] Nicholas, *Exigit*, p. 239 (lines 14–18): "Sequitur quinta conclusio quod intellectus et visus vel aliqua quaecumque alia potentia sensitiva numquam sunt ejusdem objecti, vel duae potentiae quaecumque quia semper actus unius potentiae vel est disparatus vel est magis clarus respectu ejusdem objecti, *et utroque modo sequitur distinctio ex parte rei*" (emphasis added). Nicholas draws a similar conclusion at the end of his discussion of the bright and dim patches of whiteness, p. 238 (lines 36–8) and again at pp. 239 (line 49)–40 (line 4): "Duodecima conclusio est quod quot sunt conceptus tot sunt formalitates inexistentes vel realitates; nam plures conceptus vel se habent ad invicem sicut conceptus clarus et conceptus obscurus, et tunc arguunt diversas realitates vel formalitates; vel se habent ad invicem sicut duo conceptus disparati ut conceptus bonitatis et aeternitatis, et tunc multo magis habent arguere diversas res seu formalitates."

with his simultaneous and related desires to found a probabilistic epistemology and to shore up the moral decay he sees everywhere around him
at the University of Paris. On the one hand, Nicholas seeks to define the
conditions within which intellectually defensible statements can be made
about the world and, more to the point, in opposition to the opinions of
Aristotle and Averroes. On the other hand, having finally undermined
Aristotle's authority, he hopes to show the limits of any purely human
authority, that little, perhaps nothing, can be learned from the natural
appearances.[52]

Within the contexts of Nicholas' epistemology in which it is probable
that everything that appears exists, appearances constitute a path we can
follow in our quest for the subjectively existing thing.[53] Nicholas posits
subjective being as something like an anchor or foundation around which
these appearances can be arrayed and understood. Although any given
subjectively existing thing is a unity, a singular thing, it has many different
appearances. It can, after all, be seen from any number of positions,
under any number of circumstances, and from each of these positions
and under each of these circumstances, it will appear differently to the
viewer. A patch of whiteness (to use Nicholas' example) can be seen
from close up or from afar, in a strong or in a weak light. It can, in short,
appear brighter or dimmer. Since everything that appears is true, each
and every one of these appearances discloses some truth about the white
patch. "Whiteness" contains as part of its formal definition every single
appearance it might disclose to the perceiver, every single perspective from
which it might be viewed. Since the white patch can sometimes appear to
be black, Nicholas contends that the singular subjectively existing thing

---

[52] Grellard, "*Sicut specula sine macula*," (forthcoming) reads this double role as reflecting an evolution
in Nicholas' thought as he realized the phenomenalist implications of his theory of appearances.
The problem with this thesis, as I see it, is that it disconnects Nicholas' discussion "Whether
everything that appears exists" from the larger moral and pedagogical goals that he announces
in his prefaces, and transforms it into an analysis of how quite a lot of knowledge about the
world can be gathered from the natural appearances. Questions of evolution aside, Grellard's final
analysis of the "*esse obiectivum*" agrees with mine.

[53] To avoid potential confusion, it is important to note that medieval usage of the terms "subjective"
and "objective" differs markedly from our own usage. When Nicholas refers to a subjective being,
he means the thing existing in the world (what we might refer to as the objectively existing thing).
When he talks about objective beings, he means our various cognitive grasps of the subjectively
existing thing. For a brief discussion of the medieval understanding of these terms, see Christian
Knudsen, "Intentions and Impositions," in Kretzman, *et al.* (eds.), *Cambridge History*, pp. 490–1.
Martin Heidegger, "The Age of the World Picture," in *The Question Concerning Technology and
Other Essays*, trans. William Lovitt (New York: Harper Torchbooks, 1977), pp. 147–53, locates
the shift to our modern understanding of subject and object in Descartes' decision to make man
the foundation of his metaphysic, that is, to define the knowing subject as the ground of all
knowledge claims.

can embody and encompass opposed traits. "Contraries," Nicholas notes, "co-exist."[54]

How can we determine whether any given appearance fully or only partially discloses the subjectively existing thing? One appearance, Nicholas contends, is "more perfect and clearer than another" if it more fully reveals the subjective thing, if it brings us closer to the subjective thing's ultimate unity and identity. How can we determine when an appearance does this? Since there is no awareness of things beyond what appears, Nicholas' only response is to offer a criterion in terms of what appears. In language that clearly echoes his earlier discussion of when an individual is allowed to hold ideas that differ from those of the crowd, Nicholas suggests that whenever the appearance of something does not change, no matter when or how long we look at it, then we can assume that the appearance discloses a fixed subjective being.[55]

If appearances make our knowledge of the world possible, they also mark the limit of what we can know about that world. The recognition of this limit points to the other role that the appearances play in Nicholas' thought, one that returns us to his moral critique of the university and his belief that little certainty can be derived from the natural appearances. In one respect, Nicholas seems to follow Aureol's lead. Since every cognitive act terminates in an appearance, we can only see and know real beings insofar as they appear, under the mode of appearing being. But unlike Aureol, Nicholas asks how and to what extent real being is disclosed through its appearances. Nicholas describes something like an inferential-deductive process. Having grasped one objective being, we employ it as a subjective being "in relation to other subsequent objective beings." It serves as the ground against which other beings are arrayed and understood. Having grasped the objective being "man," for example, we can use it as the basis for judging which subsequent appearances are

---

[54] Nicholas, *Exigit*, p. 239 (lines 32–6): "Nona conclusio est quod ubi est albedo clarissime ibi est omnis albedo inferioris gradus; nam inspiciendo ad illud ubi, paulatim recedente lumine, paulatim potest videri omnis albedo infra illam albedinem, immo etiam nigredo magis poterit videri recedente lumine ubi est maxima albedo, et sic contraria et simul." See also, p. 262 (lines 10–19): "Et secundum istum modum dicendi posset sustineri probabiliter quod albedo et nigredo sunt unum in esse subjectivo; nam pone sunt centum visus ordinati secundum perfectius et imperfectius; supremus videt rem et secundum esse objectivum imponit nomen albedo; infimus videbit ita obscure quod illud vocabit nigredinem quod supremus vocabat albedinem, et tamen idem sunt in esse subjectivo. Sic suo modo dicatur ad intelligendum modum positionis quod albedo et nigredo non differunt in esse subjectivo, sed bene differunt in esse objectivo. Et si sic dicatur, ita poterit dici de quibuscumque rebus quod omnes res sunt una res in esse subjectivo, licet diversificetur esse objectivum secundum quod venit apud nos."

[55] Nicholas, *Exigit*, p. 232 (lines 6–10): "Nunc quando non mutatur visio ad quodcumque se divertat et quomodo existens et realiter illud sibi apparet imponit illud nomen et dicit quod ibi est vera albedo habens esse fixum vel subjectivum; quando non sic imponit nomen et appellat illud imaginem sicut quando homo videtur in speculo . . ."

compatible or incompatible, essential or accidental. As we grasp additional objective beings, we might discover one that appears to be even more fundamental than the one we initially selected to serve as our ground. At times, Nicholas treats this process as a relatively straightforward matter. We move closer to the real subjectively existing thing through a process of comparison in which we select more and more basic objective beings to serve as our interim organizing subjective being.[56]

As the logic of Nicholas' analysis plays itself out, however, it soon becomes clear that this process never moves us beyond what appears. In the final analysis, inferences about what appears can only tell us about the appearances themselves. To begin with, it is an open question in Nicholas' manuscript whether any humanly knowable appearance fully discloses and reveals the thing in its simple perfection. Nicholas even suggests at one point that, despite the probabilism with which he frames his epistemology, certitude may be unattainable.[57] It is precisely this inability to move beyond what appears that opens up the possibility of multiple competing interpretations. Suppose someone sees a patch of dim whiteness (which he will call "black") and considers it, not as it incompletely reveals whiteness, but in and for itself. In this case, blackness is no longer treated as an objective being that truthfully, though incompletely, reveals a subjectively existing whiteness. Rather, blackness itself is now treated as the subject to which these various dim appearances are predicated. The more clearly an intellect grasps this blackness itself, "the more evident it will be to them that blackness is distinguished from whiteness."[58]

Roles reverse. Initially, subjective beings stood as absolute foundations around which appearances were predicated and understood. Now they

---

[56] Nicholas, *Exigit*, p. 264 (lines 34–42): "Et considerandum quod apud unum hominem secundum diversos intellectus est unum esse objectivum quod est quasi esse subjectivum respectu aliorum esse objectivorum subsequentium ut, cum aliquis non habituatus vidit primo Socratem, habuit unum esse objectivum confusum quia multa esse objectiva confundit in se; nam postea comparet eum ad Platonem et habet unum esse objectivum, videlicet homo, post comparans ad asinum habuit aliud esse objectivum, scilicet animal et sic de aliis."

[57] Nicholas, *Exigit*, p. 232 (lines 34–6): "Et forsan finaliter oporteret quod non habemus plenam certitudinem de rebus, immo solum eam habet intellectus primus qui est mensura omnium intellectuum."

[58] Nicholas, *Exigit*, pp. 262–63 (lines 44–6): "Tunc imaginor quosdam intellectus alterius modi quorum aspectus non erit directus ad esse subjectivum rei, sed ad ista esse objectiva. Nunc esse objectivum quod unus appellat nigredo iste videbit, et quanto habet visum clariorem, tanto magis videbit illud esse objectivum in esse propinquo sibi; et quia in esse suo objectivo distinguebatur ab aliis esse objectivis, quanto clarius videbitur, tanto magis apparebit, quod distinguitur ab alio esse objectivo, scilicet albedine quod est esse objectivum respectu primorum, sed est esse subjectivum respectu secundorum. Et de istis secundo cognoscentibus procedit ratio, scilicet quod quanto clarius cognoscent, tanto magis apparebit eis nigredo distingui ab albedine secus est in primis cognoscentibus, immo si intenderetur cognitio, finaliter devenirent ad unum esse subjectivum."

have become relative entities, entities whose existence depends upon the appearances themselves and how we choose to understand their interconnections. If we consider blackness in its relation to whiteness, we posit one subjective existent. If we consider it in and for itself, we posit two subjective existents (one for whiteness, one for blackness). Externalizing the appearances, transforming them into features of the world, strips Nicholas' thought of any definitive grounding, of any immovable centre. Or, to put it a bit differently, every appearance can serve as a centre or foundation around which we can construct some set of probable judgments, around which some set of appearances can be understood. Nicholas does not view this outcome as problematic. It is this very decentring that energizes his various critiques, that ultimately displaces or upsets any claim to an absolute intellectual authority, be it by the community or by the individual. Any given account of subjective being can only be more or less probable with respect to a given set of appearances whose relations demand that we posit *this* underlying entity, this sort of organization. Even assuming that everything that appears exists and that everything that appears to be true is true, the best we can hope for are more or less probable theories.

### PERSPECTIVE, PROBABILITY, PRAYER

In the end, Nicholas' valorization of the self-assertive, logically-minded individual with his personal grasp of concepts is merely a moment of stability in a broader program of dislocations and displacements. Having personally derived and analyzed commonly accepted concepts, perhaps having even derived and analyzed new and original concepts, the individual certainly becomes an authority, a third party. Removed from the community, he finds himself in a much better position to judge which theories are more probable than others. Regardless, this authority is far from absolute and itself begins to dissolve within the very methodological strategy that made it possible in the first place. Although he can determine which arguments are more probable than others, in the final analysis, probability has nothing to do with truth. Quite often the more probable opinion is false and Nicholas himself admits that many of his assertions must be false because they contradict truths of the Catholic faith.[59] Nevertheless, he contends that his statements are more probable than the statements of others insofar as they "are made in conformity

---

[59] Nicholas, *Exigit*, p. 184 (lines 41–6): "Item tu non potes concludere per tuum medium nisi istam conclusionem: verisimile est quod non sit bona tua doctrina etc.; dico quod, etsi vera sit tua conclusio, non ex hoc destruitur quin possit esse vera quia etiam secundum Aristotelem nihil prohibet quaedam falsa esse probabiliora quibusdam veris."

with the natural appearances." Nicholas is not asserting some version of the doctrine of the double truth. He is not arguing that there is a set of natural truths set up in opposition to the truths of faith. There is only one set of truths and we, lost as we are among the natural appearances, are inherently unable to discern them for ourselves.[60] This does not mean that the standards and procedures appropriate to speculative activity must be violated, that theological or some other less than logical standards should be invoked to fill in those moments where speculative standards fail to move us beyond mere probability. Speculative activity must conform itself to its object, to the natural appearances, and to the possibilities and limitations inherent to the appearances.

As a result, Nicholas severs any connection whatsoever between theory and truth. One theory is judged to be more probable than another if it more convincingly accounts for what appears in terms of whatever regulative ideals we have set for ourselves, such as the principle of the good or the cognitive ideal of certitude. But even these regulative ideals can be disputed, replaced or refined. When this happens, a theory that once seemed more probable might suddenly appear to be less probable, perhaps even absurd. For centuries Aristotle's ideas seemed probable, even self-evident. In the wake of the *Exigit* (or so Nicholas contends), they might well seem less probable and someday the probability of Nicholas' own ideas will themselves be undermined.[61] Nicholas never suggests that this process of theory assertion and replacement slowly improves our epistemic relation to the world. Successive theories do not provide us with increasingly accurate accounts of what really exists behind or within the appearances. It makes no sense to even discuss what lies behind the appearances. For all practical purposes nothing lies behind them. Even the putative existence of subjective beings ultimately depends upon how we organize appearances. One theory is judged more probable than another only in terms of the regulative ideals we have set for ourselves, in terms of how we have organized any given constellation of appearances with respect to those ideals. Knowledge does not progress, it circulates endlessly.

---

[60] Weinberg, *Nicolas of Autrecourt*, pp. 115–17. On the thirteenth-century origins of this concept see Richard C. Dales, "The Origin of the Doctrine of the Double Truth," *Viator* 15 (1984), 169–79. Funkenstein, *Theology*, p. 151, notes that Nicholas' contemporary, the English Dominican Robert Holcot, asserted that Aristotelian rules of inference "are sometimes invalid when transcending the domain of creation." Hester Gelber, *Exploring the Boundaries of Reason* (Toronto: Pontifical Institute of Mediaeval Studies, 1983), pp. 26–8, summarizes Holcot's reason for holding this doctrine, adding that Holcot later refined this position in his quodlibetal debates.

[61] Nicholas, *Exigit*, p. 187 (lines 30–3): ". . . nam etsi appareant probabiliora longe, mihi videtur, positis ab Aristotele; tamen sicut multo tempore visa sunt esse probabilia dicta Aristotelis quorum probabilitas nunc forsan diminuetur, sic veniet unus qui tollet probabilitatem ab istis."

Knowledge cannot progress because everything about Nicholas' epistemology works to undermine every foundation, every starting point,
every frame of reference. Externalizing the appearances does not merely
dissolve subjective being into its appearances, it also effectively serves to
dissolve the individual into those same appearances. Nicholas, for example, will argue that what is clear and evident to the intellect is true. This
hypothesis must be assumed, he contends, because we have no knowledge
of "first principles or anything else knowable except because we know
them clearly and evidently."[62] But what appears clearly and evidently to
one person, say, with a stronger intellect, will not appear to someone
with a duller intellect. A duller individual, for example, might correctly
assert that it is better to enjoy bodily delights, while the brighter individual will correctly conclude that intellectual delights are better. They do
not contradict each other, Nicholas says, because what each one says is
true insofar as it refers to the appearances that they receive. The brighter
individual can honestly say to the duller, "You have known nothing
which I have known."[63] It follows, similarly, that God knows none of
the things we know because his intelligence is infinitely more perfect
(hence it presupposes infinitely more perfect cognitive objects) than our
intelligence.

Seen in this light, the logic of appearances is a logic of differentiation, a
logic that individuates knowers into their particular perspectives. A bright
person's perspective differs from a dull person's and the judgments they
make will necessarily reflect their unique perspectives. Nicholas does not
believe that this leads to a radical subjectivism in which "whatever appears
to me is true." At certain moments, Nicholas appeals to a hierarchy of
intellects (from dullest to brightest) in order to avoid a complete rela-
tivization of truth and to provide some sort of epistemic foothold. The
individual who suggests that bodily delights are greater than intellectual
delights is correct insofar as his judgment refers solely to what appears to
him. "But," Nicholas quickly adds, "to complete the statement it must
be added that intellectual delights do not occur in him with their full

---

[62] Nicholas, *Exigit*, p. 235 (lines 39–48): "Juxta ista ponam primam conclusionem quod si de aliquo
intellectus possit dicere: hoc est verum, oppositum illius quod clare et evidenter cognoscitur non
potest inesse, ita quod universaliter et conversive quicquid est clarum et evidens intellectui est
verum. Probatur haec conclusio; nam si ita esset quod cum cognitione clara et evidenti possit
stare oppositum illius quod venit in cognitionem, sequeretur quod de nullo intellectus posset
esse certus, cujus oppositum retinebatur in hypothesi. Probatur consequentia quia nec de primis
principiis nec de quibuscumque cognoscibilibus habemus certitudinem nisi quia clare et evidenter
ea cognoscimus. Unde nullum actum experimur nos habere circa principia nisi cognitionem
claram."

[63] Nicholas, *Exigit*, p. 240 (lines 14–16): "Sexta decima conclusio est quod si sint duo, quorum unus
habeat intellectum perfectiorem alio, poterit dicere alii: nullius rei cujus habui notitiam habuisti
notitiam . . ."

being."[64] The brighter person more fully grasps the subjective truth of the matter and, it would therefore seem, his authority must be that much greater. At one point Nicholas suggests that subjective being can itself be known. After all, subjective beings are finite things and, therefore, it only makes sense that there must be some very clear and very evident, though still somewhat imperfect, appearance "beyond which, if progress were made in knowing the thing more clearly, the thing would be known according to its subjective being." And so Nicholas asserts that the brightest intellect will know the thing most intimately, that is, it would know the thing "according to its subjective being."[65]

Whatever stabilization the limit case of the brightest intellect provides for Nicholas' epistemology, it is a stabilization that in principle cannot provide any solid foundation for the rest of us. The entire tenor of Nicholas' thought works to indefinitely defer such a complete grasp of the existing thing. Any given intellect knows according to its specific capacities and abilities. We have already seen a version of this idea in our analysis of perspectivist thought. Roger Bacon, following Boethius (following Aristotle) contended that the object is known according to the mode of the knower. Bacon defended his tripartite division of the brain and its cognitive faculties precisely because we cognize objects in different ways. Different modes of knowing external objects require different cognitive faculties within the sensible soul.[66] Nicholas takes this idea, radicalizes it and, in so doing, utterly dissolves the unity of the intellect. Not only does each faculty have its own unique grasp of the cognitive object, each and every cognitive act must have its own object. No cognitive act can know more than one cognitive object. Such a possibility would undermine the regulative ideal of certitude because then the act of knowing a bright whiteness might also grasp a dim whiteness, that is, know a dim whiteness as bright and, therefore, know it incorrectly. This absolute segregation of cognitive acts eventually compels Nicholas to assert that each individual consists of a potentially infinite number of discrete intellects, one intellect for every intelligible concept, every appearance we

---

[64] Nicholas, *Exigit*, p. 233 (lines 22–7): "Ei autem qui dicit quod delectationes tactus sunt majores quam delectationes intellectus, dicemus quod verum dicit habita relatione ad illud quod sibi apparet; sed subjunctio complementi sermonis erit quod delectationes intellectus non perveniunt ad ipsum in suo plene esse, sed in eo quod habet de eis esse diminutum; alteri apparet simpliciter absque tali diminutione."

[65] Nicholas, *Exigit*, p. 242 (lines 30–6): "Et si res sit finita, tunc non videtur, cum unum objectum sit perfectius et clarius alio, licet sint ejusdem rei, quod in talibus circa eandem rem finitam sit procedere in infinitum. Quodlibet enim esse objectivum videtur deficere a perfectione quam habet res in se secundum esse subjectivum quod habet. Tunc secundum hoc est dare aliquod esse objectivum finitum supra quod, si procederetur clarius cognoscendo rem, res cognosceretur secundum esse subjectivum."

[66] See above, chapter 3, p. 90.

grasp. Since each intellect can only know one object, additional intellects are needed to account for our grasp of the difference between any two intellectual acts, and so on in an endless "third man" styled regress.[67] Not only does Nicholas' philosophy work to individualize people in terms of their unique perspectives, it even works to fragment the individual himself into an endless collection of individualized perspectives.

And it is here that Nicholas' hyper-logicism, his drive to draw out every conceivable implication, reaches something like a crescendo as he entirely undoes, not only the individual's cognitive unity, but even his temporal unity, his identity over time. At this point it becomes difficult to even describe the one who sees as an individual. Nicholas notes that as we mature our cognitive powers gradually gain in strength and as we age our powers decline. If every cognitive act, every intellect, corresponds to a specific cognitive object, then it seems to follow that separate intellects must be posited for each and every one of these changes over time. A young man's intellect must, for example, differ from an old man's intellect. "It even seems," Nicholas continues, "that, just as someone by understanding more clearly or less clearly, changes from one day to the next and from one hour to the next, and similarly in other functions, accordingly a change is produced in his faculties."[68] The individual in no way stands over and against the field of appearances. In a very real sense, the identity of the one who sees is constituted in and through what appears, multiplied, fragmented and forever deferred through the appearances. There is no humanly accessible viewpoint outside what appears and no cognitive act that can move us beyond them. Perhaps everything that appears is true, but there is no way, when all is said and done, to determine how they are true, how they relate to and how they reveal what exists.

In the end there can only be exhaustion and the recognition of the futility of all speculative endeavour. As Nicholas' analysis of terms unfolds, he inevitably falls into contradictions. He asserts at one point that if we

---

[67] Nicholas, *Exigit*, p. 254 (lines 19–29): "Sed videtur difficile si tot sint intellectus quot conceptus, quia tunc videtur quod nullus intellectus poterit ponere differentiam inter aliqua duo quia nullus unus intellectus cognoscit aliqua duo. Et dico quod sufficit quod ab aliquibus intellectibus copulatis ad invicem et cum aliquo uno supposito sunt intellecta extrema, et tunc inexistit quidam intellectus cognitivus differentiae quae est inter extrema. Unde sicut corporalia quae sunt in supposito habent [quam] quamdam copulationem ad invicem et quemdam ordinem sic isti intellectus habent quamdam copulationem consecutionis cujusdam naturalis, et forsan posset dici quod ubi sunt isti tres intellectus, scilicet duo extremorum et tertius intellectus differentiae fundantur in eadem essentia animae, et hic considera amplius."

[68] Nicholas, *Exigit*, p. 253 (lines 34–8): "Unde sicut si haberet oculum juvenis videret ut juvenis, ita si haberet intellectum juvenis intelligeret ut juvenis, immo videtur quod sicut aliquis de die in diem et de hora in horam transmutatur in intelligendo magis clare vel minus clare et sic in aliis operationibus, secundum hoc etiam fiat transmutatio in virtutibus."

know something clearly and evidently, we know it just as God knows it. Later, he contends that man and God have no common cognitive objects.[69] Contradictions like these, however, speak to Nicholas' broader goals. Certainly Nicholas sought to undermine scholastic Aristotelianism, to demonstrate that it was far from self-evident, but the critique of Aristotle itself has a larger target. Although Nicholas sets his atomistic cosmology against Aristotle's cosmology, argues that it is more probable than Aristotle's, he never claims it is true. In virtue of its very object and starting point, speculative activity can never lead to truth. The natural appearances forever forestall any attempts to move beyond them, to acquire a knowledge of how things really are. As a result, speculative activity can have no terminus, no end point and to pursue it is necessarily to pursue it for its own sake. The institutionalized pedagogy of the medieval university, organized as a series of commentaries on Aristotle's works, had effectively masked the inherent futility of all natural speculation. And so, to return to the image we began with, Nicholas can look about him and see men grown old and grey as they study Aristotle and Averroes for ten, for twenty, for thirty years, now puffed up with every sort of arrogance, imagining they know much, when really they know nothing at all. Unbridled speculation leads to every sort of vice, to pride, to vanity and to curiosity, as it leads its practitioners further from God and a life of charity.

As a treatise, the *Exigit* remains unfinished, a fitting symbol for the practice of natural philosophy as Nicholas describes it. Nicholas' moral critique of his contemporaries and the moral rejuvenation he believes his critiques can accomplish mesh perfectly with the philosophical content of his work, with its actual incompletion and its theoretical incompletability. In the final analysis, the most original medieval cosmological and epistemological treatise becomes an eminently practical work, a useful treatise, a manual that leads its readers into the endless and endlessly contradictory morass of the natural appearances only to demonstrate the futility of all speculative activity. If the probable status of all natural reasoning serves to liberate the philosopher from any intellectual authority, from the works of Aristotle and official university pedagogy, it also liberates him from the need to speculate at all and from the demands of his own intellectual authority. Speculative freedom becomes a freedom from speculation once the philosopher recognizes that such investigations no longer concern themselves with truth. Nicholas' work turns back on itself to reveal a deeply conservative undercurrent. If truth cannot be discovered among

[69] Nicholas, *Exigit*, pp. 239 (lines 5–8) and 240 (lines 35–7). Leonard Kennedy, *The Universal Treatise of Nicholas of Autrecourt*, pp. 27–8, notes some of Nicholas' contradictory statements concerning the nature of singularity.

the appearances, then all that is left, Nicholas suggests, is to return to the Bible, the study of Scripture, so that scholars will seem like "divine men." They will no longer devote their entire lives to logical discourse, but will "purify their hearts," live chastely and without envy, as they teach "the divine law to the people, diffusing the rays of their goodness on every side, so as to appear, in the sight of the most glorious Prince of all nature, like spotless mirrors, and images of His goodness."[70]

[70] Nicholas, *Exigit*, p. 182.

# CONCLUSION:
## VISION, PROMISE, DEFERRAL

From speculation to preaching, Nicholas of Autrecourt's work returns us to where we began, to Dominican friars as they attempt to balance the need for study with the demands of their religious calling, with the demand to preach. It is a curious, oddly symbolic, return. Nicholas envisions the return to preaching as an escape from the snares of speculation and the natural appearances, but the experience of preachers tells a different story. Preachers, trained as they were to always think of themselves as if on public display, in many ways most fully embodied the medieval experience of vision and its effects. Peter of Limoges addressed this experience in his popular preaching manual, the *Tractatus moralis de oculo*, when he articulated the practice of medieval religious life in the language of perspectivist optics. In doing so, he simultaneously articulated the problems that those practices had generated for the religious as explicitly visual problems, as problems arising from a distinction between what appears and what really exists, between seeing and being seen. These are precisely the same sorts of problems that occupied the minds of many fourteenth-century theologians like Peter Aureol and Bernard of Arezzo. In the final analysis, Nicholas' turn from speculation to preaching is a turn to the very practices that had problematized the relation between self and self-presentation, between appearance and reality, in the first place.

Seen in this light, the epistemological controversies that raged throughout Europe's universities during the first half of the fourteenth century, controversies that centred around vision and the relation between what appears and what exists, can be read as philosophical elaborations of problems arising from within medieval religious life itself. Too often, historians interpret these fourteenth-century controversies as signs of a "dissolution of the medieval outlook," as a falling away from the supposedly magisterial accomplishments of the thirteenth century and, to be more precise, of writers like Thomas Aquinas and Bonaventure.[1] Broadening

---

[1] Gordon Leff, *The Dissolution of the Medieval Outlook* (New York: Harper & Row, 1976). Even Blumenberg's powerful analysis of the modern age as "the second overcoming of Gnosticism,"

the contexts within which we think about and make sense of the problems that absorbed the attention of university scholars can help us to rethink the varied trajectories, breaks and continuities that make up later medieval intellectual and religious life. Peter of Limoges' *Tractatus*, for example, suggests a radically different reading of fourteenth-century debates about vision and knowledge, one that sees them as reflections of, perhaps even responses to, such central facets of religious life as public preaching, private confession and a growing concern with spiritual vision, with seeing and being seen. These concerns did not originate in the wake of Bacon's popularization of Alhacen's perspectivist theories, but rather in confessional pastoralia dating from as early as the late eleventh century. While the science of optics may have provided Peter with a technical terminology to describe the practices of that religious life, those practices themselves had already generated an awareness of the spiritual and epistemological problems that would eventually demand the attention of natural philosophers and theologians.

Attention to the broader contexts in which medieval intellectual life played itself out should also serve as something like a warning against overstating (and overly streamlining) the impact that innovations in scholastic natural philosophy exerted outside the universities. Noting the influence that Bacon's perspectivist optics had within the university, historians in recent decades have attempted to trace its influence on other areas of later medieval cultural life, on art and on literature. Art historians, for example, have contended that the popularity of Bacon's optics led to "a transformation in the whole visual field in the later Middle Ages, an 'image-explosion.'" The dissemination of perspectivist theory, in other words, not only fuelled an increase in the number of images produced, but even transformed the way in which images were manufactured and used.[2] Other historians, interested in the rise of linear perspective as an artistic practice in fifteenth-century Italy, have sought to make sense of Bacon's writings as the first term in a series of steps passing directly through

*Legitimacy*, pp. 125–203, makes similar assumptions about fourteenth-century theological nominalism and voluntarism. For a reassessment of Blumenberg's account of the "epochal threshold between the Middle Ages and modernity," see Elizabeth Brient, *The Immanence of the Infinite, Hans Blumenberg and the Threshold to Modernity* (Washington, DC: The Catholic University Press of America, 2002). For a general overview and critique of the literature of a later medieval "decline," see Howard Kaminsky, "From Lateness to Waning to Crisis: The Burden of the Later Middle Ages," *Journal of Early Modern History*, 4.1 (2000), 85–125, and for fourteenth-century intellectual culture in particular, Hobbins, "The Schoolman as Public Intellectual," 1308–21

[2] Michael Camille develops these ideas in two related essays, "The Eye in the Text: Vision in the Illuminated Manuscripts of the Latin Aristotle," in *View and Vision*, pp. 129–45, especially p. 143, and "Before the Gaze: The Internal Senses and Late Medieval Practices of Seeing," in Robert S. Nelson (ed.), *Visuality Before and Beyond the Renaissance* (Cambridge: Cambridge University Press, 2000), pp. 197–223, especially p. 206.

Giotto's early fourteenth-century frescos and culminating in the artistic works of Masaccio and Piero della Francesca, and in Alberti's treatise on the practice and function of artistic perspective, *On Painting*.[3]

Without denying the possibility that Bacon's optical theories exerted some influence on artistic production, there are real problems with verifying these sorts of claims. Often there is simply no direct evidence of such a connection.[4] Where there is evidence for some sort of awareness of visual theory, the results are equally indecisive. Alberti, for example, acknowledges that there are two radically opposed kinds of visual theory, intromission and extramission, and then simply sidesteps the question of which one is true as a theoretical nicety irrelevant to the artist.[5] Something similar happens in literature. While some medieval poets explicitly incorporated ideas from perspectivist optics into their work,[6] others found it more useful to draw inspiration from pre-existing traditions. Dante, for example, accepted the truth of intromissionist theories of vision and yet, when imagining the effect that the beloved's glance has on her lover or how God is present to the beatified in heaven, he was more than happy to deploy more traditional extramissionist models of vision.[7] Mystical visionary experiences, likewise, were often described and depicted in explicitly Augustinian, not Baconian, terms.[8] In fact, it is worth repeating that even among university theologians matters were not so clear cut.

---

[3] For two different accounts, see Edgerton, *Heritage*, pp. 23–107 and Panofsky, *Perspective as Symbolic Form*, pp. 53–66.

[4] Edgerton, *Heritage*, pp. 82–7, asserts the link through an imaginary, albeit evocative, dialogue between Petrarch and Giotto. For an interesting comparison case concerning the relation between innovations in science and art, it is useful to think of the now discredited notion that Einstein's relativity theory directly influenced Picasso's development of cubist art. See Arthur I. Miller, *Einstein, Picasso: Space, Time and the Beauty that Causes Havoc* (New York: Basic Books, 2001), who argues that both men's work can be seen as independent responses to broader social and cultural forces.

[5] Leon Battista Alberti, *On Painting*, I.5, ed. Cecil Grayson (London: Penguin Books, 1972), p. 40. Anthony Grafton, *Leon Battista Alberti: Master Builder of the Italian Renaissance* (Cambridge: Harvard University Press, 2000), pp. 124–5, stresses the practical aspects of Alberti's treatise. The most convincing account of Alberti's "use" of medieval optical theory is Joel Snyder, "Picturing Vision," *Critical Inquiry* (Spring 1980), 514–26.

[6] Suzanne Conklin Akbari, *Seeing Through the Veil: Optical Theory and Medieval Allegory* (Toronto: University of Toronto Press, 2004), surveys the use of optical theory in medieval literature from Guillaume de Lorris' *Roman de la Rose* through Chaucer. She makes no reference to Peter of Limoges.

[7] Richard Kay, "Dante's Empyrean and the Eye of God," *Speculum*, 78.1 (January 2003), 41–3.

[8] Cynthia Hahn, "*Visio Dei*: Change in Medieval Visuality," in Nelson (ed.), *Visuality*, pp. 169–96, connects a thirteenth-century transformation in the nature and use of images to a resurgence of Augustinian notions about vision. On the role of images and mysticism in the later Middle Ages, see Craig Harbison, "Visions and Meditations in Early Flemish Painting," pp. 87–118 and Jeffrey Hamburger, "The Visual and the Visionary: The Image in Late Medieval Monastic Devotions," in *The Visual and the Visionary: Art and Female Spirituality in Late Medieval Germany* (Cambridge: The MIT Press, 1998), pp. 111–48.

Both Peter Olivi and William Ockham directly opposed central aspects of perspectivist theory, and the entire tradition of intuitive cognition itself found its roots in Augustinian ideas.

It would be self-defeating at this point, not to mention simply wrong, to deny perspectivist optics an important place in later medieval cultural and religious life. But it is equally self-defeating to misidentify that importance. Natural philosophy neither created nor entirely determined the specific possibilities and anxieties that medieval men and women experienced concerning vision and its effects. Rather, as Peter of Limoges' *Treatise* and the writings of fourteenth-century scholastic thinkers and poets so amply testify, that theory was selectively deployed to make sense of those possibilities and anxieties, to make sense of the mounting emphasis that religious life and practice placed on the relation, not to mention on the distinction, between what appears and what exists. This is the broader cultural and religious discourse within which to make sense of transformations in later medieval pictorial practices, a discourse that neither overly defines lines of influence, nor seeks to understand the concerns of early fourteenth-century artists in terms taken from later centuries. Rather than reading fifteenth- or sixteenth-century notions of realism, naturalism and even mathematical science back onto early fourteenth-century religious paintings, it may be more useful to attempt to understand them through contemporary religious concerns with self and self-presentation, with individual and audience.[9]

Of course, medieval men and women, preachers and scholars, penitents and confessors, were not the first people to worry about the relation between their public and private lives. They certainly would not be the last. In recent decades, Renaissance and early modern historians have been exploring what Stephan Greenblatt refers to as the Renaissance practice of "self-fashioning," a growing self-consciousness among people living during the sixteenth century "about the fashioning of human identity as a manipulable, artful process."[10] In later work, Greenblatt has gone so far as to argue that during this period "[t]here is no layer deeper, more authentic, than theatrical self-representation."[11] Quite simply, there was

---

[9] For a critique of the category of "realism" as applied to fourteenth-century portraiture, see Stephen Perkinson, "*Portraire, Contrefaire*, and *Engin*: The Prehistory of Portraiture in Late Medieval France" (PhD diss., Northwestern University, 1998). Michael Baxandall, *Painting and Experience in Fifteenth-Century Italy: A Primer in the Social History of Pictorial Style*, 2nd edn. (Oxford: Oxford University Press, 1988), pp. 56–71, notes the connections between the concern with self-presentation in medieval preaching manuals and the use of gesture to convey meaning in Renaissance art.

[10] Stephan Greenblatt, *Renaissance Self-Fashioning: From More to Shakespeare* (Chicago: The University of Chicago Press, 1980), p. 2.

[11] Stephan Greenblatt, "Psychoanalysis and Renaissance Culture," in his *Learning to Curse* (New York: Routledge, 1990), p. 143.

nothing to the individual but his self-presentation. Most scholars, however, have proven unwilling to reduce the Renaissance courtier to a mere surface without depth. Rather they have sought to demonstrate a growing awareness during the sixteenth century of an ontological divide between a consciously fashioned exterior and a true interior self. It is an awareness that manifests itself in the growing popularity of autobiographies in both England and in France, beginning in the late sixteenth century.[12] And it is, perhaps most famously, an awareness that Hamlet gives voice to when he contrasts the trappings of his grief – customary suit of black, tears and a dejected visage – with his real, hidden, and undeniable experience of grief.[13] I am less interested in who is right as far as the Renaissance goes, than I am in pointing out that neither account captures the medieval experience of surface and depth, appearance and truth.

Medieval people, as we have seen, recognized the manipulability of one's public facade, the potential differences between self and self-presentation. The sincerity of a penitent's tears of anguish depended upon something more than mere public display, it depended upon a true experience of contrition within his soul. Mendicant novices were trained always to adapt their self-presentation to the needs and demands of their audience. Ideally, one's self-presentation of holiness manifested a real inner holiness, but this certainly could not always be the case. In his thirteenth-century guide for Franciscan novices, David of Augsburg even suggests that there will be times when the novice must present a false front. "If you should lack interior devotion," he writes in the *De institutione novitiorum*, "at the very least humbly maintain discipline and a grave exterior demeanour out of reverence for God and as an example to others."[14] Perhaps in this case, deception is advised for the good of others, but when do such deceptions become our downfall? What if the novice gradually comes to equate the appearance of devotion with devotion itself? Humbert of Romans certainly recognized this danger.

---

[12] For England, see Michael Mascuch, *Origins of the Individualist Self: Autobiography and Self-Identity in England, 1591–1791* (Stanford: Stanford University Press, 1996) and for France, Nicholas D. Paige, *Being Interior: Autobiography and the Contradictions of Modernity in Seventeenth-Century France* (Philadelphia: University of Pennsylvania Press, 2001).

[13] Katharine Eisaman Maus, *Inwardness and the Theater in the English Renaissance* (Chicago: The University of Chicago Press, 1995), p. 1. Also, Martin, "Inventing Sincerity," pp. 1321–2. Paige, *Being Interior*, pp. 21–47, warns against precipitously interpreting this sixteenth- and seventeenth-century language as somehow indicating the sudden formation of an interiorized, modern subject. Montaigne's language of interiority, Paige suggests, pp. 23–47, is still caught up in, while simultaneously transforming, a more traditional discourse concerned with the care of the self. Reis, *Mirages of the Selfe*, pp. 470–86, provocatively, if not entirely convincingly, argues that even Descartes did not seek to create or discover the modern "subject."

[14] David of Augsburg, *De institutione novitiorum*, p. 294: "Si autem non habes devotionem interius, saltem conserva disciplinam et morum gravitatem humiliter exterius, propter reverentiam Dei et aliorum exemplum."

The good preacher must always be on guard against the possibility that the words and postures he first assumed to stimulate his audience with religious fervour, he now assumes for the adulation it brings him. We can deceive ourselves, be deceived by ourselves, as easily as we can deceive others.

None of which is meant to imply that the possibility of deception did not trouble early modern thinkers; it did, and in more radical and dramatic forms than it ever seemed to trouble Nicholas of Autrecourt or Peter Aureol.[15] In the 1670s, for example, nearly three and a half centuries after the Parisian authorities had condemned Nicholas of Autrecourt's teachings, burnt his writings and revoked his license to teach, the Cartesian-influenced Catholic theologian Nicholas Malebranche, would seemingly echo many of his predecessor's deepest concerns. "But without dwelling on the opinion we might have of [Aristotle, Descartes] and all other philosophers," Malebranche writes near the beginning of *The Search After Truth*, "let us always consider them as men; and let not the votaries of Aristotle carp if, after having trod through so many centuries in darkness without finding ourselves any further ahead than we were before, we should finally wish to see clearly what we are doing; or if after having been left to wander like blind men, we should remember that we have eyes with which to try to guide ourselves."[16]

Nicholas of Autrecourt himself had invoked the metaphor of blindness in the *Exigit*'s first prologue as part of his own intellectual assault on fourteenth-century Scholastic Aristotelianism and there certainly are passages in *The Search After Truth* in which Malebranche really does seem to follow in the footsteps of his fourteenth-century predecessor. Like Nicholas before him, Malebranche will criticize his peers for their slavish devotion to Aristotle whose "principles have been of no use for two thousand years." And for that very reason Malebranche will urge his readers, as Nicholas had already urged his own, to turn from the opinions of mere men to the natural appearances. "Let us therefore be fully convinced," Malebranche writes, "that this rule, *that one must never give complete consent, except to things as seen with evidence*, is the most necessary of all the rules in the search after truth."[17] Finally, Malebranche will consider in some detail the tremendous difficulties that this turn to nature

---

[15] The classic study is Richard H. Popkin, *The History of Scepticism from Erasmus to Spinoza* (Berkeley: University of California Press, 1979), who traces the rise of scepticism in Early Modern Europe to the intellectual challenges posed by the Reformation.

[16] Nicholas Malebranche, *The Search After Truth*, trans. Thomas M. Lennon and Paul J. Olscamp (Columbus: Ohio State University Press, 1980), p. 14. See Ted Schmaltz, *Malebranche's Theory of the Soul: A Cartesian Interpretation* (Oxford: Oxford University Press, 1996) for Malebranche's intellectual debt to and deviations from Cartesian philosophy.

[17] Malebranche, *The Search After Truth*, p. 14. The italics are in the original.

entails. The opening chapters of *The Search After Truth* are replete with examples of the seeming failure of vision, the potential pitfalls of visual evidence. Vision may well be "the most noble" of all the senses, but it has its limits and if we are to follow Malebranche's rule, if we are only to assent to things seen with complete evidence, we must learn to identify those limits.

Where seventeenth-century thinkers like Descartes and Malebranche differ from their medieval counterparts is not in the recognition that human vision is perspectival, that every perceptual encounter is defined by a set of circumstances that profoundly determines what we see, but rather in their response to that situation. For Nicholas, blindness names the human epistemological condition, names the inescapable net of circumstances that shape and limit our every perceptual interaction with the world. In the writings of Malebranche, Descartes, as well as in so many of their contemporaries, it names a state that can be overcome. Since vision in principle can never deliver clear and evident ideas about the world, there must be some other means of obtaining that knowledge that escapes the deforming tyranny of circumstances.[18] This is nowhere so clear as in the opening pages of Descartes' *Meditations* as he attempts to free himself from all inherited prejudice in order to create a firm and permanent foundation in the sciences. The various stages of doubt – from optical illusions, to dreams, to the deceiving God – are specifically designed to isolate the individual and his judgments about the world, about God and about himself, from all outside influences and circumstances. As Descartes famously concludes his "First Meditation," even if there were an all-powerful deceiving god seeking to impose false beliefs on him, Descartes would still be free to withhold his assent, to refuse to accept as true something that might possibly be false.[19]

All of which returns us to the difference between medieval and early modern conceptions of the self and to the difference between what might be referred to as the later medieval practice of self-presentation and the early modern practice of self-fashioning. The writings of Descartes and Malebranche give philosophical expression to an early modern

---

[18] Karsten Harries, *The Infinity of Perspective* (Cambridge: The MIT Press, 2001) describes this as the "principle of perspective." At p. 42, he writes, "In general form [this principle] it may be expressed as follows: to think a perspective as a perspective is to be in some sense already beyond it, is to have become learned about its limitations." Harries traces the origins of this principle to Nicholas of Cusa's *On Learned Ignorance.*

[19] Descartes, *Meditations,* "Meditation One," p. 97. Harries, *The Infinity of Perspective,* p. 123, analyzing Descartes' attempt to develop an aperspectival form of knowledge writes, "The idea of objectivity . . . is tied to the idea of a knowing that is free from perspectival distortion, an angelic, divine or ideal knowing. It is thus linked to the idea of a knower not imprisoned in the body and not bound by the senses, a pure subject."

"experience of a divided self," to a tendency evident throughout the sixteenth and seventeenth centuries to imagine the individual's inner self as detached from the world, to imagine it (if only ideally) as somehow free from or impervious to external pressures and contexts. Historians have sought to explain this sixteenth- and seventeenth-century fascination with inwardness and the dream of a radical distinction between one's public and private selves as a response to intensifying religious persecution and political centralization.[20] Similarly, if at an admittedly more theoretical level, the subject of Cartesian philosophy discovers its own individual inviolability in its hypothetical confrontation with a deceiving god's omnipotent power.[21] In either case, what matters is that the inner and outer self are more sharply defined precisely in terms of how they are known. Self-examination in Descartes' writings is no longer based on models of exterior vision (as in medieval confessional practice), but rather on the demands of logic, on those truths which cannot possibly be false and which, for that very reason, avoid the potential epistemological pitfalls posed by the circumstances.[22] It is a situation captured in the visual relations established in the metaphor of the camera obscura in which the very walls of the camera mark the absolute divide between the private and public, between the inner and outer, and in so doing mark the unique and uniquely non-visual immediacy of one's relation to oneself.[23]

Whatever forces compelled early modern writers to imagine a form of knowledge, a type of vision, a conception of our interior states, that evaded the limitations and pressures of the circumstances, those forces certainly were not at work during the thirteenth and fourteenth centuries. Indeed, quite the opposite seems to have been the case. Nicholas

---

[20] Martin, "Inventing Sincerity," pp. 1321–2, and from whom I take the expression "experience of a divided self," makes this point for early modern culture considered as a whole. For the specifically English experience, see Maus, *Inwardness*, pp. 16–17, and Elizabeth Hanson, *Discovering the Subject in Renaissance England* (Cambridge: Cambridge University Press, 1998), p. 16, who describes this development in terms of a "slide of a spiritual interiority into a strategic one."

[21] Blumenberg, *Legitimacy*, p. 196.

[22] On certainty as the criterion with which Descartes distinguishes inner from outer states, see Rorty, *Philosophy and the Mirror of Nature*, p. 58. For Malebranche's critique of Descartes on this point, see Nicholas Jolley, "Malebranche on the Soul," in Steven Nadler (ed.), *The Cambridge Companion to Malebranche* (Cambridge: Cambridge University Press, 2000), pp. 42–51.

[23] Descartes, *Meditations*, "Meditation Two," pp. 107–9, describing the infallibility with which we can know our internal states, writes, "Finally, I am the same one who senses or who notices corporeal things as though through the senses: viz., I am now seeing light, I am hearing noise, I am sensing warmth. These things are false, for I am sleeping. But certainly I seem to see, I seem to hear, I seem to be warmed. This cannot be false. It is this which in me is properly called 'to sense.' And this – taken precisely – is nothing other than to cogitate." Dalia Judovitz, "Vision, Representation, and Technology in Descartes," in Levin (ed.), *Modernity and the Hegemony of Vision*, pp. 63–86, offers the most sophisticated analysis of Descartes' rejection of visual semblance. Taylor, *Sources of the Self*, pp. 143–76, explores the ethical implications that Descartes and Locke draw from this disengaged vision of the self.

of Autrecourt's hope that his writings would redirect his peers from a futile pursuit of natural knowledge to the study of the Bible and the practice of preaching may well be a harbinger of more widespread trans-formations in fourteenth-century academic life. Theologians during the fourteenth and fifteenth centuries, in many respects following the lead of canon lawyers, came to understand themselves as essentially public fig-ures with a responsibility to apply their learning and skills to the world beyond the university.[24] Men like John Wyclif in England and Jean Gerson in France spent much of their careers engaged in public controversies, presenting their arguments and adapting their self-presentation to a wide variety of audiences, learned and not learned, religious and lay. The decline of the grand synthesizing *Summas* and rise of the occasional trea-tise or tract as the academic genre of choice during the course of the second half of the fourteenth century points to the development of the "schoolman as public intellectual."[25] These were works that addressed the great and the passing issues of the moment – legal and political cases, religious questions and questions of conscience, even the validity of Joan of Arc's mission. Most importantly, theologians like Gerson refused to treat these controversies in general or abstract terms. Rather, just as Nicholas of Autrecourt had externalized the appearances and argued that objects in the world contain as part of their self-definition every per-spective within which they might possibly be perceived, Gerson believed that the very reality of these public controversies rested in their par-ticularity, in the specific and ever changing sets of circumstances that shaped them, that shaped how they appeared.[26] It is the mindset of the preacher and the confessor, and the techniques of self-presentation and self-examination, writ large on the public sphere.[27] It is a mindset I have tried to trace through its origins in the literature of preaching and con-fession from as early as the late eleventh century, through thirteenth- and fourteenth-century academic debates about the nature of vision,

---

[24] On the thirteenth- and fourteenth-century origins of this development, see Ian P. Wei, "The Self-Image of the Masters of Theology," *Journal of Ecclesiastical History*, 46.3 (July 1995), 398–402.

[25] On the rise of the later medieval "public intellectual," and Jean Gerson as its greatest exemplar, see Hobbins' thought-provoking article, "The Schoolman as Public Intellectual," pp. 1321–31. For a more general account of the public intellectual in the pre-modern era, see Rita Copeland, "Pre-Modern Intellectual Biography," in Helen Small (ed.), *The Public Intellectual* (Oxford: Blackwell Publishers Ltd, 2002), pp. 40–61.

[26] John Van Engen, "From Practical Theology to Divine Law: The Work and Mind of Medieval Canonists," p. 894, notes that this process was already underway in the mid-thirteenth century as "sentence commentators, with no basis in Peter Lombard who never presented the matter in this way, often followed their discussion of Lombard's questions about heretical sacraments with sections on simony treated as a series of *casus* . . ."

[27] Hobbins, "The Schoolman as Public Intellectual," p. 1333, notes the connections between Gerson's conception of his public persona and his experience as a confessor.

now incorporated into the very self-conception of the later medieval theologian.

For people living during the later Middle Ages, such seemingly clear-cut distinctions between self and self-presentation, between what appears and what exists, were constantly being undermined and obviated through their endless replication. The distinction between seeing and being seen did not end with one's public activities, but reappeared within the individual's conscience itself and determined how the preacher, the mendicant, the penitent and the scholar were trained to think about themselves and the world at large. Confessional practice, for example, sought the truth buried within the penitent's soul only to discover the infinite regress of intentions, like so many partial disclosures of a truth never to be fully grasped. If people during the Renaissance recognized "that a person's thoughts and passions, imagined as properties of [a] hidden interior, are not immediately accessible to other people," medieval penitents had already discovered that, in some very real sense, these interior depths were inaccessible even to themselves.[28] Echoing Nicholas of Autrecourt's analysis of human cognitive complexity, Jean Gerson would write, "The diversity of human temperament is incomprehensible – not just in several men, but in one and the same man – and not, I say, in different years or months or weeks, but in days, hours and moments!"[29] Perhaps Hamlet could know his own grief as real and true, but medieval preachers and penitents found their own experiences to be much more opaque and difficult to assess. We know ourselves in much the same way as we know others and the world around us – through appearances that reveal as much as they conceal, as they forever lead us to still more appearances.

There were, quite simply, no means available during the Middle Ages to halt the endless proliferation of appearances. Or, and this might be a better and more accurate way of putting it, there were no satisfactory means available to them. Penitents were urged to conclude their confessions with such catch-all avowals as, "concerning every other venial and mortal sin, confessed and not confessed, I acknowledge my guilt." Academics, likewise, eagerly invoked the idea of the common course of nature in a vain attempt to avoid the problem of false intuitive cognitions. Nonetheless, these were little more than ad hoc attempts to ignore tensions that were structurally endemic to late medieval religious and intellectual life. Although medieval religious and academic practice

[28] Maus, *Inwardness*, p. 5, paints the Renaissance notion of inwardness as a form of the philosophical problem of other minds. Is it possible to infer what another thinks or feels from how they present themselves?

[29] Jean Gerson, *De perfectione cordis*, in Glorieux (ed.), *Oeuvres complètes*, vol. 8, *L'Oeuvre spirituelle et pastorale*, p. 129. Cited in Tentler, *Sin and Confession*, p. 159.

increasingly emphasized the ideal, even the necessity, of clear and complete vision (whether it be of one's audience, of one's self or of the world around us), it simultaneously failed to provide the individual with the means for acquiring that vision, failed to place him in a position from which he could clearly see himself and others. Whatever the relation between what appears and what exists, medieval people found themselves unable to ascertain it. The medieval experience of vision and its effects was, when all is said and done, an experience of vision's infinite promise and its infinite deferral. As Nicholas would put it, if we hope to explain how certitude is possible, we have no choice but to assume that what appears is true. And again, as Nicholas would quickly add, that is an assumption we can in principle never demonstrate.

# BIBLIOGRAPHY

## PRIMARY SOURCES*

Adam Wodeham. *Lectura secunda in librum primum Sententiarum.* Gideon Gál and Rega Wood (eds.). St. Bonaventure: Franciscan Institute Publications, 1990.

Alan of Lille. *Liber poenitentialis.* Jean Longère (ed.). Vol. 2. Louvain: Editions Nauwelaerts, 1965.

Alexander of Stavensby. *Quidam tractatus de confessionibus.* Powicke and Cheney (eds.), vol. 2: pp. 220–6.

Alhacen (Ibn Al-Haytham). *Opticae.* Risner (ed.) 1572.

——. *The Optics of Ibn Al-Haytham: Introduction, Commentary, Glossaries, Concordance, Indices.* A. I. Sabra (ed. and trans.). 2 vols. London: The Warburg Institute, 1989.

Angelus de Clavasi. *Summa angelica de casibus conscientiae.* Chivasso: Jacobinus Suigus, 1486.

Anon. *Hic est modus instruendi novitios in suis confessionibus faciendis.* Namur MS 87, 153rb–154va.

Ps.-Anselm. *De similitudinibus.* PL 179, cols. 1113–130.

Anselm of Bec. *Opera omnia.* Salesius Schmit (ed.). 2 vols. Stuttgart–Bad Cannstatt: F. Frommann, 1968.

——. *Memorials of St. Anselm.* R. W. Southern and F. S. Schmitt (eds.). London: Oxford University Press, 1969.

Antoninus of Florence. *Summa theologica.* Verona, 1740.

Antonius de Butrio. *Speculum de confessione.* Louvain, 1473.

Aristotle. *The Complete Works of Aristotle: The Revised Oxford Translation.* Jonathan Barnes (ed.). Princeton: Princeton University Press, 1984.

Augustine. *Confessions.* Henry Chadwick (trans.). Oxford: Clarendon Press, 1992.

Ps.-Augustine. *Speculum peccatoris.* PL 40, cols. 983–92.

——. *De vera et falsa poenitentia.* PL 40, cols. 1113–30.

Bartholomew of Chaimis. *Confessionale.* Augsburg, 1491.

Bernard of Clairvaux. *On the Song of Songs.* Killian Walsh and Irene Edmonds (trans.). 4 vols. Kalamazoo: Cistercian Publications, Inc., 1979–83.

——. *Sermones super cantica canticorum.* Jean Leclercq, C. H. Talbot and H. M. Rochais (eds.), *Sancti Bernardi opera*, vol. 2. Rome: Editiones Cistercienses, 1958.

---

* The only abbreviation of note in this bibliography is the standard *PL* which stands for J. P. Migne (ed.), *Patrologiae cursus completus: series latina.* Paris, 1844–1902, and will be cited by volume and column number.

Boethius. *De consolatione philosophiae.* Adrianus Scuto (ed.). London: Burns Oates & Washbourne, Ltd., 1925.

Bonaventure. *Commentaria in quatuor libros Sententiarum Magistri.* 4 vols. and index in vol. 5. Quaracchi: Collegii S. Bonaventurae, 1882–1902.

—. *Commentarii in Sacram Scripturam.* 2 vols. (vols. 6–7). Quaracchi: Collegii S. Bonaventurae, 1882–1902.

—. *Opera omnia.* Paris: Vivès, 1868.

Caesarius of Heisterbach. *Dialogus miraculorum.* Cologne, 1851.

—. *The Dialogue on Miracles.* H. Scott and C. C. Swinton Bland (trans.). London: G. Routledge & Sons, 1929.

Cicero. *De natura deorum.* H. Rackham (trans.). Cambridge: Harvard University Press, 1961.

Creytens, Raymond. "L'Instruction des novices dominicains au XIIIe siècle d'après le MS Toulouse 418." *Archivum Fratrum Praedicatorum* 20 (1948): 114–93.

David of Augsburg. *De institutione novitiorum.* Bonaventure, *Opera omnia,* vol. 12: 292–312.

Descartes, René. *Discourse on Method, Optics, Geometry, and Meteorology.* Paul J. Olscamp (trans.). Indianapolis: The Bobbs-Merrill Company, Inc., 1965.

—. *Meditationes de prima philosophia.* George Heffernan (trans.). Notre Dame: University of Notre Dame Press, 1990.

—. *Philosophical Letters.* Anthony Kenny (trans.). Minneapolis: University of Minnesota Press, 1970.

Diogenes Laertius. *Lives of Eminent Philosophers.* R. D. Hicks (trans.). 2 vols. Cambridge: Harvard University Press, 1950.

Durand of St. Pourçain. *Petri Lombardi Sententias theologicas Commentarium libri IIII.* Venice, 1551.

Galen. *On the Doctrines of Hippocrates and Plato.* Phillip De Lacy (ed. and trans.). Corpus medicorum graecorum, vol. 5, part 4, no. 1, sections 1–2. Berlin: Akademie-Verlag, 1980.

Gerard de Frachet. *Lives of the Brethren of the Order of Preachers.* Bede Jarett (ed.) and Placid Conway (trans.). London: Blackfriars, 1955.

Goering, Joseph (ed.). "The *Summa de penitentia* of Magister Serlo." *Mediaeval Studies* 38 (1976): 1–53.

Goering, Joseph, and F. A. C. Mantello (eds.). "*Notus in Iudea Deus*: Robert Grosseteste's Confessional Formula in Lambeth Palace MS 499." *Viator* 18 (1986): 253–73.

Goering, Joseph, and Pierre J. Payer (eds.). "The *Summa penitentie fratrum predicatorum*, A Thirteenth-Century Confessional Formulary." *Mediaeval Studies* 55 (1993): 1–50.

Grant, Edward (ed.). *A Source Book in Medieval Science.* Cambridge: Harvard University Press, 1974.

Guido de Monte Rocherii. *Manipulus curatorum.* Strassburg, 1490.

Honorius Augustodunensis, *Elucidarium. PL* 172, cols. 1109–76.

Hugh of St. Victor. *De sacramentis. PL* 176, cols. 549–78.

—. *De institutione novitiorum. PL* 176, cols. 925–52.

Hugo de Folieto. *De claustro animae. PL* 176, cols. 1017–182.

Humbert of Romans. *De vita regulari.* Joachim Berthier (ed.). 2 vols. Rome: A. Befani, 1888.

Jean Gerson. *Oeuvres complètes.* P. Glorieux (ed.). 10 vols. Paris: Desclee & Cie, 1960–1973.

John Duns Scotus. *God and Creatures: The Quodlibetal Questions.* Felix Alluntis and Allan B. Wolter (trans.). Princeton: Princeton University Press, 1975.

—. *Ioannis Duns Scoti doctoris subtilis et mariani opera omnia.* Carl Balić *et al.* (eds.). 11 vols. Vatican City: Typis Polyglottis Vaticanis, 1950–.

—. *Opera omnia.* Luke Wadding (ed.). 26 vols. Paris: Vivès, 1891–5.

John of God. *Excerpta ex Poenitentiali magistri Joannis de Deo.* PL 99, cols. 1085–198.

John of Heisterbach. *Auditorium monachale.* See Michaud-Quantin (ed.), 1964.

John Pecham. *Perspectiva communis.* David C. Lindberg (ed. and trans.), *John Pecham and the Science of Optics.* Madison: The University of Wisconsin Press, 1970.

John of Salisbury. *The Metalogicon: A Twelfth-Century Defense of the Verbal and Logical Arts of the Trivium.* Daniel D. McGarry (trans.). Berkeley: University of California Press, 1955.

Joinville & Villehardouin. *Chronicles of the Crusades.* M. R. B. Shaw (trans.). London: Penguin Books, 1963.

Kirk, G. S. and M. Schofield (eds.). *The Presocratic Philosophers.* 2nd ed. Cambridge: Cambridge University Press, 1983.

Kottje, Raymund (ed.), *Paenitentialia minora Franciae et Italiae saeculi VIII–IX.* Corpus Christianorum. Series Latina 156. Turnhout: Brepols, 1994.

Lanfranc. *Libellus de celanda confessione.* PL 150, cols. 625–32.

Locke, John. *An Essay Concerning Human Understanding.* Peter H. Nidditch (ed.). Oxford: Clarendon Press, 1975.

Malebranche, Nicolas. *The Search After Truth.* Thomas M. Lennon (trans.). Columbus: Ohio State University Press, 1980.

Marchesinus of Regio Lepide. *Confessionale.* Bonaventure, *Opera omnia,* vol. 7: 359–92.

Margery Kempe. *The Book of Margery Kempe.* B. A. Windleatt (trans.). Harmondsworth: Penguin Books, 1985.

Matthew of Cracow. *De modo confitendi et de puritate conscientiae.* Bonaventure, *Opera omnia,* vol. 7: 559–82.

McNeil, John T., and Helena M. Gamer (eds. and trans.). *Medieval Handbooks of Penance: A Translation of the Principal "Libri Poenitentiales" and Selections from Related Documents.* New York: Columbia University Press, 1938.

Michaud-Quantin, Pierre (ed.). "Deux formulaires pour la confession du milieu du XIIIe siècle." *Recherches de théologie ancienne et médiévale* 31 (1964): 43–62.

—. "L'*Auditorium monachale* de l'abbé Jean de Heisterbach." *Cîteaux* 15 (1964): 125–45.

—. "Un manuel de confession archaïque dans le manuscrit Avranches 136." *Sacris erudiri: Jaerboek voor Godsdienstwetenschappen* 17, no. 1 (1966): 5–54.

Montaigne, Michel de. *The Complete Essays of Montaigne.* Donald M. Frame (trans.). Stanford: Stanford University Press, 1965.

Muckle, J. T. (ed.). "The Personal Letters Between Abelard and Heloise." *Mediaeval Studies* 15 (1953): 47–94.

Nicholas of Autrecourt. *Exigit ordo executionis.* Reginald O'Donnell (ed.). *Mediaeval Studies* 1 (1939): 179–267.

—. *The Universal Treatise of Nicholas of Autrecourt.* Leonard A. Kennedy, Richard E. Arnold and Arthur Millard (trans.). Milwaukee: Marquette University Press, 1971.

—. *Nicholas of Autrecourt: His Correspondence with Master Giles and Bernard of Arezzo.* L. M. De Rijk (ed. and trans.). New York: E. J. Brill, 1994.

—. *Nicholas d'Autrecourt: correspondence, articles condamnés.* L. M. de Rijk (ed.) and Christophe Grellard (trans.). Paris: Librairie Philosophique J. Vrin, 2001.

Odo of Sully. *Synodicae constitutiones.* PL 212, cols. 58–68.

Peter Abelard. *The Letters of Abelard and Heloise.* Betty Radice (trans.). London: Penguin Books, 1974.

—. *Peter Abelard's Ethics.* D. E. Luscombe (ed. and trans.). Oxford: Clarendon Press, 1971.

Peter Aureol. *Commentarium in primum librum Sententiarum.* Romae: ex typographia Vaticanae Romae, 1596.

—. *Scriptum in libros sententiarum.* Eligius Buytaert (ed.). 2 vols. St. Bonaventure: The Franciscan Institute, 1952 and 1956.

Peter Damian. *Opuscula varia.* PL 145.

Peter John Olivi. *Quaestiones in secundum librum Sententiarum.* Bernardus Jansen (ed.). 3 vols. Florence: Quaracchi, 1922–6.

Peter of Blois. *De confessione sacramentali.* PL 207, cols. 1077–92.

Peter of Limoges. *Liber de oculo morali.* Augsburg, 1475.

Peter Lombard. *Sententiae in IV libris distinctae.* 3rd edn. Ignatius C. Brady (ed.). 2 vols. Grottaferrata: Collegii S. Bonaventurae ad Claras Aquas, 1971–81.

Peter Quinel. *Summula sinodi Exoniensis diocesis.* Powicke and Cheney (eds.), vol. 2: 1060–77.

Peter the Cantor. *Summa de sacramentis et animae consiliis,* Analecta mediaevalia Namurcensia, 7. Louvain: Editions Nauwelaerts, 1957.

Powicke, F. M., and C. R. Cheney (eds.). *Councils and Synods with other Documents Relating to the English Church: AD 1205–1313.* 2 vols. Oxford: Clarendon Press, 1964.

Ptolemy. *Optics.* A. Mark Smith (trans.). *Ptolemy's Theory of Visual Perception: An English translation of the Optics with Introduction and Commentary.* Transactions of the American Philosophical Society 86, part 2. Philadelphia: The American Philosophical Society, 1996.

Risner, Friedrich (ed.). *Opticae thesaurus.* Basel, 1572.

Robert Courson. *Summa.* V. L. Kennedy (ed.). "Robert Courson on Penance." *Mediaeval Studies* (1945): 291–337.

Robert of Flamborough. *Liber poenitentialis.* J. J. Firth (ed.). Toronto: Pontifical Institute of Mediaeval Studies, 1971.

Robert Grosseteste. *Concerning Lines, Angles and Figures.* David Lindberg (trans.). In Grant (ed.): pp. 385–91.

—. *Deus est.* In Wenzel (ed.) 1970.

—. *Notus in Iudea Deus.* In Goering (ed.) 1986.

Roger Bacon. *Liber primus communium naturalium fratris Rogeri.* Robert Steele (ed.). *Opera hactenus inedita Rogeri Baconi.* Fasc. II. Oxford: Clarendon Press, 1909.

—. *De multiplicatione specierum.* David C. Lindberg (ed. and trans.), *Roger Bacon's Philosophy of Nature: A Critical Edition, with English Translation, Introduction, and Notes, of "De multiplicatione specierum" and "De speculis comburentibus".* Oxford: Clarendon Press, 1983.

—. *"Perspectiva".* David C. Lindberg (ed. and trans.), *Roger Bacon and the Origins of Perspectiva in the Middle Ages: A Critical Edition and English Translation of Bacon's "Perspectiva" with Introduction and Notes.* Oxford: Clarendon Press, 1996.

# Bibliography

—. *Three Treatments of Universals by Roger Bacon.* Thomas Maloney (ed. and trans.). Binghamton: Medieval and Renaissance Texts and Studies, 1989.

Tanner, Norman P. (ed. and trans.). *Decrees of the Ecumenical Councils.* 2 vols. Washington: Georgetown University Press, 1990.

Thomas Aquinas. *In Metaphysicam Aristotelis commentaria.* M.-R. Cathala (ed.). Turin: Marietti, 1935.

—. *Opera omnia.* 25 vols. Parma: Petri Fiaccadori, 1852–73.

—. *Summa contra gentiles.* Anton C. Pegis (trans.). Notre Dame: University of Notre Dame Press, 1955.

—. *Summa theologiae.* P. Caramello (ed.). Turin–Rome: Marietti, 1952.

Thomas Chobham. *Summa confessorum.* F. Broomfield (ed.). Louvain: Editions Nauwelaerts, 1968.

Tugwell, Simon (ed. and trans.). *Early Dominicans: Selected Writings.* New York: Paulist Press, 1982.

Walter Chatton. *Reportatio et lectura super Sententias: collatio ad librum primum et prologus.* Joseph C. Wey (ed.). Toronto: Pontifical Institute of Mediaeval Studies, 1989.

Wenzel, Siegfried (ed.). "Robert Grosseteste's Treatise on Confession, *Deus est.*" *Franciscan Studies* 30 (1970): 218–93.

William de Montibus. *Peniteas cito peccator.* Joseph Goering (ed.), *William de Montibus (c. 1140–1213): The Schools and the Literature of Pastoral Care.* Toronto: Pontifical Institute of Mediaeval Studies, 1992: pp. 107–39.

William of Ockham. *Opera philosophica et theologica.* Gedeon Gál et al. (eds.). St. Bonaventure: The Franciscan Institute, 1967–.

William of Auvergne. *Tractatus novi de poenitentia. Opera omnia.* Vol. 2. Paris, 1674.

William of Saint-Thierry. *Guillelmi a Sancto Theodorico opera omnia*, part 3. Paul Verdeyen et al. (eds.). Corpus Christianorum, *Continuatio Mediaevalis* 88. Turnhout: Brepols, 2003.

—. *On the Nature and Dignity of Love.* Thomas X. Davis (trans.). Kalamazoo: Cistercian Publications Inc., 1981.

Witelo. *Perspectiva.* In Risner (ed.), 1572.

—. *Witelonis Perspectivae, liber secundus et liber tertius.* Sabetai Unguru (ed. and trans.). Studia Copernicana 28. Wroclaw: The Polish Academy of the Sciences Press, 1991.

—. *Witelonis Perspectivae, liber quintus: Book V of Witelo's "Perspectiva".* A. Mark Smith (ed. and trans.). Studia Copernicana 23. Wroclaw: The Polish Academy of the Sciences Press, 1983.


## SECONDARY SOURCES

Adams, Marilyn McCord. *William Ockham.* 2 vols. Notre Dame: University of Notre Dame Press, 1987.

Akbari, Suzanne Conklin. *Seeing Through the Veil: Optical Theory and Medieval Allegory.* Toronto: University of Toronto Press, 2004.

Alferi, Pierre. *Guillaume d'Ockham: le singulier.* Paris: Les Editions de Minuit, 1989.

Amundsen, Darrel W. *Medicine, Society and Faith in the Ancient and Medieval Worlds.* Baltimore: The Johns Hopkins University Press, 1996.

Anciaux, Paul. *La Théologie du sacrement de pénitence au XIIe siècle.* Louvain: Nauwelaerts, 1949.

Bakker, Paul J. J. M. (ed.). *Chemins de la pensée médiévale: études offertes à Zénon Kaluza*. Turnhout: Brepols, 2002.

Bauer, Gerhard. *Claustrum animae: Untersuchungen zur Geschichte der Metapher vom Herzen als Kloster*. Munich: W. Fink, 1973.

Baxandall, Michael. *Painting and Experience in Fifteenth Century Italy: A Primer in the Social History*. Oxford: Clarendon Press, 1972.

Benton, John F. "Consciousness of Self and Perceptions of Individuality." Robert L. Benson and Giles Constable (eds.), *Renaissance and Renewal in the Twelfth Century*. Boston: Harvard University Press, 1982: pp. 263–95.

Bériou, Nicole. "La Confession dans les écrits théologiques et pastoraux du XIIIe siècle: médication de l'ame ou démarche judiciare?" Ecole Française de Rome: pp. 261–82.

Biernoff, Suzannah. *Sight and Embodiment in the Middle Ages*. New York: Palgrave Macmillan, 2001.

Biller, Peter. "Confession in the Middle Ages." In Biller and Minnis (eds.) (1998): pp. 3–33.

Biller, Peter, and A. J. Minnis (eds.). *Handling Sin: Confession in the Middle Ages*. Woodbridge: The Boydell Press, 1998.

Blumenberg, Hans. *The Genesis of the Copernican World*. Robert M. Wallace (trans.). Cambridge: The MIT Press, 1987.

—. *The Legitimacy of the Modern Age*. Robert M. Wallace (trans.). Boston: The MIT Press, 1983.

Boehner, Philotheus. "*Notitia intuitiva* of Non-Existents According to Peter Aureoli." *Franciscan Studies* 8 (1948): 388–416.

—. "The *notitia intuitiva* of Non-Existents According to William Ockham." *Collected Articles on Ockham*. Eligius Buytaert (ed.). St. Bonaventure: The Franciscan Institute, 1958.

Boler, John F. "Intuitive and Abstractive Cognition." Kretzman, Kenny and Pinborg (eds.): pp. 460–78.

Bossy, John. *Christianity in the West*. Oxford: Oxford University Press, 1985.

Boyle, Leonard. "The *Summa confessorum* of John of Freiburg and the Popularization of the Moral Teaching of St. Thomas and some of his Contemporaries." *St. Thomas Aquinas (1274–1974): Commemorative Studies*. Toronto: Pontifical Institute of Mediaeval Studies, 1974: pp. 245–68.

—. "The Fourth Lateran Council and Manuals of Popular Theology." Thomas J. Heffernan (ed.), *The Popular Literature of Medieval England*. Knoxville: The University of Tennessee Press, 1985: pp. 30–43.

Brakel, J. van. "Some Remarks on the Prehistory of the Concept of Statistical Probability." *Archive for the History of Exact Sciences* 16, no. 2 (1976): 119–36.

Brett, Edward Tracy. *Humbert of Romans: His Life and Views of Thirteenth-Century Society*. Toronto: Pontifical Institute of Mediaeval Studies, 1984.

Brient, Elizabeth. *The Immanence of the Infinite, Hans Blumenberg and the Threshold to Modernity*. Washington, DC: The Catholic University Press of America, 2002.

Brooke, Odo. *Studies in Monastic Theology*. Kalamazoo: Cistercian Publications Inc., 1980.

Burckhardt, Jacob. *The Civilization of the Renaissance in Italy*. Vol. 2. S. G. C. Middlemore (ed.). New York: Harper & Row, 1929.

# Bibliography

Bynum, Caroline Walker. *Docere verbo et exemplo*. Missoula: The Scholar's Press, 1979.

—. *Jesus as Mother: Studies in the Spirituality of the High Middle Ages*. Berkeley: University of California Press, 1982.

—. *The Resurrection of the Body in Western Christianity: 200–1336*. New York: Columbia University Press, 1995.

Camille, Michael. "The Eye in the Text: Vision in the Illuminated Manuscripts of the Latin Aristotle." In *View and Vision*, vol. 2: pp. 129–45.

—. "Before the Gaze: The Internal Senses and Late Medieval Practices of Seeing." Nelson (ed.) (2000): pp. 197–223.

Caplan, Harry. "Classical Rhetoric and the Mediaeval Theory of Preaching." *Classical Philology* 28, no. 2 (1933): 73–96.

Carruthers, Mary. *The Book of Memory: A Study of Memory in Medieval Culture*. Cambridge: Cambridge University Press, 1990.

Chenu, M.-D. *La Théologie comme science au XIIIe siècle*. Paris: Librairie Philosophique J. Vrin, 1957.

—. *Toward Understanding Saint Thomas*. A.-M. Landry and D. Hughes (trans.). Chicago: Henry Regnery Company, 1964.

Clark, David L. "Optics for Preachers: The *De oculo morali* by Peter of Limoges." *Michigan Academician* 9, no. 3 (1977): 329–43.

Colish, Marcia. "Systematic Theology and Theological Renewal in the Twelfth Century." *Journal of Medieval and Renaissance Studies* 18, no. 2 (1988): 135–156.

—. *Peter Lombard*. Vol. 2. Leiden: E. J. Brill, 1994.

Copeland, Rita. "Pre-Modern Intellectual Biography." Helen Small (ed.), *The Public Intellectual*. Oxford: Blackwell Publishers Ltd, 2002: pp. 40–61.

Courtenay, William. *Adam Wodeham: An Introduction to His Life and Writings*. Leiden: E. J. Brill, 1978.

—. "Inquiry and Inquisition: Academic Freedom in Medieval Universities." *Church History* 58, no. 2 (1989): 168–81.

Crary, Jonathan. *Techniques of the Observer: On Vision and Modernity in the Nineteenth Century*. Cambridge: The MIT Press, 1991.

Crosby, Alfred W. *The Measure of Reality: Quantification and Western Society, 1250–1600*. Cambridge: Cambridge University Press, 1997.

D'Avray, D. L. *The Preaching of the Friars: Sermons Diffused from Paris Before 1300*. Oxford: Clarendon Press, 1985.

Dales, Richard C. "The Origin of the Doctrine of Double Truth." *Viator* 15 (1984): 169–79.

Dear, Peter. *Discipline and Experience: The Mathematical Way in the Scientific Revolution*. Chicago: The University of Chicago Press, 1995.

Déchanet, Jean. *Guillaume de Saint-Thierry: aux sources d'une pensee*. Paris: Editions Beauchesne, 1978.

—. *William of St. Thierry: The Man and his Work*. Richard Stachann (trans.). Spencer: Cistercian Publications, 1972.

Delumeau, Jean. *Sin and Fear: The Emergence of a Western Guilt Culture, Thirteenth–Eighteenth Centuries*. Eric Nicholson (trans.). New York: St. Martin's Press, 1990.

Denery, Dallas G. "The Appearance of Reality: Peter Aureol and the Experience of Perceptual Error." *Franciscan Studies* 55 (1998): 27–52.

Dewey, John. *The Quest For Certainty*. New York: G. P. Putnam & Sons, 1980.

# Bibliography

Diekstra, F. N. M. "The *Supplementum tractatus novi de poenitentia* of Guillaume D'Auvergne and Jacques De Vitry's Lost Treatise on Confession." *Recherches de théologie ancienne et médiévale* 61 (1994): 22–41.

Duby, Georges. "Solitude: Eleventh to Thirteenth Century." Georges Duby and Phillippe Aries (eds.), *A History of Private Life.* Vol. 2. Cambridge: Belknap Press, 1987.

Duggan, Lawrence, G. "Fear and Confession on the Eve of the Reformation." *Archiv für Reformationsgeschichte* 75 (1984): 153–75.

Dumont, Stephen D. "Theology as a Science and Duns Scotus' Distinction between Intuitive and Abstractive Cognition." *Speculum* 64 (1989): 579–99.

Ecole Française de Rome. *L'Aveu: antiquité et moyen-age.* Rome: Ecole Française de Rome, 1986.

—. *Faire croire: modalités de la diffusion et de la reception des messages religieux du XIIe au Xve siècle.* Rome: Ecole Française de Rome, 1981.

Edgerton, Samuel Y., Jr. *The Heritage of Giotto's Geometry: Art and Science on the Eve of the Scientific Revolution.* Ithaca: Cornell University Press, 1991.

Elkins, James. *The Poetics of Perspective.* Ithaca: Cornell University Press, 1994.

Emery, Kent and Joseph Wawrykow (eds.). *Christ Among the Medieval Dominicans: Representations of Christ in the Texts and Images of the Order of Preachers.* Notre Dame: University of Notre Dame Press, 1998.

Evans, G. R. *Old Arts and New Theology: The Beginning of Theology as an Academic Discipline.* Oxford: Clarendon Press, 1980.

—. *Getting It Wrong: The Medieval Epistemology of Error.* Leiden: Brill, 1998.

Foucault, Michel. *Discipline and Punish: The Birth of the Prison.* New York: Vintage Books, 1977.

Funkenstein, Amos. *Theology and the Scientific Imagination.* Princeton: Princeton University Press, 1983.

Garber, Daniel, and Sandy Zabell. "On the Emergence of Probability." *Archive for the History of Exact Sciences* 21, no. 1 (1979): 33–53.

Gehl, Paul. "Mystical Language Models in Monastic Educational Psychology." *Journal of Medieval and Renaissance Studies* 14, no. 2 (1984): 219–43.

—. "*Competens silentium*: Varieties of Monastic Silence in the Medieval West." *Viator* 18 (1987): 125–60.

Gelber, Hester. *Exploring the Boundaries of Reason.* Toronto: Pontifical Institute of Mediaeval Studies, 1983.

Glorieux, P. "Le *Tractatus novus de poenitentia* de Guillaume d'Auvergne." *Miscellanea moralia in honorem eximii domini Arthur Janssen.* Louvain: É. Nauwelaerts, 1949: pp. 551–65.

Goering, Joseph. "The Internal Forum and the Literature of Penance and Confession." W. Hartmann and K. Pennington (eds.). *History of Medieval Canon Law.* Washington, DC: Catholic University Press of America, 2001: pp. 1–75.

Goering, Joseph, and Daniel S. Taylor. "The *Summulae* of Bishops Walter de Cantilupe (1240) and Peter Quinel (1287)." *Viator* 26 (1995): 576–94.

Gougaud, Louis. *Dévotions et pratiques ascétiques du Moyen Âge.* Paris: Desclée de Brouwer, 1925.

Gracia, Jorge (ed.). *Individuation in Scholasticism: The Later Middle Ages and the Counter-Reformation.* Albany: State University of New York Press, 1994.

# Bibliography

Grafton, Anthony. *Leon Battista Alberti: Master Builder of the Italian Renaissance.* Cambridge: Harvard University Press, 2000.

Grant, Edward. *The Foundations of Modern Science in the Middle Ages: Their Religious, Institutional and Intellectual Contexts.* Cambridge: Cambridge University Press, 1996.

—. "Medieval Natural Philosophy: Empiricism without Observation." Cees Leijenhorst, Christoph Lüthy and J. M. M. H. Thijssen (eds.). *The Dynamics of Aristotelian Natural Philosophy from Antiquity to the Seventeenth Century.* Leiden: Brill, 2002: pp. 141–68.

Greenblatt, Stephan. "Psychoanalysis and Renaissance Culture." *Learning to Curse.* New York: Routledge, 1990: pp. 131–45.

—. *Renaissance Self-Fashioning: From More to Shakespeare.* Chicago: The University of Chicago Press, 1980.

Grellard, Christophe. "Introduction." In Nicholas d'Autrecourt (2001): pp. 7–72.

—. "Amour du soi, amour du prochain. Nicholas d'Autrecourt, Jean Buridan et l'idée d'une morale laïque (autour de l'article condamné no. 66)." Bakker (ed.) (2002): pp. 215–51.

—. "*Sicut specula sine macula*: la perception et son objet chez Nicolas d'Autrecourt." Anca Vasiliu (ed.), *Image et representation dans la pensée médiévale.* Paris: Vrin, forthcoming.

Groupe de la Brussière. *Pratiques de la confession: des pères du désert à Vatican II.* Paris: Les Editions du Cerf, 1983.

Gurevich, Aaron. *The Origins of European Individualism.* Katharine Judelson (trans.). Oxford: Blackwell Publishers Ltd., 1995.

Gy, Pierre-Marie. "Le Précepte de la confession annuelle (Latran IV, c. 21) et la détection des hérétiques." *Revue des sciences philosophiques et théologiques* 58 (1974): 444–50.

—. "Les Bases de la pénitence moderne." *La Maison Dieu* 117 (1974): 63–85.

—. "Les Définitions de la confession après le quatrième concile du Latran." Ecole Française de Rome (1986): pp. 283–95.

Hackett, Jeremiah. "Philosophy and Theology in Roger Bacon's *Opus maius.*" James R. Long (ed.), *Philosophy and the God of Abraham.* Toronto: Pontifical Institute of Mediaeval Studies, 1991: pp. 55–69.

Hacking, Ian. *The Emergence of Probability.* Cambridge: Cambridge University Press, 1975.

Hahn, Cynthia. "*Visio Dei*: Change in Medieval Visuality." In Nelson (ed.) (2000): pp. 169–96.

Hamburger, Jeffrey. *The Visual and the Visionary: Art and Female Spirituality in Late Medieval Germany.* Cambridge: The MIT Press, 1998.

Hamilton, Sarah. *The Practice of Penance, 900–1050.* Woodbridge: The Boydell Press, 2001.

Hamm, Bernt. "Normative Centering in the Fifteenth and Sixteenth Centuries." *Journal of Early Modern History* 3.4 (1999): 307–54.

Hanson, Elizabeth. *Discovering the Subject in Renaissance England.* Cambridge: Cambridge University Press, 1998.

Harries, Karsten. *The Infinity of Perspective.* Cambridge: The MIT Press, 2001.

# Bibliography

Haskins, Charles Homer. *The Renaissance of the Twelfth Century*. Cambridge: Harvard University Press, 1929.

Hatfield, Gary C., and William Epstein. "The Sensory Core and the Medieval Foundations of Early Modern Perceptual Theory." *Isis* 70 (1979): 363–84.

Heidegger, Martin. "The Age of the World Picture." *The Question Concerning Technology and Other Essays*. William Lovitt (trans.). New York: Harper Torchbooks, 1977: pp. 115–54.

Heimsoeth, Heinz. *The Six Great Themes of Western Metaphysics and the End of the Middle Ages*. Ramon J. Betanzos (trans.). Detroit: Wayne State University Press, 1987.

Hinnebusch, William A. *The History of the Dominican Order: Origins and Growth to 1500*. Staten Island: Alba House, 1965.

Hobbins, Daniel. "The Schoolman as Public Intellectual: Jean Gerson and the Late Medieval Tract." *The American Historical Review*. 108.5 (2003): 1308–337.

Ivins, William M. Jr. *On the Rationalization of Sight: With an Examination of Three Renaissance Texts on Perspective*. New York: Da Capo Press, Inc., 1975.

Jay, Martin. *Downcast Eyes: The Denigration of Vision in Twentieth-Century French Thought*. Berkeley: University of California Press, 1993.

—. "Scopic Regimes of Modernity." Hal Foster (ed.), *Vision and Visuality*. New York: The New Press, 1993: pp. 3–23.

Jolley, Nicholas. "Malebranche on the Soul." Steven Nadler (ed.), *The Cambridge Companion to Malebranche*. Cambridge: Cambridge University Press, 2000: pp. 31–58.

Jonas, Hans. "The Nobility of Sight: A Study in the Phenomenology of the Senses." *The Phenomenon of Life: Toward a Philosophical Biology*. Chicago: The University of Chicago Press, 1982: pp. 135–56.

Judovitz, Dalia. "Vision, Representation, and Technology in Descartes." Levin (ed.) 1993: pp. 63–86.

Kaluza, Zénon. *Nicolas d'Autrecourt: l'ami de la vérité*. Histoire Littéraire de la France. Tome 42, fasc. 1 (1995).

—. "Voir: la clarté de la connaissance chez Nicholas d'Autrecourt." In *View and Vision*, vol. 1: pp. 89–105.

Kaminsky, Howard. "From Lateness to Waning to Crisis: The Burden of the Later Middle Ages" *Journal of Early Modern History*. 4.1 (2000): 85–125.

Kay, Richard. "Dante's Empyrean and the Eye of God," *Speculum* 78:1 (January 2003): 37–65.

Kaye, Joel. *Economy and Nature in the Fourteenth-Century: Money, Market Exchange, and the Emergence of Scientific Thought*. Cambridge: Cambridge University Press, 1998.

Kennedy, Leonard. "Late-Fourteenth-Century Philosophical Scepticism at Oxford." *Vivarium* 23, no. 2 (1985): 124–151.

—. "Philosophical Scepticism in England in the Mid-Fourteenth Century." *Vivarium* 21, no. 1 (1983): 35–57.

Knudsen, Christian. "Intentions and Impositions." Kretzman *et al.* (eds.): pp. 479–95.

Kretzman, Norman. *The Metaphysics of Theism: Aquinas' Natural Theology in "Summa contra gentiles" I*. Oxford: Clarendon Press, 1997.

Kretzman, Norman, Anthony Kenny and Jan Pinborg (eds.). *The Cambridge History of Later Medieval Philosophy*. Cambridge: Cambridge University Press, 1982.

# Bibliography

Kretzman, Norman, and Eleonore Stump (eds.). *The Cambridge Companion to Aquinas*. Cambridge: Cambridge University Press, 1993.

Ladner, Gerhart B. *Images and Ideas in the Middle Ages: Selected Studies in History and Art*. Vol. 2. Rome: Edizioni di Storia e Letteratura, 1983.

Lea, Henry Charles. *A History of Auricular Confession and Indulgences in the Latin Church*. 3 vols. London: Swan Sonnenschein & Co., 1896.

Leclerq, Jean. *The Love of Learning and the Desire for God*. C. Misrahi (trans.). New York: Fordham University Press, 1962.

Leff, Gordon. *The Dissolution of the Medieval Outlook: An Essay on Intellectual and Spiritual Changes in the Fourteenth Century*. New York: Harper & Row, 1976.

Leff, Michael C. "Boethius' *De differentiis topicis*, Book IV." Murphy (ed.) (1978): pp. 3–34.

Levin, David Michael (ed.). *Modernity and the Hegemony of Vision*. Berkeley: University of California Press, 1993.

—. *Sites of Vision: The Discursive Construction of Sight in the History of Philosophy*. Cambridge: The MIT Press, 1997.

Lindberg, David C. "The Genesis of Kepler's Theory of Light: Light Metaphysics from Plotinus to Kepler." *Osiris* 2nd series, 2 (1986): 5–42.

—. "Roger Bacon and the Origins of *Perspectiva* in the West." Edward Grant and John E. Murdoch (eds.), *Mathematics and its Applications to Science and Natural Philosophy in the Middle Ages: Essays in Honor of Marshall Clagett*. Cambridge: Cambridge University Press, 1991: pp. 249–68.

—. "Science as Handmaiden: Roger Bacon and the Patristic Tradition." *Isis* 78 (1987): 518–36.

—. *Theories of Vision from Al-Kindi to Kepler*. Chicago: The University of Chicago Press, 1976.

Little, Lester K. "Les Techniques de la confession et la confession comme technique." In Ecole Française de Rome (1981): pp. 87–99.

Lochrie, Karma. *Covert Operations: The Medieval Uses of Secrecy*. Philadelphia: University of Pennsylvania Press, 1999.

Longère, Jean. *La Prédication médiévale*. Paris: Etudes Augustiniennes, 1983.

Lynch, John E. "The Knowledge of Singular Things according to Vital du Four." *Franciscan Studies* 29 (1969): 271–301.

MacDonald, Scott. "Theory of Knowledge." Kretzman and Stump (eds.): pp. 160–95.

MacIntyre, Alasdair. *After Virtue: A Study in Moral Theory*. Notre Dame: University of Notre Dame Press, 1981.

Maier, Anneliese. "Das Problem der *species in medio* und die neue Naturphilosophie des 14 Jarhunderts." *Freiburger Zeitschrift für Philosophie und Theologie* 10 (1963): 3–32.

Mansfield, Mary. *The Humiliation of Sinners: Public Penance in Thirteenth-Century France*. Ithaca: Cornell University Press, 1995.

Martin, John. "Inventing Sincerity, Refashioning Prudence: The Discovery of the Individual in Renaissance Europe." *The American Historical Review* 102, no. 5 (1997): 1309–42.

Mascuch, Michael. *Origins of the Individualist Self: Autobiography and Self-Identity in England, 1591–1791*. Stanford: Stanford University Press, 1996.

Maus, Katharine Eisaman. *Inwardness and the Theater in the English Renaissance.* Chicago: The University of Chicago Press, 1995.

McGrade, Arthur Stephen. "Seeing Things: Ockham and Representationalism." Christian Wenin (ed.), *L'Homme et son univers au moyen age.* Louvain-La Neuve: Editions de l'Institute Superieur de Philosophie, 1986: pp. 591–7.

Meens, Rob. "The Frequency and Nature of Early Medieval Penance." Biller and Minnis (eds.): pp. 35–62.

Merleau-Ponty, Maurice. "Eye and Mind." James M. Edie (ed.) and Carleton Dallery (trans.), *The Primacy of Perception.* Evanston: Northwestern University Press, 1964: pp. 12–42.

Metz, Christian. *The Imaginary Signifier: Psychoanalysis and the Cinema.* Celia Britton (trans.). Bloomington: Indiana University Press, 1982.

Michaud-Quantin, Pierre. "La *summula in foro poenitentiali* attribueé a Berenger Fredol." *Studia Gratiana* 11 (1967): 147–67.

—. "A propos des premières *Summae confessorum*: theologie et droit canonique." *Recherches de théologie ancienne et médiévale* 26 (1959): 264–306.

—. *Sommes de casuistique et manuels de confession au moyen âge (XII–XVI siecles),* Analecta Mediaevalia Namurcensia, 13. Louvain, 1962.

Miller, P. Isaac. "Singularity in Medieval Minds: Augustine, Scotus, Cusa." PhD Thesis, University of California, Berkeley, 1997.

Montford, Angela. "Fit to Preach and Pray: Considerations of Occupational Health in the Mendicant Orders." R. N. Swanson (ed.), *The Use and Abuse of Time in Christian History.* Woodbridge: The Boydell Press, 2002: pp. 95–110.

Morenzoni, Franco. "Parole du prédicateur et inspiration divine d'après les *Artes predicandi.*" Rosa Marie Dessì and Michel Lauwers (eds.), *La Parole du prédicateur: Ve – Xve siècle,* vol. 1. Nice: Centre d'Etudes Médiévales, 1997: pp. 271–90.

Morris, Colin. *The Discovery of the Individual: 1050–1200.* London: SPCK, 1972.

Mulchahey, M. Michèle. *First the Bow is Bent in Study: Dominican Education before 1350.* Toronto: Pontifical Institute of Mediaeval Studies, 1998.

Murphy, James J. *Rhetoric in the Middle Ages: A History of Rhetorical Theory from Saint Augustine to the Renaissance.* Berkeley: University of California Press, 1974.

Murphy, James J. (ed.). *Medieval Eloquence: Studies in the Theory and Practice of Medieval Rhetoric.* Berkeley: University of California Press, 1978.

Murray, Alexander. "Confession as a Historical Source in the Thirteenth Century." R. H. C. Davis and J. M. Wallace-Hadrill (eds.), *The Writing of History in the Middle Ages: Essays Presented to Richard William Southern.* Oxford: Clarendon Press, 1981: pp. 275–322.

—. "Confession Before 1215." *Transactions of the Royal Historical Society.* 6th series, 3 (1993): 51–81.

—. "Counseling in Medieval Confession." Biller and Minnis (eds.): pp. 63–78.

Nelson, Robert (ed.). *Visuality Before and Beyond the Renaissance.* Cambridge: Cambridge University Press, 2000.

Newhauser, Richard. "Towards a History of Human Curiosity: A Prolegomenon to its Medieval Phase." *Deutsche Vierteljahrsschrift für Literaturwissenschaft und Geistesgeschichte.* 56.4 (1986): 559–75.

—. "Der *Tractatus moralis de oculo* des Petrus von Limoges und seine *exempla.*" Walter Haug and Burghart Wachinger (eds.). *Exempel und Exempelsammlungen,* Tübingen: Max Niemeyer Verlag, 1991: pp. 95–136.

# Bibliography

—. "Nature's Moral Eye: Peter of Limoges' *Tractatus moralis de oculo*." Susan J. Ridyard and Robert G. Benson (eds.), *Man and Nature in the Middle Ages*, Sewanee Mediaeval Studies 6. Sewanee: University of the South Press, 1995: pp. 125–36.

—. "Jesus as the First Dominican? Reflections on a Sub-theme in the Exemplary Literature of Some Thirteenth-Century Preachers. Emery (ed.) (1998).

Newman, Martha G. *The Boundaries of Charity: Cistercian Culture and Ecclesiastical Reform, 1098–1180*. Stanford: Stanford University Press, 1997.

O'Carrol, Maura. "The Educational Organisation of the Dominicans in England and Wales 1221–1348: A Multidisciplinary Approach." *Archivum fratrum praedicatorum* 50 (1980): 23–62.

Oakley, Francis. *Omnipotence, Covenant and Order*. Ithaca: Cornell University Press, 1984.

Oakley, Thomas P. "Some Neglected Aspects in the History of Penance." *The Catholic Historical Review* 24, no. 3 (1938): 293–309.

Oberman, Heiko. *The Harvest of Medieval Theology: Gabriel Biel and Late Medieval Nominalism*. Cambridge: Harvard University Press, 1963.

Ong, Walter. *Ramus, Method and the Decay of Dialogue*. Cambridge: Harvard University Press, 1958.

Ottoson, Per-Gunnar. *Scholastic Medicine and Philosophy: A Study of Commentaries on Galen's "Tegni" (ca. 1300–1450)*. Naples: Bibliopolis, 1984.

Paige, Nicholas D. *Being Interior: Autobiography and the Contradictions of Modernity in Seventeenth-Century France*. Philadelphia: University of Pennsylvania Press, 2001.

Panofsky, Irwin. *Perspective as Symbolic Form*. Christopher S. Wood (trans.). New York: Zone Books, 1991.

Pasnau, Robert. *Theories of Cognition in the Later Middle Ages*. Cambridge: Cambridge University Press, 1997.

Payen, Jean Charles. "La Pénitence dans le contexte culturel des XIIe et XIIIe siècles: des doctrine contritionistes aux pénitentiels vernaculaires." *Revue des sciences philosophiques et théologiques* 61 (1977): 399–428.

Payer, Pierre J. "The Humanism of the Penitentials and the Continuity of the Penitential Tradition." *Mediaeval Studies*, no. 46 (1984): 340–54.

Pelikan, Jaroslav. *The Christian Tradition: A History of the Development of Doctrine*. 5 vols, *The Growth of Medieval Theology (600–1300)*. Chicago: The University of Chicago Press, 1978.

Perkinson, Stephen. "*Portraire, Contrefaire*, and *Engin*: The Prehistory of Portraiture in Late Medieval France." PhD diss, Northwestern University, 1998.

Perler, Dominik. "Peter Aureol vs. Hervaeus Natalis on Intentionality." *Cahiers de l'Institute du Moyen Age Grec et Latin* 61 (1994): 227–62.

Peters, Edward. "*Libertas inquirendi* and the *vitium curiositas* in Medieval Thought." George Makdisi, Dominique Sourdel and Janine Sourdel-Thomine (eds.). *La Notion de liberté au moyen age. Islam, Byzance, Occident*. Paris: Les Belles Lettres, 1985: pp. 89–98.

Pinborg, Jan. "Radulphus Brito on Universals." *Cahiers de l'Institut du Moyen Age Grec et Latin* 35 (1980): 56–142.

Popkin, Richard H. *The History of Scepticism from Erasmus to Spinoza*. Berkeley: University of California Press, 1979.

Poschmann, Berhhard. *Penance and the Annointing of the Sick*. Francis Courtney (trans.). London: Burns & Oates, 1964.

# Bibliography

Ranft, Patricia. "The Concept of Witness in the Christian Tradition." *Revue Benedictine* 102, nos. 1–2 (1992): 9–23.

Reiss, Timothy J. *Knowledge, Discovery and Imagination in Early Modern Europe.* Cambridge: Cambridge University Press, 1997.

—. *Mirages of the Selfe: Patterns of Personhood in Ancient and Early Modern Europe.* Stanford: Stanford University Press, 2003.

Robertson, D. W. "A Note on the Classical Origin of 'Circumstances' in the Medieval Confessional." *Studies in Philology* 43 (1946): 6–14.

Ronchi, Vasco. *The Nature of Light: An Historical Survey.* V. Barocas (trans.). London: Heineman Educational Books, Ltd., 1970.

Rorty, Richard. *Philosophy and the Mirror of Nature.* Princeton: Princeton University Press, 1980.

Rusconi, Roberto. "De la Prédication à la confession: transmission et controle de modèles de comportment au XIIIe siècle." Ecole Française de Rome (1981): pp. 67–85.

Sabra, A. I. "The Astronomical Origin of Ibn al-Haytham's Concept of Experiment." *Actes du XIIe Congrès International d'Histoire des Sciences*, vol. 3a. *Paris, 1968.* Paris: Albert Blanchard, 1971: pp. 133–6.

—. "Sensation and Inference in Alhazen's Theory of Visual Perception." Peter K. Machamer and Robert G. Turnbull (eds.), *Studies in Perception: Interrelations in the History of Philosophy and Science.* Columbus: Ohio State University Press, 1978: 160–85.

Sambursky, S. *Physics of the Stoics.* London: Routledge and Kegan Paul, 1959.

Sayili, Aydin M. "The Observation Well." *Actes du VIIe Congrès d'Histoire des Sciences.* Jerusalem, 1953: pp. 542–50.

Schleusener-Eichholz, Gudrun. "Naturwissenschaft und Allegorese: Der *Tractatus de oculo morali* des Petrus von Limoges." *Frühmittelalteriche Studien* 12 (1978): 258–309.

Schmaltz, Tad M. *Malebranche's Theory of the Soul: A Cartesian Interpretation.* Oxford: Oxford University Press, 1996.

Schmitt, Jean-Claude. "Entre le texte et l'image: les gestes de la prière de Saint Dominique." Richard Trexler (ed.), *Persons in Groups: Social Behavior as Identity Formation in Medieval and Renaissance Europe. Medieval and Renaissance Texts and Studies.* Binghamton: Medieval and Renaissance Texts and Studies, 1985: pp. 195–218.

—. "La 'Decouverte de l'individu': une fiction historiographique?" Paul Mengal (ed.). *La Fabrique, la figure et la feinte: fictions et statut des fictions en psychologie.* Paris: Vrin, 1989: pp. 212–36.

Scott, T. K. "Nicholas of Autrecourt, Buridan and Ockhamism." *Journal of the History of Philosophy* 9, no. 1 (1971): 15–41.

Serene, Eileen. "Demonstrative Science." In Kretzman *et al.* (eds.): pp. 496–517.

Simon, Gérard. *Le Regard, l'être et l'apparence dans l'optique de l'antiquité.* Paris: Editions du Seuil, 1988.

—. *Sciences et savoirs aux XVIe et XVIIe siècles.* Paris: Presses Universitaires du Septentrion, 1996.

—. "La Théorie Cartésienne de la vision, réponse à Kepler et rupture avec la problematique médiévale." Joël Biard and Roshdi Rashed (eds.), *Descartes et la moyen age.* Paris: J. Vrin, 1997: pp. 107–17.

Siraisi, Nancy G. *Medieval and Early Renaissance Medicine: An Introduction to Knowledge and Practice*. Chicago: The University of Chicago Press, 1990.

Smith, A. Mark. "Getting the Big Picture in Perspectivist Optics." *Isis* 72 (1981): 568–89.

—. "The Psychology of Visual Perception in Ptolemy's *Optics*." *Isis* 79 (1988): 189–207.

Snyder, Joel. "Picturing Vision." *Critical Inquiry* 6, no. 3 (Spring 1980): 514–26.

Soler, Albert. "Ramon Llull and Peter of Limoges." *Traditio* 48 (1993): 93–105.

Spencer, H. Leith. *English Preaching in the Late Middle Ages*. Oxford: Clarendon Press, 1993.

Stafford, Barbara. *Visual Analogy: Consciousness as the Art of Connecting*. Cambridge: The MIT Press, 1999.

Stump, Eleonore. *Aquinas*. New York: Routledge, 2003.

Swanson, R. N. *Religion and Devotion in Europe, c. 1215–c. 1515*. Cambridge: Cambridge University Press, 1995.

Tachau, Katherine. "The Problem of the *Species in medio* at Oxford in the Generation after Ockham." *Mediaeval Studies* 44 (1982): 394–443.

—. "Some Aspects of the Notion of Intentional Existence at Paris, 1250–1320." Sten Ebbesen and Russel L. Friedman (eds.), *Medieval Analyses in Language and Cognition*. Copenhagen: The Royal Danish Academy of Sciences and Letters, 1999: pp. 333–53.

—. *Vision and Certitude in the Age of Ockham*. Leiden: E. J. Brill, 1988.

Taylor, Charles. *Sources of the Self: The Making of the Modernity*. Cambridge: Harvard University Press, 1989.

Tentler, Thomas N. *Sin and Confession on the Eve of the Reformation*. Princeton: Princeton University Press, 1977.

—. "The Summa for Confessors as an Instrument of Social Control." Charles Trinkaus and Heiko A. Oberman (eds.), *The Pursuit of Holiness in Late Medieval and Renaissance Religion*. Leiden: E. J. Brill, 1974: pp. 103–37.

Thijssen, J. M. M. H. *Censure and Heresy at the University of Paris, 1200–1400*. Philadelphia: University of Pennsylvania Press, 1998.

—. "John Buridan and Nicholas of Autrecourt on Causality and Induction." *Traditio* 43 (1987): 237–55.

—. "The Quest for Certain Knowledge in the Fourteenth Century: Nicholas of Autrecourt against the Academics." Juha Shivola (ed.), *Ancient Scepticism and the Sceptical Tradition*. Helsinki: The Philosophical Society of Finland, 2000: pp. 199–223.

Thijssen, J. M. M. H. and Jack Zupko (eds.). *The Metaphysics and Natural Philosophy of John Buridan*. Leiden: Brill, 2001.

Thompson, Augustine. *Revival Preachers and Politics in Thirteenth-Century Italy: The Great Devotion of 1233*. Oxford: Clarendon Press, 1992.

Tugwell, Simon. "Humbert of Romans's Material for Preachers." Thomas L. Amos, Eugene A. Green and Beverly Mayne Kienzle (eds.), *De ore Domini: Preachers and the Word in the Middle Ages*. Kalamazoo: Medieval Institute Publications, 1989: pp. 105–17.

Van Engen, John. "From Practical Theology to Divine Law: The Work and Mind of Medieval Canonists." *Proceedings of the Ninth International Congress of Medieval Canon Law*. Vatican: Biblioteca Apostolica Vaticana, 1997: pp. 873–96.

—. "Dominic and the Brothers: *Vitae* as Life-forming *exempla* in the Order of Preachers." Emery and Wawrykow (eds.) (1998): pp. 5–25.

Vanneste, Alfred. "La Théologie de la pénitence chez quelques maitres parisiens de la prèmiere moitié du XIIIe siècle." *Ephemerides theologicae lovanienses* 28 (1952): 24–58.

Vescovini, Federica Gabriella. "Vision et réalité dans la perspective au XIVe siècle." *View and Vision*, vol. 1: 161–80.

*View and Vision in the Middle Ages.* 2 vols. Micrologus. Turnhout: Brepols, 1997.

Vitz, Evelyn Birge. *Medieval Narratology and Modern Narratology: Subjects and Objects of Desire.* New York: New York University Press, 1989.

Wallace, William A. *Causality and Scientific Explanation.* Vol. 1. Ann Arbor: The University of Michigan Press, 1972.

Wei, Ian P. "The Self-Image of the Masters of Theology at the University of Paris in the Late Thirteenth and Early Fourteenth Centuries." *Journal of Ecclesiastical History* 46:3 (1995): 398–431.

Weinberg, Julius. *Nicolas of Autrecourt.* 2nd edn. New York: Greenwood Press, 1969.

—. *Ockham, Descartes and Hume.* Madison: The University of Wisconsin Press, 1977.

Whitehead, Christiana. "Making a Cloister of the Soul in Medieval Religious Treatises." *Medium aevum* 67 (1998): 1–29.

Wippel, John F. "Thomas Aquinas and the Axiom 'What is Received is Received According to the Mode of the Receiver'." Ruth Link-Salinger (ed.), *A Straight Path: Studies in Medieval Philosophy and Culture.* Washington: The Catholic University of America Press, 1988: pp. 279–89.

Wilson, Catherine. "Discourses of Vision in Seventeenth-Century Metaphysics." Levin (ed.) (1997): pp. 117–38.

Wolfson, Harry Austryn. "The Internal Senses in Latin, Arabic, and Hebrew Philosophical Texts." *Harvard Theological Review* 28 (1935): 69–133.

Wolter, Allan B. "John Duns Scotus (b. ca. 1265; d. 1308)." Gracia (ed.) (1994): pp. 271–98.

—. *The Philosophical Theology of John Duns Scotus.* Ithaca: Cornell University Press, 1990.

Wood, Rega. "Adam Wodeham on Sensory Illusions with an Edition of *Lectura secunda, prologus, quaestio 3.*" *Traditio* 38 (1982): 213–52.

—. "Intuitive Cognition and Divine Omnipotence in Fourteenth-Century Perspective." Anne Hudson and Michael Wilks (eds.), *From Ockham to Wyclif.* Oxford: Basil Blackwell, 1987: pp. 51–61.

Zupko, Jack. "Buridan and Skepticism." *Journal of the History of Philosophy* 31.2 (April 1993): pp. 191–221.

—. "On Certitude." Thijssen and Zupko (eds.) (2001): pp. 165–82.

# INDEX

# Index

# Index

*Cambridge Studies in Medieval Life and Thought*
*Fourth series*

Titles in series

*Also published as a paperback

Printed in Great Britain
by Amazon